GA DOCUMENT EXTRA is a new type of publications. Each issue is dedicated to an architect and documents the latest works through photographs, drawings and lively interviews. Each issue contains three chapters.
The first chapter illustrates the architect's past, present and future through and in-depth interview at his/her atelier. The second chapter focuses on recently built projects illustrated with abundant color and black-and-white photographs and interviews. The third chapter introduces projects currently in progress in order to examine the architect's philosophy for the future.

いま、世界の第一線で活躍する建築家群像に、写真、図面、インタヴューで迫り、その過去・現在・未来を三部構成で紹介するGA DOCUMENT EXTRA ドキュメント・エクストラ。
第1章では、彼らの創造の拠点であるアトリエに彼らを訪ね、まんべんなくルポルタージュ。建築を志すに至った動機、過去から現在への変遷、そして今、建築の現在に向けて何を思うか、赤裸々に語ってもらう。
第2章では最近実現した代表作を、豊富な図面と写真で紹介。それぞれの作品についてルポルタージュ。
第3章では、現在進行中のプロジェクトを中心に、明日に向けての建築思考をインタヴュー。

07 JEAN NOUVEL
ジャン・ヌヴェル

WORKS
Lyon Opera／Tours Congress Center／Lille-Centre Euralille／Fondation Cartier／Galeries Lafayette
PROJECTS
Court House, Nantes／Swatch-mobile Factory／Saitama Arena／Tenaga Nasional Park／Lucerne Cultural and Congress Center

144 total pages, 72 in color　¥2,903

10 BERNARD TSCHUMI
ベルナール・チュミ

WORKS
Parc de la Villete／Glass Video Gallery／Le Fresnoy National Studio for the Contemporary Arts／Architecture and Event Exhibition, MOMA
PROJECTS
Interface／Bridge-city／Metropont／CAPC／ZKM Center for Art and Media Technology／National Library of France／School of Architecture／Lerner Student Center／Renault Master Plan／Letzipolis—Department Store

160 total pages, 64 in color　¥2,848

08 RICHARD MEIER
リチャード・マイヤー

WORKS
Museum of Contemporary Art, Barcelona／Swissair North American HQ／The Hague City Hall／The Gagosian Gallery／Exhibition and Assembly Building, Ulm／Espace Pitôt, Montpellier／Museum of TV & Radio, Beverly Hills
PROJECTS
US Courthouse & Federal Building, Islip & Phoenix／Euregio Office & Retail Building, Basel／Getty Center, Los Angeles／Rachofsky House, Dallas

192 total pages, 8 in color　¥2,903

11 ÁLVARO SIZA
アルヴァロ・シザ

WORKS
Santa Maria Church of Marco de Canavezes／Galician Center for Contemporary Art／Main Library, University of Aveiro／Faculty of Architecture, University of Oporto／Rectory of University of Alicante／Expo'98 Portuguese Pavilion
PROJECTS
Manuel Cargaleiro Foundation／Restaurant of Ocean Swimming Pool／Contemporary Art Museum of Oporto／Faculty of Media Science, Santiago University／Cultural Center of the Precinct of Revellin

160 total pages, 64 in color　¥2,848

09 MORPHOSIS
モーフォシス

WORKS
6th Street House／Blades House／Landa House／Sun Tower／Vistor's Center at ASE Design Center
PROJECTS
Diamond Ranch High School／Wagramerstrasse Housing／The Prado Museum Competition／Long Beach International Elementary School／Hypo Alpe Adria Center

144 total pages, 40 in color　¥2,848

PLANNED ISSUES　編集中

NORMAN FOSTER

FRANK O. GEHRY

RICARDO LEGORRETA

Japanese and English text／Size: 300×228mm

表記価格に消費税は含まれておりません。

Main Library, University of Aveiro, Aveiro, Portugal, 1995　アヴェイロ大学図書館

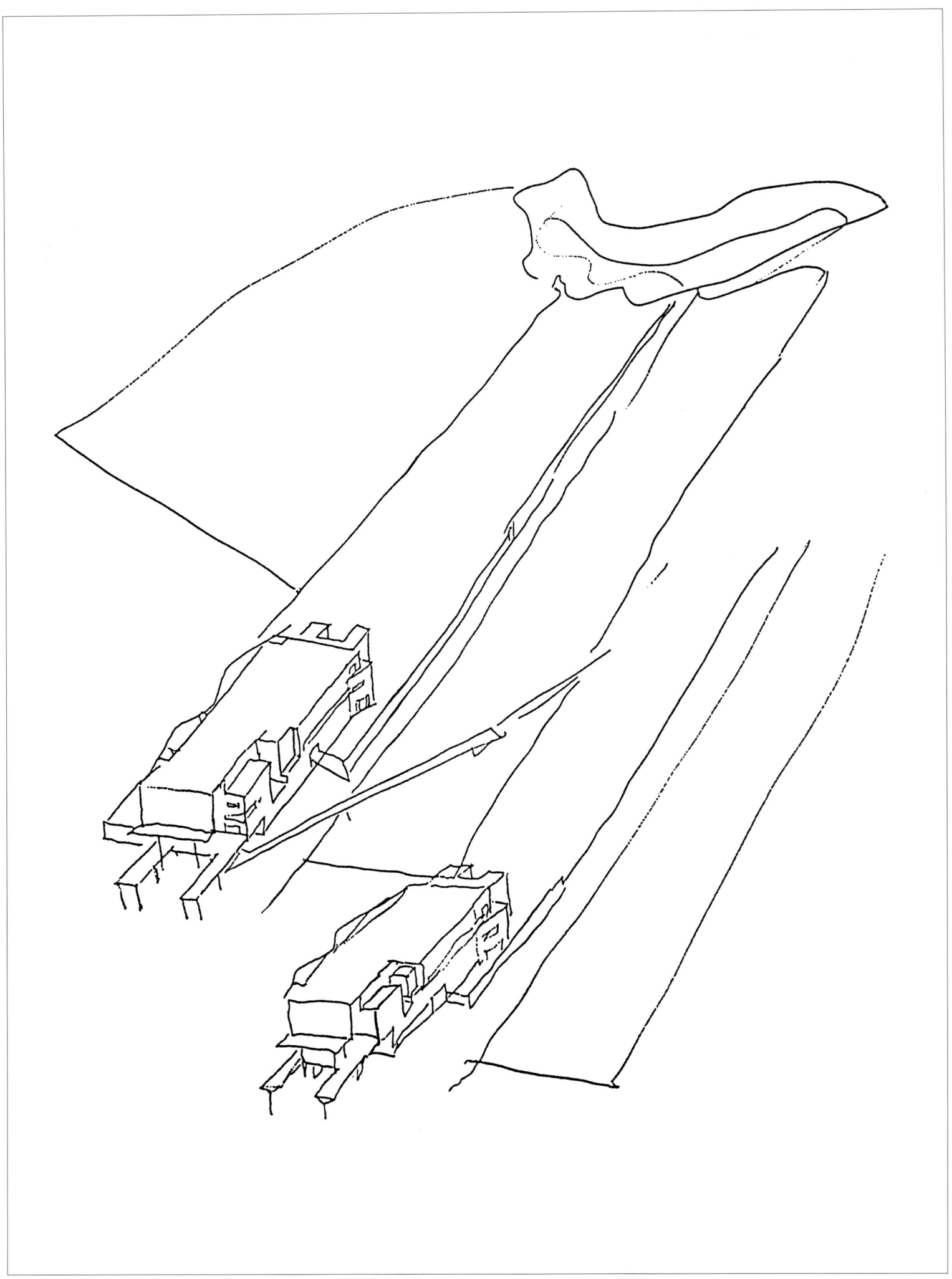

GA DOCUMENT EXTRA 11
ÁLVARO SIZA

ÁLVARO

GA DOCUMENT EXTRA 11

SIZA

Interview with Álvaro Siza, Oporto, Portugal, June, 1998

企画・編集・撮影：二川幸夫　　インタヴュー：二川由夫

Edited and Photographed by Yukio Futagawa　　Interview by Yoshio Futagawa (GA)

A.D.A. EDITA Tokyo

Copyright ©1998 A.D.A. EDITA Tokyo Co., Ltd.
3-12-14 Sendagaya, Shibuya-ku, Tokyo 151-0051, Japan
All rights reserved. No part of this publication may be reproduced,
stored in a retrieval system, or transmitted, in any form or by any means,
electronic, mechanical, photocopying, recording, or otherwise,
without permission in writing from the publisher.

Copyright of photographs:
© 1998 GA photographers: Yukio Futagawa and Associated Photographers
Copyright of drawings:
© 1998 Álvaro Siza Arquitecto, Lda
Copyediting: Yoshio Futagawa, Takashi Yanai
Design: Gan Hosoya

Printed and bound in Japan

ISBN4-87140-231-2 C1352

CONTENTS
目次

STUDIO
8 STUDIO

WORKS

36 Santa Maria Church of Marco de Canavezes, Marco de Canavezes
マルコ・ドゥ・カナヴェーゼスの教会

50 Galician Center for Contemporary Art, Santiago de Compostela
ガリシア現代美術センター

70 Main Library, University of Aveiro, Aveiro
アヴェイロ大学図書館

82 Faculty of Architecture, University of Oporto, Oporto
ポルト大学建築学部

102 Rectory of University of Alicante, Alicante
アリカンテ大学管理／教室棟

118 Expo'98 Portuguese Pavilion, Lisbon
Expo'98　ポルトガル・パヴィリオン

PROJECTS

132 Manuel Cargaleiro Foundation, Lisbon
マヌエル・カルガレイロ財団

140 Restaurant of Ocean Swimming Pool, Leça da Palmeira
レサのスイミングプール・レストラン

146 Contemporary Art Museum of Oporto, Oporto
ポルト現代美術館

156 Faculty of Media Science, Santiago University, Santiago de Compostela
サンティアゴ大学情報科学学部

164 Cultural Center of the Precinct of Revellin, Ceuta
レヴェリン文化センター

STUDIO

Office of Álvaro Siza Arquitecto, Oporto, Portugal　アルヴァロ・シザ事務所

GA: Where were you born?
Álvaro Siza: I was born in Matosinhos, a town near Oporto. There is in effect a continuity between Matosinhos, Oporto and other nearby towns.
GA: This was true at the time you were born?
Siza: Yes, although the relationship is much stronger now. Matosinhos became more important in the 1940s. In the 19th century it was the harbor of Oporto. Before it was in the river at the center of Oporto, but there was a problem so they moved the harbor to Matosinhos. Before then it was really just a small village, a fisherman's village. At the time of the second world war, it became a harbor centered around the fishing of sardines, and they built a lot of factories to process the sardines and that created a lot of money for the town. In wartime they sold a lot of sardines.

Today this industry is almost gone. It has collapsed. There are even limitations on the fishing. There are a lot of people who work in Oporto who live in Matosinhos also because it's less expensive.
GA: Can you tell me about your family?
Siza: My father was an electrical and mechanical engineer. He directed a sugar refinery factory. My mother stayed at home as did most women at the time. She educated her children until we were five. When I had the idea of what to do, I painted and sculpted. I began drawing as a child at around eight years old or so. I used to do drawings and designs of stories. Cartoons. I like designing things, and painting and sculpture. But my father wasn't very supportive of this because at the time it was difficult to be an artist. It wasn't comfortable to have a son who was a painter or a sculptor. So when the time came I decided to study architecture. The school I went to was basically Beaux Arts. My plan was to begin in architecture and then change to sculpture without conflicts. But it happened that I liked architecture. It wasn't due to pressure from my family but the school of architecture was at a very interesting moment because when I entered there was a big change in the curriculum. There was a new director, Carlos Ramos, an architect from Lisbon, a very intelligent person and talented architect. He brought in a new crop of teachers from a younger generation. He was intelligent enough to attract the best. One of them was Fernando Távora. He was my teacher and he invited me to work for his office. This was the my first office job. I worked there maybe two years. It was there that I did my first building.
GA: This happened in school?
Siza: Yes. I entered school in 1949. I was sixteen. In 1953 I finished the first four years of the course. Back then it was a school of arts. We had four years of general courses along with art and design, and then in 1953 we had competitions and we had to make a certain score to become an architect. After that we had to do a thesis as a final examination. I did my thesis very late because I began working in 1951 which was before I finished school. My thesis was these houses which I did from 1954 to 57. Before this I had small projects for my family. I began working in 1951. In 1953 I began working with Távora. I worked about two years and then I was already doing these first houses.
GA: How was Távora's office.
Siza: At the time it was a fantastic ambiance. He was very young. Just ten years older than me. In fact, he had began working around this time. So the relation between the students and him was very close. There was no wall. In his office he was making some famous projects. I worked for instance on the market in Vila da Feira which was a very interesting project, and he also did some houses.

At the time, there was a movement towards vernacular architecture in Portugal. They studied all aspects of vernacular architecture. This was partly provoked by the

---

GA：ご出身はどちらですか。
アルヴァロ・シザ：ポルトに近い，マトジィニョスの町で生まれました。マトジィニョス，ポルト，そしてその周辺の町々は実質的には繋がっているのです。
GA：生まれた頃から既にそうだったのですか。
シザ：ええ，しかも，その繋がりは今よりも強いものでした。マトジィニョスは1940年代にはもっと重要な町だったのです。19世紀は，ポルトの港としての役割を果たしていました。それ以前は，港はポルトの中心部を流れる川のなかにあったのですが，不都合が生じて，マトジィニョスへ移されたのです。それまではただの小さな村，漁村でした。第二次大戦当時は鰯漁を中心とする漁港となり，サーディンの加工工場が沢山つくられ，町に多くのお金を落としました。戦時にはサーディンがよく売れたのです。

今では，こうした工場はほとんど消え去りました。急激に衰えてしまったのです。漁業にも限界があります。マトジィニョスに住んで，仕事場はポルトという人が大勢います。生活費が安いこともあるのでしょうね。
GA：シザさんのご家族はどんな方々だったのですか。
シザ：私の父は，電気機械関係のエンジニアでした。砂糖の精製工場を経営していたのです。母は当時の女性のほとんどがそうであったように，家を守っていました。私たち兄弟は5歳まで，母に教育を受けたのです。何をしようかと自分で考え始めたときには，既に絵を描いたり，彫刻をつくったりしていましたね。8歳ごろにはドローイングを描き始めていました。物語や風刺漫画の筋をつくり，絵を描いたりしていたものです。しかし，父はこれにはあまり感心していませんでした。当時は芸術家であるのは困難なことでしたから，画家や彫刻家の息子を持つのは，自慢できることではなかったのです。そういうわけで，時期が来ると，建築を勉強することに決めました。私が進んだ学校は基本的には美術学校で，まず建築を始め，その後で，父と衝突せずに彫刻に変わるというのが私の計画でした。ところが，たまたま建築が好きになってしまったのです。家族からの圧力のせいではなく，入学した当時，カリキュラムが大幅に変更され，建築学部は非常に面白い時期にあったのです。新しい学部長が就任していました。リスボン出身のカルロス・ラモスという人で，非常に知的で才能のある建築家です。若い世代から成る一群の教師を引き連れてきていました。優れた人たちを惹きつけるだけの知性を持っていたのですね。彼らのなかの一人にフェルナンド・ターヴォラがいたのです。彼は私の先生で，自分の事務所で働くように勧めてくれ，それが私にとって最初の仕事になりました。そこで2年間働いたのではなかったかと思います。最初の建物を設計したのもこの事務所でのことでした。
GA：それは在学中のことなのですか。
シザ：そうです。私は1949年に入学しました。16歳でした。1953年にこの課程の最初の4年間を修了したのです。さっき言いました美術学校です。美術とデザインの一般課程が4年間ありました。それから，1953年に，建築家になるためにはある程度の点を取る必要がある設計競技がいくつかありました。その後，最終試験として，卒業論文を仕上げなければならないのですが，私が卒論を仕上げたのはかなり遅くなってからです。というのは，学校を終える前，1951年には既に働き始めていましたから。卒論は，1954年から57年にかけて設計した，これらの住宅でした。その前に，家族のために小さなプロジェクトをやっています。1951年に働き始め，1953年にはターヴォラと仕事を始めました。2年間ほど働きましたが，そのころ既に，これらの小さな住宅を始めていたのです。
GA：ターヴォラの事務所はどんな所でしたか。
シザ：当時は，空想的な雰囲気がありました。彼はとても若く，私より10歳上だけで，ちょうど仕事を始めたばかりでした。それもあって学生との関係はとても親密で，間を隔てる壁のようなものは何もありません。事務所では，い

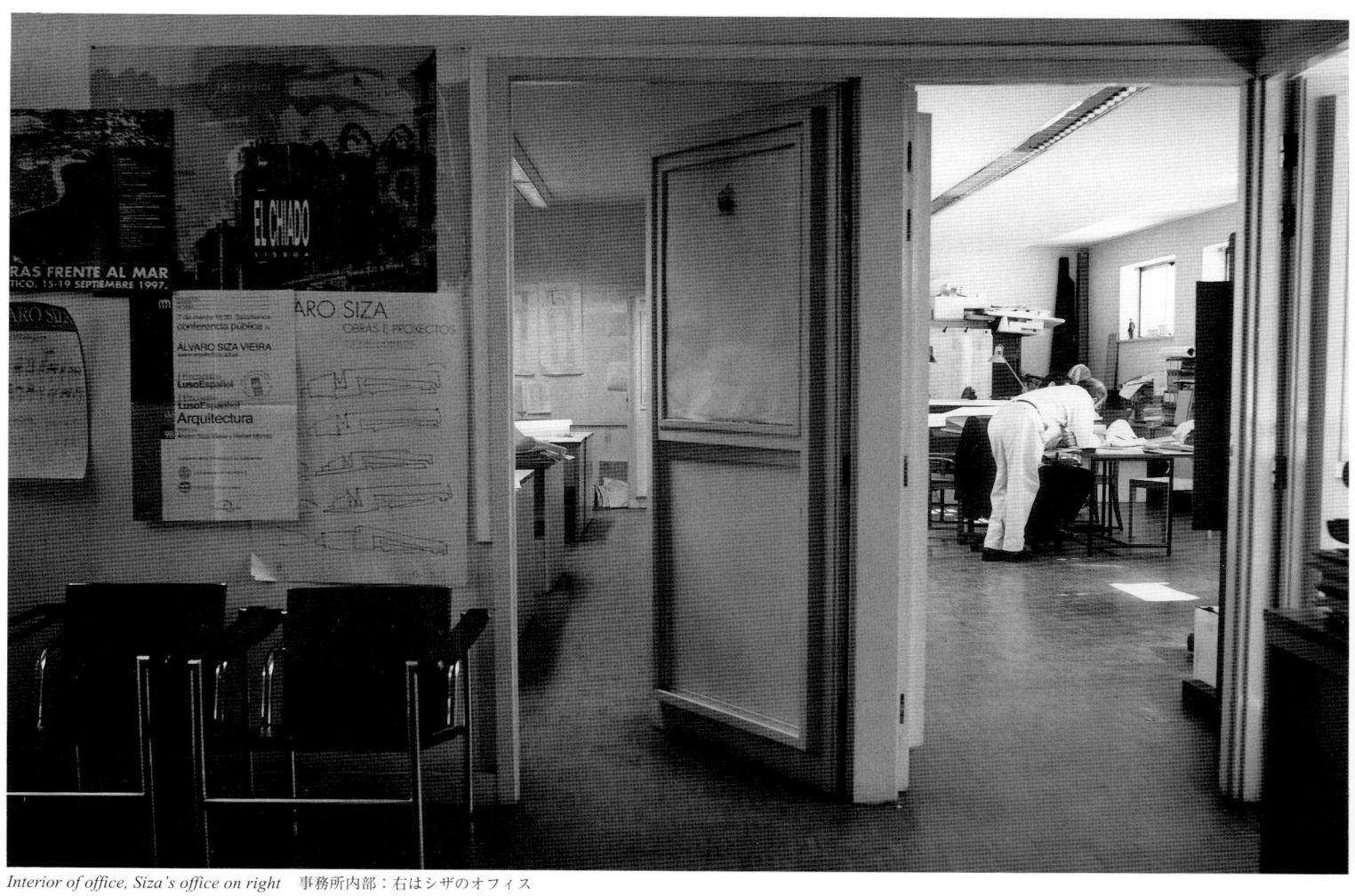

Interior of office, Siza's office on right　事務所内部：右はシザのオフィス

Interior of office　事務所内部

opening of the country. Because after WWII the regime could not remain closed as it was. The model of fascism had fallen. So there was an era of opening and it allowed more information about what was going on in architecture in Europe to enter Portugal. There was more contact and more openness. There were more foreign teachers and political control was less severe. Távora was the Portuguese member of CIAM. So we had direct contact with people like Team Ten. It was a moment of self reflection and autocriticism. We were highly influenced by what was going on in Italy, like Neo-Realism and neo-empiricism. He brought all of these discussions back to the students and to the office. I remember talking to him just coming back from CIAM meetings. For instance, once he came back from France, and told us about the Maison Jaoul. He was extremely excited about it and was describing the project and all of its details. It was a very exciting time for me in school and also outside of school working with him at his office. It was very clear in the way he addressed the projects as an individual architect, but also paid a lot of attention to his collaborators. He was not a dictator in the office. I remember he would listen very patiently to the opinion of his collaborators. And in fact, the first important project I had was through Távora. He was working in Matosinhos, and I was working in his firm. The project was the swimming pool. He helped me to develop it. The work was going very slowly. I think he understood that I was deeply interested and obsessed by this project. And he said, maybe it's better if I develop this project alone. So this was my first project, and he consented that I work alone on this.

GA: Can you tell me who else was a big influence on your development as an architect?

Siza: When I entered the school I knew nothing. I didn't necessarily want to become an architect. And there was no one in my family who studied architecture. My father was interested in art and literature but not especially in architecture. We used to go to Spain as a family during holidays, and I remember he liked very much to go to museums. But I remember the first time I was in Barcelona with my family, I was very impressed with Gaudí. I was not yet in school for architecture, but I decided to see all the buildings by Gaudí. My father was not interested so he would not go, so architecture was not a main interest for him. I was very interested in Gaudí because when I compared the buildings in real life to the photographs of this famous architecture I said this was like sculpture. In fact I think I was more interested in it as sculpture than as architecture. When I arrived and saw it with my own eyes, I saw that this sculpture was actually houses and had all of the elements of a regular houses: doors, windows, baseboards. So this in a way opened the world of architecture up to me. Before I could see the work as sculpture, but now I could see it as architecture.

But still when I entered school I had no information. I remember one of my first contacts with a teacher of architecture, the director, Carlos Ramos. He looked at my work, and he told me, maybe you should buy some books of architecture and see what is going on in architecture because I can see that you have no information. And so I asked my father to buy four or five magazines of architecture. What they sold here at the time was *l'architecture d'aujourd'hui*. I didn't know what was in those first magazines. My father could not help me much. But by chance, one was a monographic issue was on Walter Gropius and another was on Alvar Aalto. Alvar Aalto was not known in Portugal yet. Of course among the teachers the biggest figure was Le Corbusier. And during my first years in school there was a lot of attention paid to Le Corbusier in Brazil. When I saw Alvar Aalto, I was astonished by it. Maybe it was as intense as when I first saw Gaudí. I

くつかの有名なプロジェクトを設計していました。たとえば，私はヴィラ・ダ・フェイラのマーケットを手伝いましたが，これはとても面白い仕事でしたし，また，住宅もいくつかやっていました。

あの頃，ポルトガルではヴァナキュラー建築運動が起こっていました。彼らはヴァナキュラー建築のあらゆる面を研究していましたね。こうした運動が生まれたのには，国が開放されたことにも一因があります。第二次大戦後，政治体制は，以前のように閉ざされたものであるわけにはいかなくなったわけですから。ファシズム体制は崩壊し，開かれた時代になったことにより，ヨーロッパからの情報が以前より多くポルトガルに入ってくるようになりました。外との接触が増し，ずっと開放的になりました。外国人教師が増え，政治的な規制も緩和されたのです。ターヴォラはＣＩＡＭのポルトガル人メンバーでしたから，チーム・テンのような人たちと直接会うことができました。それは，自分でよく考え，自己批判を行う季節とも言うのでしょうか。私たちは，イタリアで進行していたことに，ネオ＝リアリズムや新経験主義に大きく影響されていたのです。ターヴォラはこうした議論のすべてを学校やオフィスに持ち帰り話してくれました。ＣＩＡＭの会議から帰ったばかりの彼と話したときのことを覚えています。たとえば，あるとき，フランスから帰国して，ジャウル邸について話してくれたのです。彼はその住宅にとても感動していて，建物とそのあらゆるディテールについて説明してくれたものです。学校にも，彼のオフィスでの仕事にも，私は夢中になっていましたね。ターヴォラは作品を一人の建築家として表現していることはもちろんでしたが，一方で，協働者に対し非常な神経をつかってもいました。オフィスの独裁者ではなかった。協働者の意見を忍耐強く聞いていました。事実，私の最初の重要なプロジェクトはターヴォラを通してきたものです。彼はマトジニョスで仕事をしていて，私は彼の事務所で働いていた。その仕事というのはスイミングプールでした。仕事の進み具合はとてもゆっくりしていて，彼は，私がこの仕事に打ち込み，とりつかれているのを理解していたのではないかと思います。それで，彼はこう言いました。このプロジェクトは，君一人で進めた方がよいかもしれない。そんなわけで，これが私の最初のプロジェクトになり，彼も私が一人で進めることを認めてくれたのです。

GA：建築家としての成長過程で，大きな影響を受けた方がいらっしゃいますか。

シザ：入学当時は，建築について何も知りませんでした。必ずしも建築家になりたいとは思っていなかったのです。それに，家族や親戚には建築を勉強した人は一人もいません。父は美術や文学に関心がありましたが，建築に対して特にということはなかったのです。休暇にはよく家族でスペインに行きました。父は美術館に行くのが大好きでしたが，家族と初めてバルセロナを訪ねたとき，私にはガウディがとても印象的でした。まだ建築の学校には通っていなかったころでしたが，ガウディの建物を全部見ることに決めました。父は興味を持たなかったので，一緒には行きませんでしたね。つまり，建築は彼にとって主な関心事ではなかったのです。私はガウディに強く惹かれました。この有名な建築の写真と現実の建物を比較したとき，これは彫刻に似ていると思ったからです。事実，私には建築としてよりも彫刻としての関心の方が強かったのです。建物の建っている場所に着いて，自分の目で建物を見たとき，この彫刻には，普通の住宅が備えているあらゆるエレメントが備わり内包されているのだと分かりました。扉，窓，幅木。つまり，ある意味でこのことが私に建築の世界を開いてくれたのです。その前までは，私はこれを彫刻として見ていましたが，このとき，建築として見ることが出来たわけです。

しかし，入学した当座は依然として，何の知識もなかったのです。建築の先生に，学部長のカルロス・ラモスだったのですが，初めて会ったときのことを覚えています。彼は私の作品を

showed my colleagues but nobody like it because it was very different from Le Corbusier. No doubt the building that impressed me the most was his design for the dormitories in Boston, the curved dormitories. Then we had a certain amount of information, mainly through Távora and his connections to CIAM. And also there was this discussion about vernacular architecture. And Távora, very soon began speaking and writing texts about vernacular architecture, and the need for architecture to relate to the country, the culture of the country. He also wrote on the difference between the various cultural and geographical origins. So very soon he was contemporary with the renovation of the main ideas of the modern movement of the time. CIAM was in Holland at the time and there was Team Ten. A little later we began having contact with Spain, mainly Barcelona. So the Portuguese magazine *Arquitectura* was at the time very very interested in supporting the movements of architects in Spain, and some architects in Lisbon. It was a way of contact between architects and also the public. One of the directors of the magazine was Nuno Portas, and he began contact with Spain. And in fact it was an invitation through Portas that I was for the first time invited for a Congress in Barcelona, where the big figures were Bohigas, Correa, Studio Per, and Bofill, and other architects from other regions. There was Moneo from Madrid, some from Seville, Peña from Pais Basco. They met and showed their projects and discussed them and I was from then on invited to this congress. This was also the time when more architects were interchanged at schools and schools were changing rapidly. Today it's good to see that students have this kind of contact with important figures in architecture. This was important for the advancement of culture, even in terms of cultural autonomy so that there is not this feeling of isolation and also shock when the rest of the world is finally exposed to you. I can tell you also that the number of magazines coming to Portugal exploded at the end of the 1950s. We began receiving everything. At the time there was a very good Japanese magazine, although I don't remember the name. It had translations in English. Many many people started to buy this. It was a generation of architects in Japan that owed a lot to Corbusier but also was looking toward tradition. The magazine would not only feature totally modern things but also other things. It was really influential at that time.

It was a strange moment for me because it may be the first time an international critic came to look at my work. He came to Portugal to make a book which was published but unhappily I could not buy it. It was a book about the younger generation. He went to all of the countries and when he visited Portugal he visited the Restaurant Boa Nova which I had just finished. He said this had Japanese influence. I never had thought this. Maybe he thought this because of the scale and dimensions and the woodwork and also some influence of things that were going on at the time. Especially Frank Lloyd Wright, and of course Frank Lloyd Wright was very very influenced by Japan as were a lot of architects at the time. Japanese influenced Western art beginning in the 19th Century and then in architecture too. It was an incredible influence. But in Portugal this influence goes back much further. Back to the 16th century. There was a lot of influence from China or India, as well as Japan.
GA: Let's go back to your first project. Your very first project was a house for your family.
Siza: Yes. These are not published. The first work I ever did was a kitchen for my grandmother.
GA: What was it like?
Siza: If I looked back at it today, I'd say that the main influence was definitely Bauhaus furniture. So it's related I'm sure

Boa Nova Restaurant, 1958–63
ボア・ノヴァ・レストラン
Leça da Palmeira, Portugal

Main level

Upper level: entrance

View from southeast 南東より見る

Entrance エントランス

Approach アプローチ

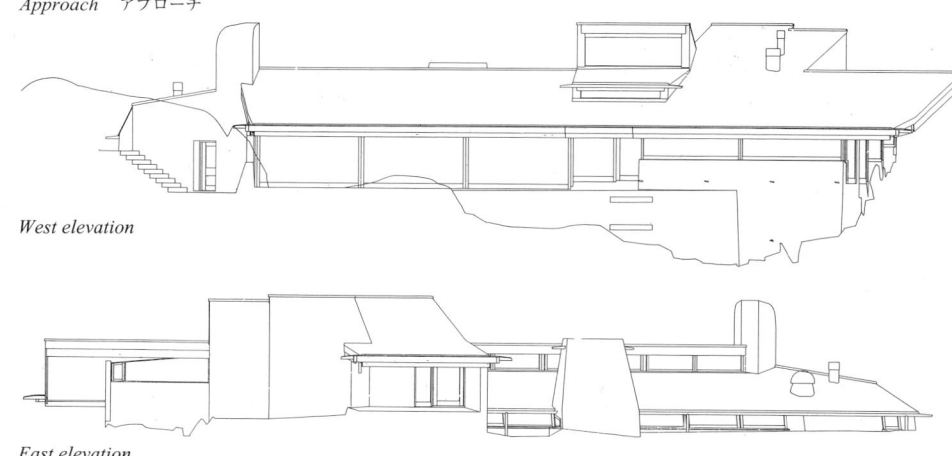

West elevation

East elevation

View of Atlantic Ocean from entrance エントランスより大西洋を見る

East view 東より見る

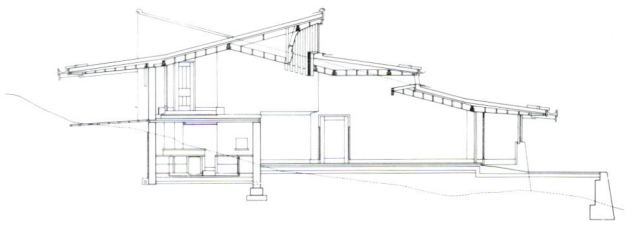
Section: entrance hall

Restaurant レストラン

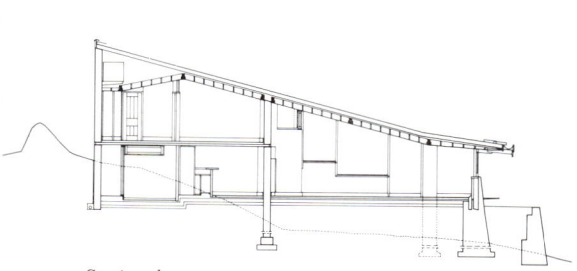
Section: bar

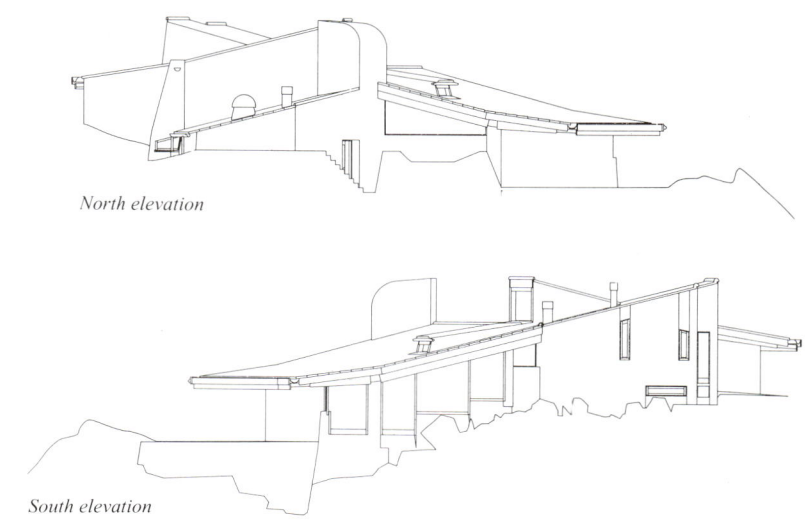
Entrance hall エントランス・ホール

North elevation

South elevation

with what I saw in that magazine on Walter Gropius.

GA: But at the time you had not yet seen the Bauhaus work in person. You knew them just from images.

Siza: That's right. My first trips abroad were to Spain when modern architecture was not really on my mind. Besides it was not yet a heavy influence and it wasn't easy to find. It wasn't my mood at the time. I never went outside of Spain until maybe I went to Paris in around 1960 or 1962. I didn't travel that much at a young age. Then I began going on trips to Paris and other school trips to Venice. Traveling is a very important way to learn and young students today are very fortunate in being able to make these kinds of trips at a young age. You have to see and experience directly because you cannot experience architecture through magazines. There are some fantastic photographs but it is not the same.

GA: So at the time you designed Boa Nova you had never seen a real Aalto building in your life. That's amazing.

Siza: No. I had only seen the magazines. When I made Boa Nova, Aalto had already had a strong influence in Europe and in Portugal in particular, because his architecture related to this new interest in vernacular architecture in Portugal. Alvar Aalto has a strong relationship to the vernacular architecture of his country. He also made a lot of trips to Spain and you can see how important the south of Spain and Africa and Greece was to the architecture of Alvar Aalto. You can see it in his many travel sketches.

So there was a natural connection to his work. There was a connection in terms of the economic and political climate in Finland and Portugal. The yet undeveloped industries of Finland after the war etc. His work exemplified the importance of high craftsmanship of woodwork and other crafts. There are many reasons why Aalto was much admired by architectural circles in Portugal and not only academic reasons. It was important because this modernity of Alvar Aalto was full of themes also. The results of the investigation of vernacular architecture were quickly distorted by many for two main reasons. It was easy to take vernacular forms to make altruistic images. And this relationship with Alvar Aalto, of course, was important to maintain a line which didn't have traditionalism or regionalism as its goal.

GA: Can we talk about the important projects in your development as an architect?

Siza: The Boa Nova restaurant was an important project for me. It was along with the road along the sea. Perhaps I was looking at the work of the restaurant and considered that the solution was too direct a translation with the accidents of landscape. If you look at the profile of the restaurant, it is almost a direct parallel to the profile of the rocks. I made the project about the site. Designing each rock in a way. Or referring directly to the rocks. After I finished I found it too much dependent on the landscape if I can say that. The swimming pool was in the same sort of site but I was after an entirely different kind of relationship with the landscape. It was a more wide open landscape than the rocks at the restaurant. It was more horizontal. The relationship between the building and the landscape is much more essential. The main base of the design is where the concrete walls meet and come against the rocks. So this made the choice of where to put these walls the critical moment of the design. It was an architecture made of the natural world and artificial intervention.

GA: Is this a traditional thing? To put a swimming pool at the shore? Because I saw similar buildings to this in the Canary Islands.

Siza: No. I don't think so. Here the site was interesting because there was already this natural pool created by the rocks. But in some points it was dangerous. Then the municipality decided to use these rocks to

ちょうど完成したばかりの，私が設計したボア・ノヴァ・レストランを見に来ました。これには日本の影響が見られると彼は言っていましたね。私はそんなことは考えたこともなかったのです。たぶん，スケールとディメンション，木部の構成，それに当時進行していたことのいくらかの影響からそう考えたのだと思います。その影響というのは特にフランク・ロイド・ライトですが。そしてもちろん，当時の多くの建築家がそうであったように，ライトも日本から大きな影響を受けていたわけです。日本の西欧美術に対する影響は19世紀に始まり，次に建築にも影響を与えました。信じられないような影響です。しかし，ポルトガルでは，これはさらに以前からのことなのです。16世紀に遡ります。中国やインドと並んで日本からの影響が多くありました。

GA：シザさんの最初の作品に話を戻したいのですが。一番はじめは，ご家族の住宅でしたね。

シザ：そうです。本に掲載されてはいませんが，最初につくったのは，祖母の台所でした。

GA：どんなものだったのですか。

シザ：今，見たら，主要な影響はまさしくバウハウスの家具からだったと説明するでしょうね。つまり，ワルター・グロピウスを特集した雑誌で見たものと関係があるのは確かです。

GA：しかし，当時はまだバウハウスの作品をご自分の目で見てはいなかった。写真からだけ知っていらした。

シザ：その通りです。最初の海外旅行はスペインで，まだ近代建築のことは，実際には心にありませんでした。加うるに，それはまだ強い影響力を持っていませんでしたし，見つけるのも簡単ではなかったのです。当時はまだ私の気持ちのなかに入ってくるものではなく，また，1960年か1962年頃にパリに行くまで，スペインの他に国外に出ることはありませんでした。若い時は旅をあまりしていないのです。そのうちに，パリに行き始め，他にも学校の旅行でヴェニスに行きました。旅は，学ぶのにとても重要な方法です。今の学生は，若い歳でこうした旅行が出来ますから恵まれていますね。実際に見て経験する必要があります。雑誌では建築を経験出来ないのですから。すばらしい写真はありますが，本物と同じではない。

GA：ボア・ノヴァを設計された時はまだ，アアルトの建物を実際には見たことがなかったわけですね。これにはちょっと驚かされます。

シザ：雑誌でしか見ていませんでした。ボア・ノヴァを設計したとき，アアルトはヨーロッパでは既に強い影響力を持ち，彼の建築が，ヴァナキュラー建築に対する新たな関心ともつながるものがあったためポルトガルでは特に影響が大きかったのです。アルヴァ・アアルトは母国のヴァナキュラー建築と強い関係を持っています。スペインにも何度も旅行していますし，スペイン南部，アフリカ，ギリシャがアルヴァ・アアルトの建築にとっていかに重要であったかが分かるはずです。それはアアルトの夥しい数の旅のスケッチのなかに見ることが出来る。

つまり，彼の作品とは自然なつながりがあったのです。フィンランドとポルトガルの政治的経済的状況が似ていたのです。戦後フィンランドのまだ遅れていた工業開発等々。彼の作品は，木工や他の工芸品についての質の高い職人気質の重要性を実証するものです。ポルトガルの建築家サークルのなかで，アアルトが何故非常に賞賛されたかには多くの理由があり，単にアカデミックな理由だけではないのです。アルヴァ・アアルトの近代性には多くの主題が含まれていることからも重要だったのです。ヴァナキュラー建築の研究成果は，主に2つの理由から，多くの人によってまたたくまにゆがめられてしまいました。愛他主義的なイメージをつくるにはヴァナキュラーな形態を使うのが簡単だったこと。そしてもちろん，このアルヴァ・アアルトとの関係が，伝統主義も地方主義も目標としない路線を維持するのには重要だったことからです。

GA：建築家として成長されて行く過程での，主要作品についてうかがいたいのですが。

create an inexpensive swimming pool. And in fact an engineer, a very good engineer, a brother of Távora, began this project. He told the mayor of the town that he needed an architect because the site is very delicate. He chose me to be the architect. What I suggested when they presented the project to me was to create the walls only as the limits of the swimming pool and related them strongly with the rocks. This was my proposal immediately. Then by addition they wanted to make the baths and changing rooms. So the program became more complex. But it all started from this idea of using the rocks to make this inexpensive pool.

It was a very good exercise for me to understand what landscape and topography demanded and I didn't want to make more demands than this that were required for the project. So this work is much more essential in its expression than the Boa Nova restaurant where you find all of these excesses of the first work of a young architect. It was also a very good exercise in that the site was very exigent for architecture. In winter the sea is very strong. So an architecture that was too delicate and not essential enough in itself would have been destroyed. It was a very good exercise for the beginning of my career.
GA: Your career started very early when compared with other architects. Usually an architect might train for years and then make a first project at 30 or so in the earliest course.
Siza: I was very anxious to build. When I made this decision to pursue architecture instead of painting or sculpture, I was more interested in building than in making drawings. So the relation of the project was very much dependent on working on the site. I had this anxiety to build, and I was very lucky to have this relationship with Távora. It was extremely generous of him to let me participate in the work of his office.
GA: My guess is that it wasn't just luck, but that Távora recognized your talent.
Siza: Maybe he saw something in my work. I don't know. But I didn't have a very good record at the school. I would say in fact that I was a little below average in my standing as a student, except in mathematics and history for instance. My projects were not very good. When Távora was my teacher the 4th year was when I received my first good marks in studio. I can understand this because as I told you I had very little exposure to architecture in the beginning and I wasn't very interested in the representation of architecture. The way I represented it was also not the fashion of the times. So my drawings were not agreeable. I was really thinking about the space and the volumes. And I'm sure that they were not very good. But I was making an effort towards the real thing, built work in space. As anyone else who was just beginning I'm sure I was making big mistakes. It's a fact that the schools of architecture did support beautiful drawings. First year students didn't make good drawings. If they already could do this they wouldn't be in school. So I know that Távora saw in my poor drawings something other than the attempt to make beautiful drawings.
GA: Let's go on to your next significant project.
Siza: Of course it's difficult for me to tell what is a significant project or not. For me my work is like one whole project. All of them are important to me. For instance this group of housing by the sea in Caxinas which has completely disappeared was very important. It was a whole group of houses along the sea in a fisherman's village north of Oporto. It was becoming more of a tourist area and tourists are from the interior of Portugal and most of the buildings they were building were interiorized and hidden. At the same time there is the vernacular architecture of the fishermen, which are mostly small houses painted white. This relates to Arab architecture. You can see this type of architecture

シザ：ボア・ノヴァ・レストランは私にとって重要な作品でした。海岸沿いに走る道路に面した場所です。たぶん，レストランの建物について考えていて，この解は，風景の偶発的出来事へと翻訳することに向けようと判断したのです。レストランの輪郭を見ると，岩の輪郭とほとんど直接平行しています。この建物を敷地についてのものとしてつくっている。ある意味で，一つ一つの岩をデザインしています。あるいは直接岩を参照している。完成後，言うなれば，あまりに岩に依存していることを発見しました。スイミングプールも同じ性格の敷地のなかにありますが，風景との全く違った種類の関係を探しています。レストランの岩場よりももっと広く開放的な風景です。もっと水平的な。建物と風景との関係はさらに本質的なものになっています。設計上の主要な基盤はコンクリートの壁が出会い，岩とぶつかるところです。ですから，これらの壁をどこに配置するかの選択が，デザイン・プロセスの決定的な瞬間になりました。これは自然界と人工的な介入からつくられた建築なのです。
GA：海の側にスイミングプールを配置するのは伝統的なことなのですか。カナリア諸島でもこれと同じような施設を見たのですが。
シザ：いやそうは思いません。ここでは，岩のつくった自然のプールが既にありましたから，敷地そのものが面白いものだったのです。しかし，いくつかの点でそれは危険でもあった。そこで市当局はこれらの岩を利用して経済的にスイミングプールをつくることに決めたのです。そんなわけで，ターヴォラの兄弟で非常に優秀なエンジニアがこの計画に着手しました。彼は，敷地がかなり微妙なものなので，建築家の協力が必要だと市長に話したのです。彼は私を建築家に選びました。この計画案を見せられたときの私の提案は，スイミングプールの境界としてのみ壁をつくり，それを岩と強固に関係づけることでした。これが，私が即座に考えた計画でした。次に，それに加えて，バスと更衣室の設置を求めてきました。このため，プログラムは前より複雑なものになりました。しかし，これはすべて，安価なスイミングプールをつくるために岩を利用するというアイディアから出発しています。

これは，風景と地形が要求するものとは何かを理解するのにとても良い練習でしたし，このプロジェクトに求められた要求以上のものをつくりたくはなかったのです。ですからこの作品はその表現の点で，若い建築家の処女作ゆえの過剰が見られるボア・ノヴァ・レストランよりはるかに実質的なものになっています。また，敷地が建築にとって非常に厳しいものであったことも良い訓練になりました。冬の海はとても荒れます。ですから，あまりに繊細で，それ自身が十分に実質的なものでない建物は倒壊してしまうでしょう。私のキャリアの始まりとして，これはとても良い修業だったのです。
GA：他の建築家に比較して，キャリアをかなり早くからスタートされましたね。建築家は何年かの訓練を受けた後，早くて30歳くらいで最初の作品をつくるのが普通です。
シザ：実際に建てることにはとても不安がありました。絵や彫刻の代わりに，建築を追求することに決めたとき，絵を描くことよりも建てることに興味があったのです。つまり，このプロジェクトとの関わりは敷地での作業にかなり依存していたのです。建てることに対する不安がありましたから，ターヴォラとのつながりがあることは幸運でした。彼のオフィスで，この仕事に参加させてくれたのは，とても寛大なことだったと思います。
GA：私の推察では，単なる幸運ではなく，ターヴォラはあなたの才能に気づいていたのだと思います。
シザ：私の作品に，何かを見つけていたのかも知れません。私には分かりません。しかし，学校での成績が特に良いわけではなかったですし，実際，学生としての成績は，数学や歴史などを除いては，平均の少し下でした。私のつくるプロジェクトは特に優れていたわけではあり

Ocean Swimming Pool, 1958–63
レサのスイミングプール
Leça da Palmeira, Portugal

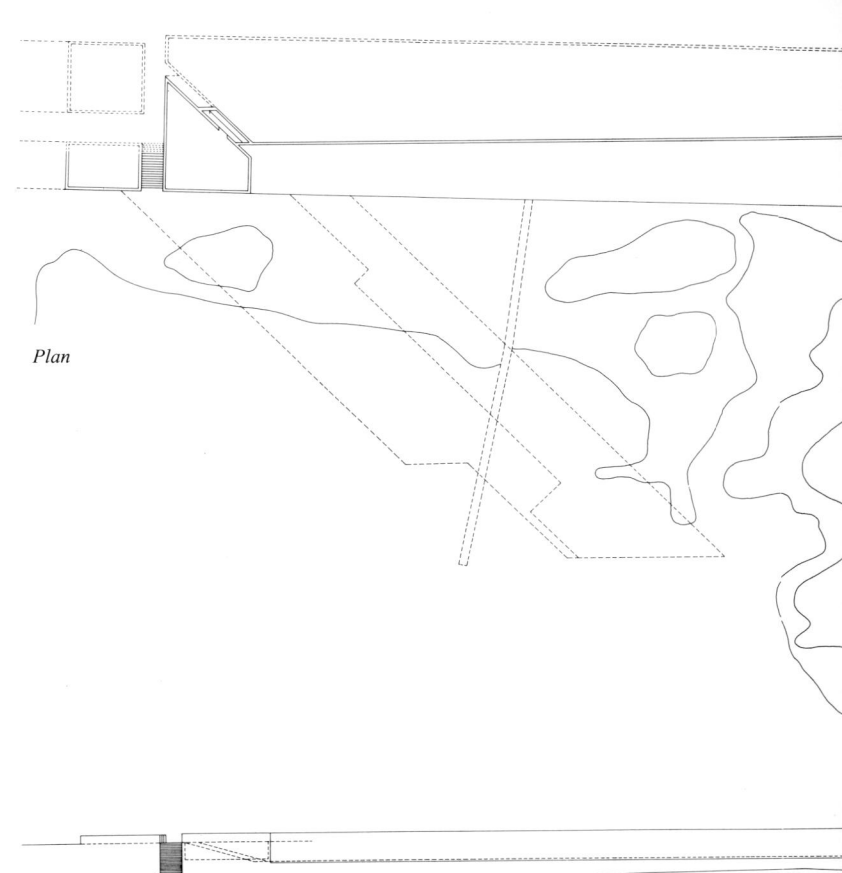

Plan

Elevation

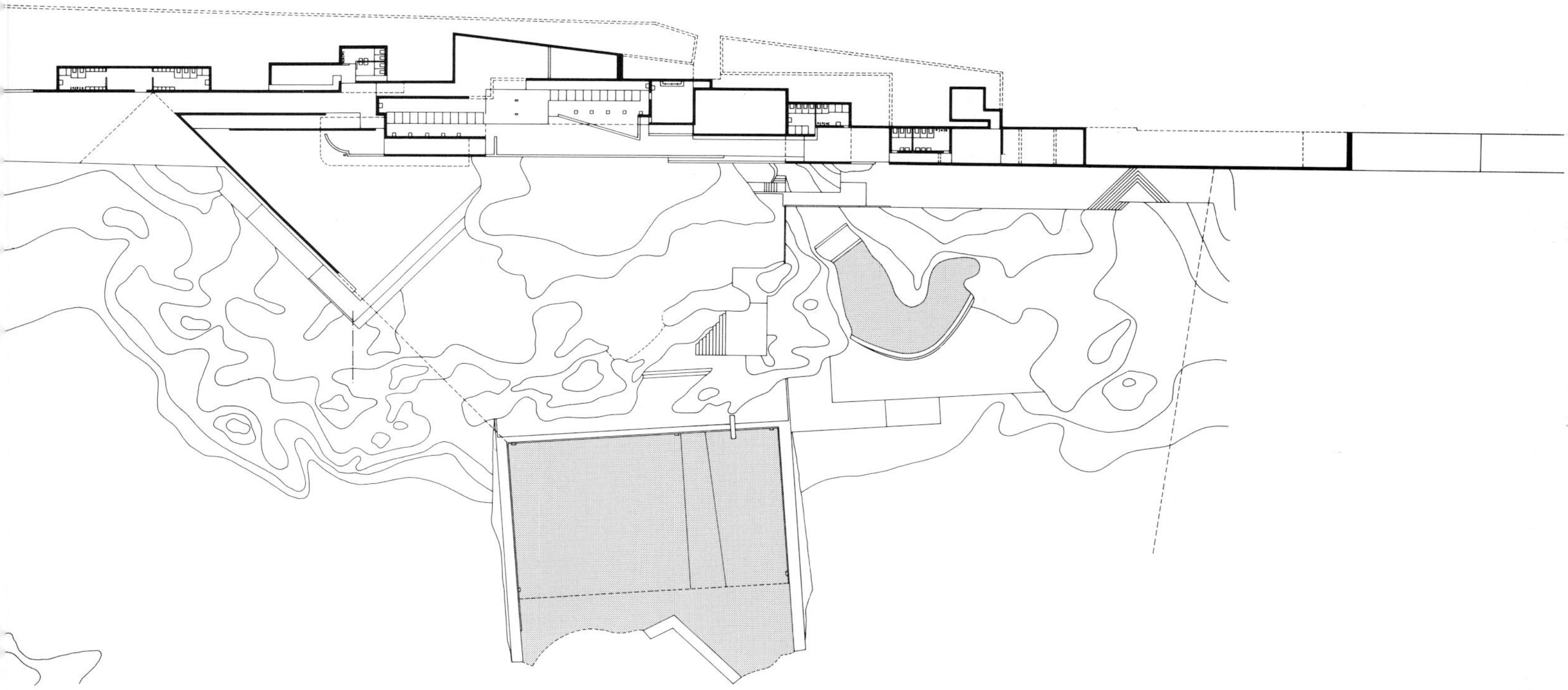

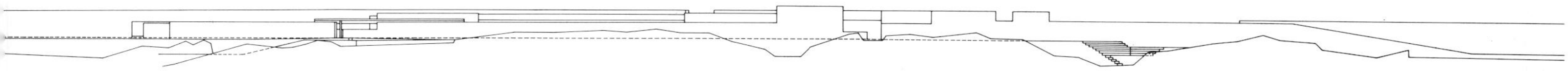

all along the coast of Portugal. But the interior is rather different. So there was a mix of this fisherman's house and the newer housing for tourists from the country who came for the summer or for the holidays. It was the beginning of the appearance in the territory of the north of houses built by immigrants. Very extravagant designs with lots of colors. Very naïve designs, some of which recalled the architecture of Switzerland. But this was a time that was alive and changing. So when I made this project I had been going to Barcelona. It was the time of Venturi and Scott Brown, *Complexity and Contradiction in Architecture* and later *Learning from Las Vegas*. It was within this debate that I tried to explore the social changes that were going on and consider them in the project. In a way it was a failure because it was interrupted after the construction of four or five houses and they were completely changed. The changes were much further than what I wanted to have. I wanted to create a relationship between tradition and innovation. But it was not time to create something like this. It came at a time when architecture could not be assessed immediately but had to be looked at later. But nevertheless it was a good experience.

GA: What happened after that?

Siza: After the revolution there was this strong movement of people mainly in Lisbon. People living in the center of town, the historical center, that were in the process of expulsion. And with revolution there was a time of transformation. And these urban movements were very powerful in terms of their influence in these transformations. The government created a service to support these people when they organized into associations. They began a program that included the process of expropriation, projects and financing for construction. And some groups, namely in Oporto, consisted of professors and students of the school of architecture. Not too many architects were involved because these projects, while extremely stimulating, were very hard and didn't pay well. But it was an extremely exciting time. So we had contact with these people. Many of us wanted to be part of this transformation in a different way. We didn't want to be part of repeating speculative housing, but something new and something related to history and tradition and something that also related to the new ideas in architecture. And so this mixing of idealistic wishes and financial greed and so on was a very exciting moment for architecture in Portugal. I was responsible for one of the teams working in Oporto. We were working on sites around the historical center where they used to be small worker's housing inside the blocks of the town. Lines of small houses. Now we were planning to develop those by connecting two or three or adding something to make them more a part of the town, participating in the town. Actually at recent time these kinds of places were occupied by over half of the populations so in a way they were the real town. So by the 1970s these areas changed dramatically, although they still exist in some places today. But this project was kind of an explosion of these places and human life inside of the blocks. We were trying to remake the tissue that was destroyed by former expropriations to make parking or speculative housing and so on. And we worked a lot during the first phase. We decided to put together a new architecture that had not yet existed. There were many obstacles. We had a difficult but very exciting time. There were bombs in motorcars. Lots of political changes. Inquests and accusations. Collapses of governments and even the public works programs. Then came a long long period of not working in Oporto. This was one of the major reasons why I began working outside of Portugal.

GA: If this had not happened, do you think you would have stayed here to work exclu-

ませんでした。ターヴォラが先生だったとき，4年になって，スタジオで初めて良い点をとったくらいです。このことは納得できます。何故なら，お話ししたように，最初は，建築についてよく知りませんでしたし，建築表現にもあまり関心がなかったのですから。それに私の表現方法は当時の流儀ではなかった。ですから私の図面は受け入れられにくかったともいえます。私は空間とヴォリュームについて真剣に考えていました。うまく行っていなかったことは確かですが。しかし，現実のもの，現実の空間のなかに建つ作品に向けて努力を注いでいました。始めたばかりの人が誰でもそうであるように，私も大きな間違いを犯したことは確かです。事実，学校は美しい図面を奨励していましたし，一年生には良い図面は描けません。もし既にそれが出来ていたら，学校にはいないでしょう。ですから，ターヴォラが私の下手な図面のなかに，美しい図面を描こうというのとは別な何かを見ていたことは分かっています。

GA: 次にくる重要な作品に話を進めましょう。

シザ: もちろん，どれが重要な作品で，どれがそうでないかをお話しするのは，私には難しいことです。私にとって自分の作品は丸ごと一つのようなものです。全部が大切なのです。たとえば，カシーナスの海辺にあったこの一群の住宅はすべて今は存在しませんが，大変重要なものでした。ポルトの北にある漁村の一角で，海沿いに並ぶ住宅の集合体だったのです。ここはだんだんに観光地となって行き，ツーリストはポルトガルの内陸から来て，彼らの建てる建物はほとんどが内向きで，外部からは隠されていました。同時にそこには漁師のヴァナキュラー建築もあり，そのほとんどが，白く塗られた小さな家です。これはアラブ建築とつながっています。このタイプの建築は，ポルトガルの海岸沿いにずっと見られます。しかし内陸部のものはかなり違っている。つまり，漁師の家と夏や休暇を過ごしに来るツーリストのための新しいハウジングが混在していたのです。それは移住者たちによって建てられた北部の住宅がこの領域に出現した始まりでした。たくさんの色を使った過剰なデザインでした。非常に素朴なデザインで，そのいくつかはスイスの民家を想わせます。しかしこれは活発で変わりつつある時代のことです。このプロジェクトを進めていた間に，私はバルセロナに行っていました。ヴェンチューリとスコット・ブラウン──『建築の多様性と対立性』，そしてその後の『ラスヴェガスに学ぶ』の時代だったのです。この論議のなかに，進行中の社会変化を探そうと試み，それらをプロジェクトのなかでよく考えてみました。ある意味でこのプロジェクトは失敗でした。4つか5つの住宅が完成すると中断され，まったく別なものに変更されてしまいましたから。変更は私が思っていたものよりはるかに大幅なものでした。伝統と革新の間の関係をつくりだしたいと思いました。しかし，そのようなものを創造するような時代ではなかった。それは，こうした建築が即座に評価され得ず，その判定には時を待たねばならない時代に登場してしまったのです。にもかかわらず，それは良い経験でした。

GA: その後は，どうなりましたか。

シザ: 革命の後，主にリスボンで，人々の間に大きな運動が生まれました。街の中心部，歴史的中心に住む人たち，排除される過程にあった人たちの間でです。そして革命と共に変革の時代が訪れました。これらの都市運動は，こうした変革のなかにおける影響力という点で非常に力がありました。彼らが共同体として組織されると，政府はこれらの人たちに対する支援機関をつくりました。土地の収用，計画立案，建設資金の用意のプロセスを含むプログラムを始めたのです。そのいくつかのグループは，言い換えればポルトのグループは，建築学部の教授や学生で構成されていました。それほど多くの建築家がこれに参加したわけではありません。これらのプロジェクトは非常に刺激的である一方で，仕事はとても厳しく，支払いも良いわけではなかったからです。しかし，実に胸の踊るような時期でした。ですから，私たちはこうした

sively in Portugal?.
Siza: I think so. Because Oporto's architecture became known for these problems relating to housing. This period of evolution and transformation became a topic of interest for much of Europe, and many architects came here to see the architecture and the events surrounding it. Many of them ignored the design; they came to see the revolution. There were some big hopes about the potential of the changes that could occur here. Hopes and also fears.

There was a big interest in this work. Not only made by me but by some other architects. Also for several architects this work was the beginning of their practices in architecture. I can mention for you for instance that Souto de Moura worked also on this project. Then the second reason I was not contracted after this, was because it was considered politically incorrect. So then I needed to find work, and these works were known. My first invitation came through this theme of participation and a few things that were done in Portugal.

At the same time I began work to stay active in Portugal and I began working with cooperatives. There was still support for associations of inhabitants which formed these cooperatives. I still work with some of these. The work is slow. There are a lot of financial problems and other obstacles.

Then in Berlin I went to work in areas where there were a lot of conflicts and this idea of participation was going on. With Professor Hamer in Kreusberg, where more than half the population was Turkish. And then in Holland I was invited in this participation process in Haia where also 50% of the population were immigrants and there were conflicts and difficulty in the dialogue. Only later was I invited for competitions for other types of programs.

Housing in Schilderswijk Ward, Hague, Netherlands, 1986

During this time I suffered from a label of only working on these types of projects. It was a time when certain architects specialized in museums, or hospitals, which is absurd. The best museums and the best hospitals were not designed by specialists. They were made by designers who loved and were obsessed with architecture. Architecture is not a field of specialization.
GA: The Banco Pinto and Sotto Mayor was another breakthrough project for you. How did you get the commission for this project?
Siza: This was before the revolution when I got this commission for this bank. It was a moment when I and some other architects were invited to make buildings for the prestige of the banks. By that time, I had done some private houses and the swimming pools. The private houses were in north Portugal and they were considered good architecture. But I never got invitations for designing institutional buildings or even housing. It was just houses and nothing more. And then some banks were trying to enhance their prestige and also beginning to organize their collections of art, it was considered a good investment at the time which was around the end of the 1960s and the beginning of the 1970s. They invited some architects that were considered to be of quality, to make the

人たちと近づきになりました。私たちの多くは，この変革を今までとは違った方法で進めたいと思っていました。投機的なハウジングを繰り返すのではなく，何か新しい，歴史や伝統につながるもの，また建築の新しい考え方にもつながる何かに関わりたいと望んでいました。つまり，理想主義と経済的欲得の混合は，ポルトガルの建築にとって非常に面白い時代だったということです。私は，ポルトで仕事をしていたチームの一つの責任者になっていました。私たちの仕事は歴史地区の中心周縁に位置する敷地に対するものでした。ここは街区の内側にある労働者のための小さなハウジングとして使われていました。小さな住宅がつくりあげる幾つもの列。さて，私たちは，これらを，もっと街の一部として取り込まれるように，街に参加するように，二，三を接続したり，何かを加えたりすることによって，開発を進める計画を立てることになりました。実際，当時こういった種類の場所は，人口の半分以上によって占められていましたから，ある意味で現実の街でした。つまり，これらの地域は，70年代に劇的に変化しましたが，今日でもそのいくつかは依然として残っています。このプロジェクトは，これらの場所と，この街区内での生活の一種の爆発でした。駐車場や投機的なハウジングなどをつくるために以前に行われた土地の収用によって破壊された組織

Housing in Schilderswijk Ward

を再構築しようとしたのです。第一期の間，私たちは大いに働きました。まだ存在しない新しい建築を一緒に配置することに決めました。たくさんの障害がありました。困難ではありましたが，非常に刺激的な時間を送ったのです。そして自動車の爆発的普及があり，政治も大きく変わりました。査問や告発。政府が瓦解し，そ

のうちに公共計画さえも中止されました。それからポルトには何も仕事の無い，長い長い時期が来ました。ポルトガルの外で仕事を始めたのは，これが大きな理由でした。
GA：もしそうしたことが起こらなければ，ここに留まり，ポルトガルだけで仕事をされたと思いますか。
シザ：そう思いますね。というのは，ポルトの建築はハウジングに関わる問題のためによく知られるようになっていましたから。この，ポルトガルにおける発展と変貌の時代は，ヨーロッパの多くで関心の的となり，大勢の建築家が建築とそれを巡るイベントを見にここを訪ねてきました。彼らの多くはデザインについては無視していました。革命を見に来たのです。ここで発生した，変革の可能性に対するある大きな希望があったのです。希望と，そしてまた恐れと。

この仕事には大きな関心が寄せられました。私がつくったものばかりでなく，他の建築家によるものに対しても。また，幾人かの建築家にとっては，この仕事は建築実務の端緒にもなったのです。たとえば，ソウト・デ・モウラもこの計画に参加していました。この後，政府と再契約しなかった二つ目の理由は，政治的な正当性が崩れたからです。ということで，仕事を見つける必要があり，ここでの仕事は国外でも知られていたこともあって，最初の招請は，住民

bank buildings. Many architects were critical of this trend, most of them who had not themselves been invited to design public buildings. In the Bank Borges in Vila do Conde, first, I designed one in a place after it was considered not convenient. It was under this enormous 18th century convent. The convent was an enormous presence in the town. The first building for this project you entered under the convent. There was a glass roof and through it you could see the convent and this was the main way to characterize the atmosphere of the bank. A new road made this site inconvenient so they chose another site along the houses of a street in the center of town. Some of the houses dated back to the beginning of the 19th or even late 18th century. There was a market in the garden in front. But in this one I made first the renovation of one of these houses. They asked for a renovation because they didn't want to spend too much money. At the time the government called for an austerity plan. So I made this second project, and later on they changed their mind again. This time they wanted to demolish the old house on the block and build an entirely new building. So finally I designed this project. The problem was to reconciliate the situation along the street of small houses. I wanted a modest architecture but of good quality. There was also

Bouça Housing, Oporto, Portugal, 1977

the problem of the monumental scale of the convent. I tried to make something that related to the scale of the town as a public building but something that was not monumental at all. In the end it was offices, banking offices, and not an institutional building, so I didn't think a monumental scale was appropriate. I wanted to maintain the scale of the street. Here, the dimensions of the windows of the bank were very big in relation to the houses around. So we can establish some relation with the monumental through this contradiction of scale and big plain surfaces which the program allowed. Later I had the opportunity of making the whole square arrangement but then I lost it to another architect. It's not yet made.

GA: I'm curious about how you determined the form of the plan.

Siza: It came from the particular conditions of the site. One was the side passage to the square, and also I had difficulty in putting this volume with windows and openings of a different scale to the buildings next to it. I wanted to cross scales. And then I created this kind of continuity through the arc on the facade. In fact you don't see a block as you normally would, but see instead a continuity between the two elevations. That gives a different scale to the building. At street level it seems a

参加というこのテーマや，ポルトガルでのいくつかの仕事を通して来ました。

同時に，ポルトガルに積極的に留まることも考え，共同組合とも仕事を始めました。これらの共同組合を形成した住民連合への支援も依然としてありました。この関連の仕事もいくつかまだ続けていたのです。この仕事はゆっくりしたものです。資金面やその他の障害など多くの問題があるのです。

そのうちに，ベルリンの，様々な対立があり，この住民参加というアイディアが進行中の地区に仕事に行きました。住民の半分以上がトルコ人という地区で，クラウスベルグのハーメル教授と一緒の仕事でした。次に，オランダで，この住民参加のプロセスが進行しているハイアでの仕事に招かれましたが，ここでもまた住民の半分が移民という場所で，対立や意志疎通の難しさがありました。他のタイプのプログラムを持つコンペに招待されるようになったのは，もっと後になってからです。この時代は，これらのタイプの仕事専門というレッテルに悩まされました。美術館専門，病院専門という具合に一定の建築家が特定されていた時代でした。不合理なことです。最高の美術館，最高の病院は，スペシャリストによって設計されてはいない。建築を愛し，そのとりこになっているデザイナー達によって設計されたものです。建

Pinto & Sotto Mayor Bank, Oliveira de Azemeis, Portugal, 1974

築は専門技術化されるべき分野ではないのです。

GA：ピント・アンド・ソット・マヨール銀行もまた，シザさんにとって，大きな飛躍となった作品でした。この仕事をすることになったきっかけはどういうものだったのですか。

シザ：この銀行の仕事が来たのは革命前です。銀行の威信をかけた建物を設計するために私と他に幾人かの建築家が招待されたのです。その頃，私はいくつかの住宅を建て，スイミングプールを終えたところでした。住宅は北部ポルトガルにあり，建築としての評判も良かったのですが，研究所などの大きな建物はもちろん，ハウジングの設計でさえ依頼は来ませんでした。住宅だけで，それ以上のものではなかった。そのうちに，いくつかの銀行がその威信を高めようと試みたり，美術コレクションを組織化し始めました。60年代の終わりから70年代の始め頃で，そうしたことが，格好の投資と考えられた時代でした。彼らは，銀行の建物をつくるために，才能があると見なした幾人かの建築家を招待したのです。多くの建築家がこうした流れに批判的でした。その多くは公共建築の設計を依頼されなかった人たちです。

ヴィラ・ド・コンデのボルジェス銀行では，ある敷地に設計したのですが，そのあとで，その場所は不便とみなされました。そこは，この巨大な18世紀の修道院の下にあったのです。修道院は圧倒的な存在感がありました。最初の案

very small and modest building. And at the top of the tower it emerges from the immediate tissue and establishes a relationship with the monumental. So it can at the same time fit the scale of the street and in a general view relate to the monumental. That was the intention. I don't know if it is completely successful, but it was at the time very badly received. There was a group who suggested that this building was an insult to the town. This came at a moment when the building was just about finished. Then I received support from some others and it was finally finished. But overall it was not well received until it won the Mies van der Rohe Prize and then the town was proud of it. I was happy they accepted it.

GA: Do you have a different approach to projects outside of Portugal?

Siza: Even if we did not wish to make a different architecture, we have to, because the means of production is different. For example, even today, I have to design all of the details specifically for the work because we don't really have an established system of fabricated components here. We can use prefabricated details for windows for instance if we work with aluminum but if we work with wood or steel we have to design the details specifically.

When I worked in Holland I realized that I had to work with prefabricated elements for different reasons. One is the cost. The other is the responsibility for the quality. Each element furnished for the building will have the certificate for quality from the industry that produced it. If you want to design specifically, you have no protection, you have to take all the responsibility. So the way to work is more to choose the elements to serve our concept. And in fact I wound up making these choices by walking the streets and looking at buildings. We have a big variety of details, so this choice is not constrained. We could use either Dutch or imported parts. At the same time, the regulations, mainly in relations to comfort as it related to the particular climate, were rather different. The climate is much more extreme in the north. So the expression of architecture is very different.

It would not make sense just to transport the architecture of Portugal to the north since it would not be efficient or economical. Nor would it be appropriate for the climate and most importantly it would not be appropriate for the culture. If you work in a new town you must go inside the culture of the town and understand it. You can feel it, and you cannot ignore that. That's extremely stimulating and in a way your personality changes when you are there. I don't like superficial transpositions of design from one site to the other. I think that there is far more valuable potential in the local culture. It's much deeper. In Northern Europe there is a strong exchange of cultures. You know that there are many immigrants from the south that now live in the north. And now there are resorts in both the north and the south. There is this constant exchange. So in architecture it is the same. But this exchange must not be superficial. It must be deep and thoughtful. This is the reason why the towns of open countries are more interesting and stronger. So sometimes I found surprises and sometimes disappointment when working in other countries. Some would ask me why I didn't make those characteristically delicate details when I was in Berlin. Well, the answer is that although the design came from me, it is not just from me. The context in which the building was produced plays a big role in it. I would never go to work somewhere else just to simply put my personal ideas or forms there. Instead I go to work with what that place has within it already and try to extract the best architecture possible from it.

GA: You've done competitions in the United States and of course you've done work in Europe, but you've never had work in Asian countries.

は，修道院の下を入ってくるものです。ガラスの屋根があり，それを通して修道院が見える。そしてこれが，銀行の雰囲気を特徴づける主要な方法になっているのです。ところが，新しい道路によって，この敷地は不便なものとなり，銀行側は，街の中心にある通りに面した住宅に沿った別の敷地を選び直しました。住宅のいくつかは，19世紀初頭，あるいは18世紀末にさえ遡るものです。正面の庭園のなかに市場がありました。しかし，この敷地で，まず最初に私がしたのは，これらの住宅の一つを改造するというものでした。彼らは改造を依頼してきたのです。あまり多額の金を使いたくなかったのですね。当時，政府は質素な計画を推奨していました。そこで，この二番目の案をつくりました。しばらくすると，銀行側は再び考えを変えました。今度は，この区画にある古い住宅を取り壊して，全面的に新しい建物を建てることを望んだのです。そこで，私は最終的にこの案を設計したのです。問題は小さな住宅の並ぶ道路沿いの状況になじませることでした。簡素ではあるけれど，質の高い建築をつくりたかったのです。また修道院のモニュメンタルなスケールという問題もありました。公共建築として街のスケールと結び付くのあるもの，しかしモニュメンタルでは全くないものをつくろうとしたのです。結局，それはオフィス，つまり銀行のオフィスであり，インスティテューショナルな建物ではないわけですから，モニュメンタルなスケールは適切ではないと思いました。通りの持っている尺度を維持したかった。ここでは，銀行の窓のディメンションは，周囲の住宅に比べて非常に大きくなっています。つまり，プログラムが認めている大きな面とスケールとの矛盾を通してモニュメンタル性とある程度の関係をつくりあげることが出来るのです。その後，広場全体の配置構成をする機会がありましたが，その仕事は他の建築家の手に移ってしまいました。それはまだつくられていません。

GA：平面形をどのように決めて行かれるかに興味があるのですが。

シザ：敷地固有の条件から出て来るのです。一つは広場へ出る側面の通路でした。また，このヴォリュームに，隣接する建物と異なったスケールで窓や開口をとる難しさがありました。スケールの交差が欲しかったのです。次に，ファサードの弧を通してこの種の連続性をつくりだしました。事実，普通はそうであるように単一のブロックを見いだすことはありません。その代わりに二つの立面の間の連続性を見ることになります。それが建物に異なったスケールを与えている。道路レベルでは，非常に小さく簡素な建物に見えます。そしてタワーの頂部では，すぐ側の都市ファブリックから立ち上がり，モニュメンタルな関係性を確立する。つまり，それは，道路のスケールと，そして全体的な視点ではモニュメンタルなものに，同時に関係性を持つことが出来るのです。それこそが狙いでした。それが完全に成功しているかどうかは分かりませんが，当時は非常に評判が悪かった。この建物は町への侮辱であると示唆するグループがいました。建物が完成しようとしていたその時にこうした意見が出てきたのです。私を支持してくれる人も他に出てきて，なんとか建物は完成しました。しかし，この建物がミース・ファン・デル・ローエ財団の賞をとるまで，その評判は全般的に良くなかったのです。賞を取ると，町はこの建物を誇りに思うようになりました。彼らがそれを受け入れてくれて，私はうれしかったですね。

GA：ポルトガル国外のプロジェクトに対して，別のアプローチを取りますか。

シザ：違う建築をつくりたいと望まなかったとしても，そうしなければならないでしょう。生産の方法が違いますから。たとえば，今でも私は，一つの仕事ごとにすべてのディテールをデザインしなければならないのです。ここでは，部材生産の確立したシステムは現実に存在しないからです。たとえば，アルミであれば，窓のディテールにプレファブ部材を使えますが，木やスティールを使おうとしたら，ディテールを

Siza: I made plans for Macao, but no, I've never been invited to Asia. I recently had an invitation to India, in Goa, but I couldn't go because at the time I was too busy. It was a pity. I think Távora was doing this particular competition and that would have been interesting to participate in the same competition.

In Macao I made some plans for a new area next to the sea but they were never executed. As much as I know, the grid that I proposed was executed but not the block types or regulations. For instance the buildings became much higher than what I proposed. I think it was too ambitious in terms of scale. Hong Kong has completely different geographic and topographic conditions. You can make 30 floors in Hong Kong and it's nothing because of the scale of the city as a whole. Macao is much more delicate, so the plans I made for the new area, in my opinion, were more appropriate for the scale of the local topography. The concept was to create big platforms next to the sea, like islands, that would be related to the peninsula by bridges. I wanted to preserve the delicate line of the coast of Macao. There was this dialogue with new and old areas. We worked with Dutch specialists on the creation of the channels which helped to solve some water problems. There were also teams for traffic studies. It was an interesting project. But in the end they did not totally support our proposal. All the restrictions were slackened and buildings got higher and higher, pressured by speculation.

GA: Do you think you will ever accept work in Asia?

Siza: If I had the opportunity.

GA: I was thinking maybe you weren't interested in Asia.

Siza: That's not the case at all. It would be very interesting I'm sure. But only with the provision that I'm invited and that I have the time. Sometimes we are very busy here. We never have that much work because that's not my way of working, but sometimes it is very urgent in the office. This is a problem of our times, that things must be done on such tight schedules, and I think this is one of the reasons why there is such a poverty in architecture today.

GA: But some people have chosen to make large offices with associates and corporate structures. You aren't that kind of person. Could you tell me a little about the structure of your office?

Siza: That depends a lot on where your base is. In some countries, say England or Japan, there is a strong connection between industry, the production of elements, and the design. In Portugal, mainly by reasons of the state of development and the state of the economy, this is not the case. It's not easy to work like that. We are in an intermediate point where we still make most of the construction in the old way. And then still exists a contact and relationship with the hands that put up the buildings and those that design them. An architect can have more contact with the workers themselves. But this is changing today. It's not as easy to find good artisans as it was years ago. Industrialism is beginning and the import of elements is rising as Europe has transformed a lot in recent times. So we find ourselves in a kind of transitional stage. Also planning is not very rigid here, and the amount of work available for us to do can rise and fall very quickly. It is difficult to maintain a large office in this case.

GA: I'm thinking more in terms of the personal and artistic nature of our work. Maybe besides the political and economic reasons you are giving there is an essential quality in your work that doesn't translate well into a traditional office structure. But nevertheless you do have people here in your office and several projects currently underway. How do you delegate responsibility in your office.

Siza: Of course there is a sense that there is single person responsible for the concept in the end. But that doesn't mean that

特別にデザインする必要があります。

オランダで仕事をしたときに，様々な理由からプレファブ部材を使わなければならないことに気づきました。一つはコストです。もう一つは質に対する責任です。建物に組み込まれるそれぞれのエレメントは，それを生産する産業からの品質保証書がつくことになるでしょう。特別なデザインが欲しければ，保証はなく，すべての責任を自分で持たなければならない。つまり，仕事の方法は，われわれのコンセプトに活用するためのエレメントの選択に比重がかかる。事実，通りを歩いていて，建物を見て，これらの選択をしたことに心が痛むことがあります。もっとも，非常に多彩なディテールがありますので，この選択は窮屈なものではありません。オランダ製でも輸入物でもどちらも使うことが出来ました。同時に，固有の気候と結びついた快適性と主に関わる条例がかなり異なっていました。北部では気候ははるかに厳しい。それで，建築表現もかなり違ってきます。

ポルトガルの建築を北にただ持ってくることは意味がありません。有効でも経済的でもないからです。気候にも適切でないばかりでなく，最も重要な点は，文化に適合しないだろうということです。新しい街で仕事をするとすれば，その内に入って，その固有文化を理解する必要があります。それを感じることが出来ますし，それを無視することは出来ません。このことは実に刺激的ですし，ある意味で，そこにいる時は，その人のパーソナリティも変わってしまう。ある敷地から別な敷地へ表面的にデザインを転置することは好きではないのです。地方文化には，それより遙かに価値のある潜在的可能性が存在すると思います。もっと深いものです。

北ヨーロッパには，激しい文化の交流があります。南部からの大勢の移民が，今，北部に住んでいます。そして今や，北にも南にも多くのリゾートがある。こうした絶え間ない交流があります。建築の世界においても同じことがいえます。しかし，この交換は表面的なものであってはならない。深く，熟慮されたものでなければならない。これが，開かれた国の街が，そうではないところの街より興味深く，力強い理由なのです。ですから，他国で仕事をすると，時に驚きを発見し，時に失望に直面することになります。ベルリンでは，なぜこうした特徴のある繊細なディテールをつくらなかったのかと，ある人は尋ねるかもしれない。答えは，デザインは私から生まれたものですが，私からだけではないということです。建物が産み出される場のコンテクストがそのなかで大きな役割を演じている。個人的なアイディアや形態をただ置いてくるためだけにどこかある場所に出かけることは決してしないでしょう。そうではなく，その場所が既に内包しているものによって仕事を進め，そこから可能性のある最善の建築を引き出すようにしています。

GA：シザさんは，アメリカのコンペに参加したり，もちろんヨーロッパでも仕事をされているわけですが，アジア諸国での仕事はまだありませんね。

シザ：マカオの計画をつくったことがありますが，アジアの国から招聘されたことはないですね。最近，インドのゴアへ招かれたのですが，その時は忙しくて行けませんでした。残念でした。ターヴォラはこの特異な性格を持つコンペの仕事をしたと思いますが，同じコンペに参加したら楽しかったでしょうね。

マカオでは，海側の新開発地区にいくつかの計画案をつくりましたが，実施されませんでした。知っている限りでは，私の提案したグリッドは実施されましたが，ブロック・タイプ，つまり街区構成は実現しなかった。たとえば，建物の高さは私の提案したものよりずっと高くなりました。私の考えでは，それはスケールの点で野心的に過ぎると思うのです。香港はマカオとはまったく異なった地理的，地形的条件を持っています。香港では30階建てをつくることが出来ますし，高さは問題ではない。全体としての都市のスケールであるからです。マカオはもっと繊細なので，新しい地区に対する私の案は，

Meteorological Center, Barcelona, Spain, 1992

自分としては，この地方の地形的スケールには合っていると思います。コンセプトは海に隣合って，大きなプラットフォーム——島のようで，橋で半島と結びつけられることになります——をつくるというものでした。マカオの繊細な海岸線を保存したいと思いました。新しいエリアと古いエリアの間にこのような対話があります。いくつかの水の問題を解決する助けとして，運河をつくるために，オランダの専門家と一緒に仕事をしました。交通問題を研究するチームもありました。面白いプロジェクトだったのです。しかし，結局，彼らはわれわれの提案を全面的には支持しませんでした。すべての規制がゆるめられ，投機の圧力で，建物の高さはどんどん高くなって行きました。

GA：将来，アジアでの仕事を引き受けられることがあると思いますか。

シザ：機会があればですね。

GA：アジアには関心をお持ちでないかもしれないと考えていたのです。

シザ：そのようなことは全くありません。非常に興味深いだろうと確信しています。ただし，招請され，そのときに私に時間があればですが。ここでは，時々，とても忙しいのです。私たちの事務所ではたくさんの仕事をかかえることはありません。それは私の流儀ではないからです。しかし，時に，非常に急を要することもありま

す。これはわれわれの生きている時代の問題であり，つまり，このようにタイトなスケジュールで仕事をしなければならないということですが。今日の建築がかくも貧しいものである一つの理由がそれだと私は思っています。

GA：しかし，ある人たちは，アソシエイツや共同組織を持つ大事務所をつくることを選んでいます。シザさんはそうしたタイプの人ではありませんね。あなたの事務所の在り方について少しうかがいたいのですが。

シザ：それは，大きくは仕事の基盤がどこにあるかによります。ある国々では，たとえば，イギリスや日本には，産業，部材の生産，デザインの間に強力な連携があります。ポルトガルでは，主に，発展状況や経済状況の理由からこうしたものは存在しません。それが存在している場合のように仕事を進めるのは簡単ではありません。われわれは，工事の大半を依然として昔ながらの方法で進めるということとの中間点にいるのです。そして，建物を建て上げ，デザインする，手との接触と関係がまだ存在しています。建築家は現場で働く人と多く接することが出来る。しかし，これも今，変わってきています。数年前から，腕の良い職人を見つけることは簡単ではなくなっています。産業主義が始まっていて，ヨーロッパの最近の変貌に従って，輸入部材が増えている。つまり，われわれは一

種の転換点に立っているのです。また，この国では計画の策定は特に厳密というわけではなく，われわれに可能な仕事の増減は急に変動します。こうしたなかでは大事務所を維持するのは難しい。

GA：仕事が持つ，パーソナルで個人的な性格面について考えているのですが。あなたのおっしゃる政治的経済的理由に加えて，伝統的なオフィス構造にはうまく翻訳しえない本質的な性質があなたの作品にはあるかもしれません。しかし，にもかかわらず，あなたのこのオフィスにはある数の人がいて，複数のプロジェクトが進行中です。オフィスでの責任をどのように委任されているのですか。

シザ：もちろん，一人の人間が，最終的なコンセプトに責任があるという感覚はあります。しかし，これは，オフィスでの展開に他の人間が関わってはいけないということを意味しない。一人の人間が，他の協力者全員の調整に対して責任を持つべきだと私は思います。ハイテクビルの素晴らしいコンプレックスでさえ，委員会によって全体が出来得るとは思いません。多くの専門家やデザイナーが協力していることは確かですが，最終的には，全体プロセスを見，プロセスをリードする一人の人間がいるのが普通です。チームによる仕事の仕方は違うかもしれませんが，私の意見では最終的には同じことだ

there can't be other people involved in the development of an office. I think that one person has to be responsible for the coordination of all the other contributors. I think that even a wonderful complex high-tech building cannot be made entirely by committee. To be sure there are many specialists and designers involved, but in the end there is usually one person who sees the whole process and guides the process. The way a team works can be different, but in the end it is the same thing in my opinion. Of course my interest in architecture is as an art. And all of the utility of architecture is the nature of architecture, but the objective of the completed process comes back to art. Every building must have a function, must be strong, must be comfortable, but these are not things to discuss. It is unthinkable to pretend that a building can be beautiful and not functional. That's a perverse idea. It cannot be. The process of creating architecture is based on utility, functional problems, technical problems, giving a solution to programmatic problems, but in the end architecture must be free from those things. Technical quality and aesthetic quality are not necessarily opposites. In architecture they are complimentary.

GA: Now you are one of the most important figures in the architectural world, do you have any thoughts on the work of your peers?

Siza: Well, first of all I don't consider myself important. There are a lot of people today making important contributions to architecture. Sometimes they seem to be on opposite sides. But all of them are answers to special circumstances. There is no such thing as a universal answer to a problem. When I say, I don't consider myself important in the world of architecture, it's because I don't see people important in that way. Instead I see a lot of contributions that are important. We have many avenues today and they are all worth something.

And the apparently more opposite ideas to the traditional concepts in the end are the most influential because they challenge old ideas and make you think. We are forced to test our own ideas and concepts. Criticism is a central tool for architects.

Also you see that the most distant contributions are strong and important. We spoke before about Japan's influence on the students when I was in school. We can speak of African influence on European and Western arts at the beginning of the century. You can see how important it was for Le Corbusier to work in India, or Louis Kahn and how this was a benefit for Western architecture. I'm interested in the work of other architects in this way. I'm interested in seeing what they produce in different conditions, and different contexts.

GA: You mention Louis Kahn. When you were a student who else were you looking at?

Siza: Kahn's biggest contributions didn't come at the time I was student. It was almost two generations later. Those in school about ten years after me were very much influenced by Kahn and his buildings. My exposure to Kahn came when I visited some of his projects later, or else what was shown in the media. It was new way for Western architecture. In Portugal the big influence of oriental art was in the 16th and 17th century. As we had during some time very little information even from Europe in the school of architecture in respect to Asia. It really began again in the 1960s through magazines with the work of some architects influenced by Le Corbusier. And some strange things are not that strange in this light. There was a new interest in ceramics during this time. In the 1950s almost no one used this, it was not a modern material. But Le Corbusier used it in the Ministry of Education building in Brazil. In Portugal ceramics were almost no more used, but it came back through the use of Corbusier. There was the rediscovery of ceramics.

と思います。もちろん，私の関心は芸術としての建築にあります。建築の実用性すべてが建築の性格であるわけですが，全プロセスの目的は芸術に立ち返ります。建物はすべて，機能を持ち，頑丈で，居心地よくなければなりませんが，こうしたことは議論の対象ではない。建物は美しくあるべきで，機能的ではないと主張することなど考えられない。そんなものはひねくれた考えです。そうであるべきではない。建築を創造するプロセスは，実用性，機能的問題，技術的問題，プログラム上の問題に解決を与えることに基づいていますが，最終的には，建築はこうしたことから自由にならなければならない。技術的質と美的質は必ずしも対立しません。建築においては，それらは補足関係にあります。

GA：今や，シザさんは，世界の建築界で最も重要な建築家の一人です。同じような立場にある建築家の作品については，どのようにお考えですか。

シザ：まず，お断りしたいのは，私は自分を重要な存在だとは思っていないということです。多くの人たちが，現在，建築に重要な貢献をなす仕事をしています。時々，私とは正反対の側にいるように見えるものもあります。しかし，そのすべては，それぞれの状況に対して答えているわけですから，ある問題に対する普遍的な答えというものはありません。建築の世界のなかで，自分が重要な存在ではないというとき，私はそういうことで人を重要だとみてはいないということなのです。そうではなく，重要である多くの貢献をみているのです。今，私たちには多くの道があるのであり，それらはすべて，何らかの価値を持っています。

そして明らかに，伝統的なコンセプトに対するより対立的なアイディアが最終的には最も影響力を持つのだと思います。なぜなら，それらは古い考えに挑戦し，われわれを考えさせてくれるからです。自分自身の考えやコンセプトを試すことを強いられるのです。批評は建築家にとって中心的な道具です。

また，自分とは最もかけ離れた場における貢献こそが強く，重要なのです。学校時代の，学生に及ぼした日本の影響について前にお話ししましたが，今世紀はじめにおけるヨーロッパに対するアフリカの影響について指摘することも出来ます。ル・コルビュジエやルイス・カーンにとってインドでの仕事がどれだけ重要であったか，そしてこれが，西欧建築にいかに恩恵を与えたかはうかがい知ることが出来ます。こうした点において，私は他の建築家の作品に関心を持っています。異なった状況，異なったコンテクストのなかで何をつくりだしたかを見ることに興味があるのです。

GA：ルイス・カーンをあげられましたが，学生時代，他に注目された建築はありましたか。

シザ：カーンの最大の貢献になったものは，学生時代には実現していませんでした。ほとんど，二世代後に生まれたものです。私の卒業後，10年くらいして学生はカーンとその建物に強い影響を受けたのです。私がカーンの作品に接したのは，後にその建物のいくつかを実際に訪れたとき，あるいはまた，メディアを通して目にしたときでした。それは新しい西欧建築の在り方を示していました。ポルトガルでは16世紀，17世紀に東洋芸術の影響を強く受けています。学校では，アジアについても，ヨーロッパについてさえ，情報が非常に少なかった時期があるのです。実際，情報の流入は，1960年代に，ル・コルビュジエに影響された建築家の幾人かの作品を掲載した雑誌を通して再び始まったのです。いくつかの奇妙なことも，この光のもとではそれほど奇妙ではないのです。この時期に，セラミックに対する新たな関心が起こりました。1950年代はほとんど誰もセラミックを使うことはありませんでした。それは近代的な材料ではなかったのです。しかし，ル・コルビュジエはこの材料をブラジルの教育省の建物に使いました。ポルトガルでは，セラミックは，もはやほとんど使われていなかったのですが，ル・コルビュジエが使ったことによって，復活したのです。セラミックの再発見でした。

Teachers' Training College, Setúbal, Portugal, 1993

WORKS

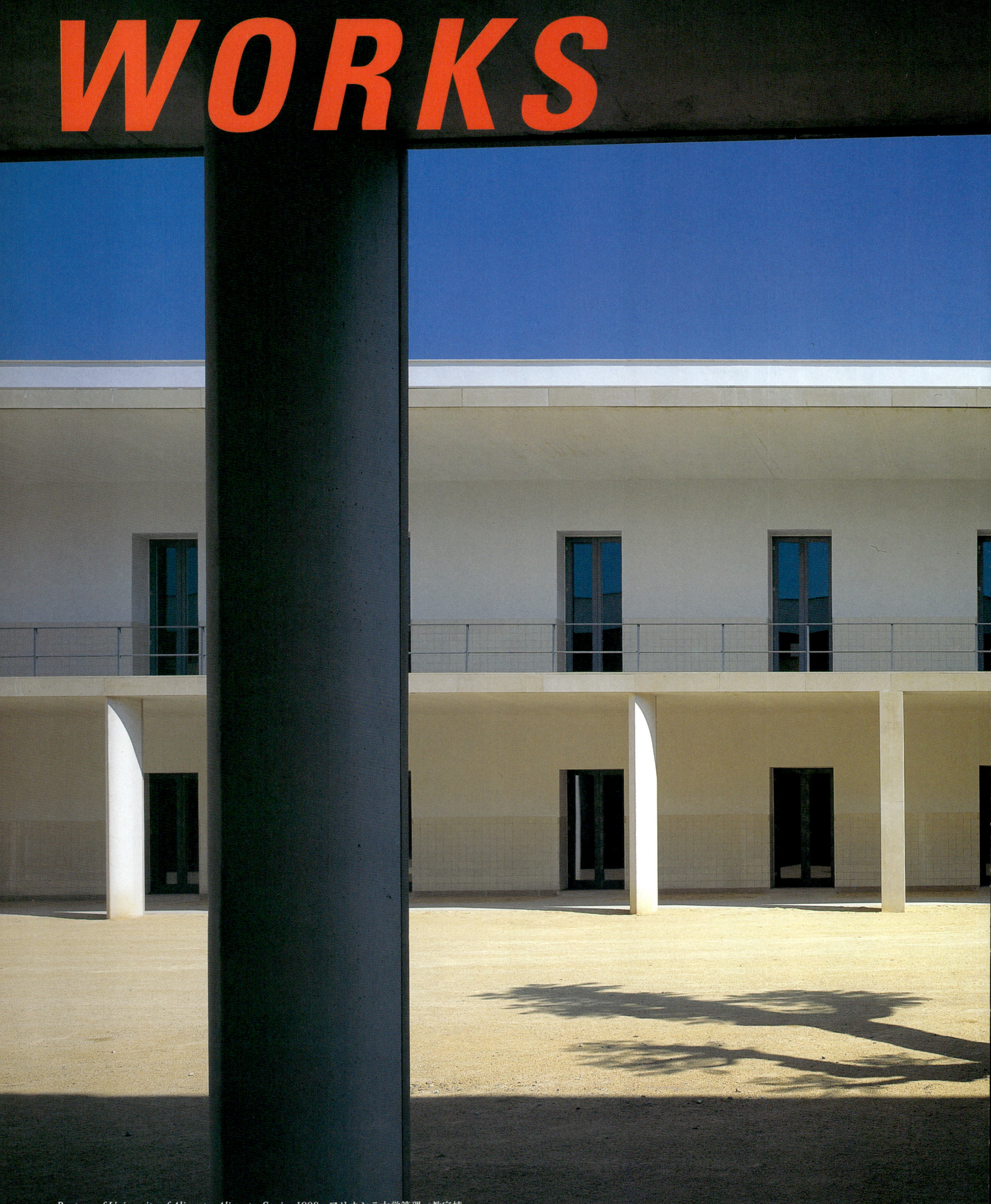

Rectory of University of Alicante, Alicante, Spain, 1998 アリカンテ大学管理／教室棟

Santa Maria Church of Marco de Canavezes
マルコ・ドゥ・カナヴェーゼスの教会

Marco de Canavezes, Portugal

Client: Paróquia de fornos Design period: 1990–93 Construction period: 1994–96
Architects: Álvaro Siza Arquitecto, Lda—Edite Rosa, principal-in-charge Project team: Miguel Nery, Tiago Falcão, Rui Castro, Paul Scott, Joana Caneiro Structural engineer: G.O.P. Mechanical engineer: G.E.T. General contractor: Empreiteros Casais Structural system: reinforced concrete structure

GA: Is this your first church design?

Álvaro Siza: Actually, I had done another project before but it was never executed. The project was not well received by the priests so it was stopped. I don't know if someday it will start again. The priest was obsessed by the symbolic elements and this always related with tradition and old models or else futurist interpretations. He wanted a very traditional approach to church architecture, loaded with clichés, that I could not accept. I had some of the same problems with this church. But the priest in this case was a very different person. He was young priest and a man of culture. He didn't have immovable preconceptions. I didn't know him. But he knew of me through some friends who were familiar with architecture. He had visited some of my works and then invited me after convincing the hierarchy to accept me. He worked with a lot of enthusiasm. Of course the construction and completion of the church owes much to this man. A good client like this is always absolutely critical for the creation of good architecture. Of course, there were difficulties nevertheless. I wanted to make a church that felt like a church and not a building with a cross in it. I wasn't interested in this primitive notion of how a symbol could determine the character of a building. It was too superficial approach and wouldn't work for me. So I tried to achieve something I could call the character of the church without adding symbols to be read. This is particularly difficult today. The liturgy has been changed a lot by the Vatican. I can give you a simple example, in early times the priest did not face the celebrants. The celebrants looked at his back. This explains the generous space of the apse that was in turn always projected onto the exterior of the building. Of course this apse is part of the character we associate with the church. But as the priest turned to the assembly, the space behind him no longer has a logic. It doesn't seem to have a purpose. That made the traditional model obsolete. In fact we see this reflected in the tendency for spaces that more or less resemble auditoriums. This was more democratic. Research on the architecture of the church has never clarified the relationship between the celebration and the space. You could say that the history of architecture can be studied through church buildings. So this is a large burden for anyone who is to design a church. In this case, my work passed through much debate and dialogue with theologians and the priest himself. I went again to church to sit through mass and see the new programmatic requirements of a contemporary ceremony and celebration. I asked a lot of questions and created many sketch propos-

GA：これは，最初に設計された教会ですか。

アルヴァロ・シザ：実は，この前に別な教会を設計しているのですが，それは実現しませんでした。その案は司祭の受けが悪く，中止になったのです。いつか再開されることがあるかどうかは解りません。司祭は象徴的なエレメントに取りつかれていて，こうしたものは常に伝統や古いモデルや，未来派の解釈などに関係しているものです。彼は教会建築に対して非常に伝統的なアプローチを求めていました。紋切り型を積み込んだようなものです。これは私には受け入れられませんでした。今度の教会でも同じような問題にいくつかぶつかりましたが，こちらの方の司祭はまったく違ったタイプの人でした。歳若い司祭で，文化人。かたくなな先入観は持っていません。私は彼を知りませんでしたが，彼の方では，建築に詳しい幾人かの友人を通して，私のことを知っていました。私の作品のいくつかを実際に見て，それから，私を受け入れることを大司祭に説得した後，依頼してきたのです。彼は非常な熱意をもって仕事に携わってくれました。もちろん，この教会が完成にこぎつけるには，多くをこの人に負っています。このような良きクライアントは，優れた建築の創造には常に絶対的に重要です。もちろん，にもかかわらず難しい問題はありました。私がつくりたかったのは，教会のように感じられる教会であり，そのなかに十字架のある建物ではなかったからです。象徴が建物の性格をいかに決定することが出来るかといった，プリミティヴな考えには興味がありませんでした。それはあまりに表面的なアプローチで，私には合いません。そこで，判読可能な象徴を付加せずに，教会という性格を喚起することのできる何かをつくりあげようとしたのです。今の時代，これはかなり難しいことです。典礼がヴァチカンによって大きく変えられてきていますから。簡単な例をあげると，初期には，司祭は参列者に向き合っていなかったのです。参列者は司祭の背中を見ていました。これが，常に建物の外へ順に張り出して行くことになった後陣の広い空間を説明しています。もちろん，この後陣はわれわれが教会を連想する際の性格の一部です。しかし，司祭が会衆の方を向くに従って，司祭の後方に広がる空間はもはや必然性を持たなくなりました。目的があるようにはみえないのです。それが，伝統的規範を時代遅れのものにしています。事実，多かれ少なかれ似たところのあるオーディトリアムの空間に，この傾向が反映されています。もちろんオーディトリアムはもっと民主的な性格のものではありますが。教会建築に対する研究は，儀式と空間の関係を明確にしてくれたことはないのです。建築史は，教会の建物を通して学ぶことが出来るともいえます。宗教儀式に関わる問題は教会を設計する誰にとっても重荷なのです。この建物では，私の設計案は，神学者や司祭との多くの論争や対話を通過してきました。再び教会に行き，ミサの間，座って，現代の典礼や礼拝式の新しいプログラムが要求するものを観察してきました。たくさんの質問をし，現代的精神に基づく典礼式のための新しい形態を見つけようと数多くのスケッチ・プロポーザルをつくりました。それについて議論を交わした神学者たちとは完全な同意には至りませんでした。この問題は，ある意味で，特殊な種類の研究といえるものです。実に興味深いものだったですね。

次に，実に陳腐な問題がありました。たとえば，十字架をデザインする難しさが解りますか。今までにつくられた何万もの十字架があります。この問題にはまったく新鮮味がありません。私は新しい宗教的シンボルを創造することには興味がないのです。伝統の重荷は非常なものです。そして改めて反復してみても滅多に成功しません。宗教美術の現代作品を集めた展覧会へ行けば，このことがよく解ります。感動するようなものは皆無です。何も心に触れてこない。それは非常に難しいことなのです。現代建築のなかで，優れた十字架のデザインを考えてみようとすると，浮かんでくるのは，ル・コルビュジエのロンシャンからラ・トゥーレット，あるい

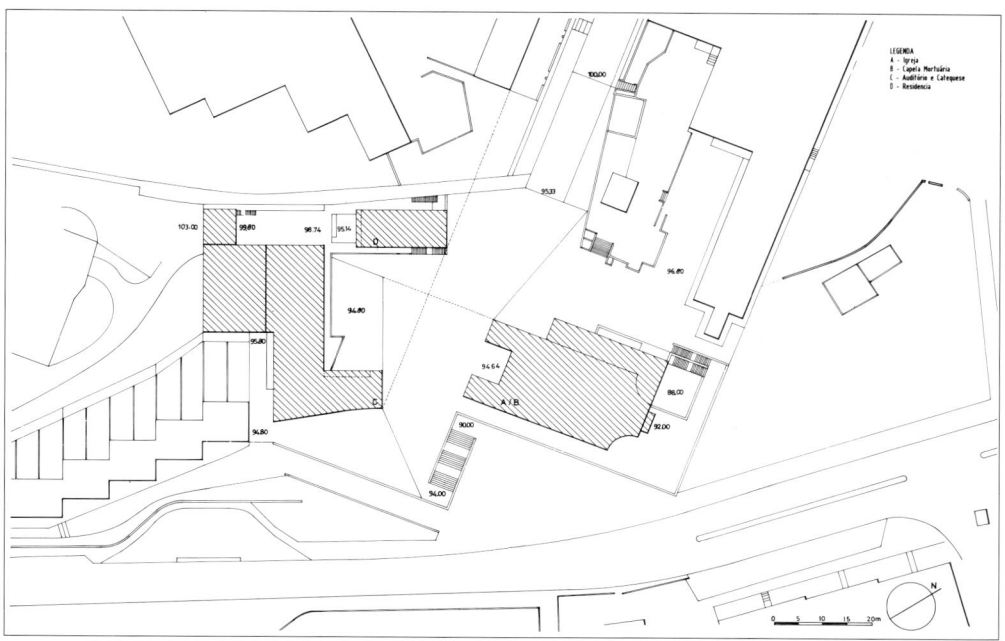

Site plan

als that tried to find a new form for the contemporary spirit of the liturgy. I could tell that the theologians who discussed it were not in complete agreement. So this problem was, in a way, a special kind of research. It was extremely interesting.

Then there were issues that were extremely banal. Can you see the difficulty of designing a cross for instance? There are millions of crosses made. The whole problem was extremely banal. I am not interested in creating new kinds of religious symbols. The burden of tradition is heavy. And new iterations are rarely successful. You can see this when you go to see contemporary exhibitions of religious art. You find nothing that is moving; nothing touches you. It is very difficult. If you try to think of a good cross in modern architecture, I can only think of the ones designed by Le Corbusier in Ronchamp or La Tourette, or the one of Barrágan and not much more. There are very few contemporary churches that have this atmosphere that is difficult to describe, that make you feel that you are in a sacred building. I think that the purpose of this project should be to insert this fraternal relation between men and this atmosphere. I tried this and through research and reflection and tests of proposals submitted to discussion I slowly began to find solutions. It was a slow process of solving problems of space and problems of light.

You think of a church mainly as a dark building. But there is much more than that. In a church you know how the vaulting opened the walls to bring in more light inside, and to make invention out of this light. You feel the presence of the light through the insertion of glass windows. But you cannot attain that without the glass windows. In the church of Marco de Canavezes light has a very important role in the definition of space. And the space of the apse is in a way pressed toward the assembly as if it follows the movement of the position of the priest. It has a kind of compressive quality. The light comes from up high, to the nave. And it is oriented in such a way that the color changes and moves throughout the day. There is light

はバラガンのものくらいで，それ以上のものはありません。聖なる建物のなかにいるのだという，説明し難いこの感覚を与えてくれる雰囲気を備えた教会は，現代建築ではごくわずかです。このプロジェクトの目的は，人々とこの雰囲気の間に，こうした兄弟愛的関係を挿入することであるべきだと考えました。私はそれを試みました。そして，研究し，考え抜き，案を討議にゆだねてテストしながら，ゆっくりと答えを見つけて行きました。空間の問題，光の問題を解いて行く，緩慢なプロセスでした。

教会というのは，だいたいがうす暗い空間だと考えると思います。しかし，それ以上のものがあるのです。教会の中に入ると，ヴォールトがより多くの光を内部に採り入れるために，そしてこの光から創造するために，どのように壁に開口をつくりあげているかが解ります。はめ込まれたガラス窓を通して光の存在が感じられる。しかし，ガラス窓なしには，これを獲得することは出来ません。マルコ・ドゥ・カナヴェーゼスの教会では，光はその空間を定義することに非常に重要な役割を担っています。そして後陣の空間は，まるで司祭の位置の動きに従うかのように会衆に向かって押しつけられているところがある。一種の圧縮された性格を持っている。光は上方高くから身廊に差し込んできます。そしてそれは，一日中，光が色を変え，動いて行くような方向に向けられている。背後にある一種の滑り板（シュート）から入ってくる光もあります。直接光ではなく，強い対比をつくることなしに，とても柔らかな光を与えています。祭壇の空間の周りに一種のオーラをつくりだしている。いずれにせよ，風景が見えるように，水平の窓もあります。この教会は，周りにいくつかの家々が点在する谷を前にした小さな丘の上にあるからです。とても豊かで美しい景色です。実は，プロジェクトを進めるためにここに来たとき，最初は町の中心に近い敷地を選んだのです。美しい，小さな広場でした。しかし，結局そこは2つの教区の境界にあたっていたので適切ではありませんでした。この教会がサービスする教区のもっと中心に建てるべきであったので，新しい敷地を見つけたのです。

GA：そこには既に，礼拝などに使われていた建物があったのですか。

シザ：最終的に決まった敷地には，小さなチャペルがありました。礼拝に使われていたこの建物は，実際は移築された18世紀の古い住宅でした。そこに行ってみたときは，パニックに襲われました。広い敷地ではなかったからです。ひどく難しいものでした。その地域となじみがなく，その歴史も理解していないとき，どのように進めて行けるかその可能性をはかることは難しいものになります。建物の設計は難しいものになる。そんなわけで，最初は私には途方もなく困難なものでした。模型をたくさんつくって研究し，敷地にも何度も行きました。結局，この細長い建物を利用することに決めました。そして，教会をこれに垂直に配置したのです。こうした分節の付け方によって，道路側から階段による，もう一方の側からは斜路によるアクセスを組み合わせることが出来ました。つまり，これらの小さなヴォリュームを，地形の持つ限界を変換するために使うことが出来たのです。葬儀用の礼拝堂を，背面からの入り口を付けて，1階の下に置くためにレベル差を利用しました。次に，鐘楼など，あらゆる問題に対処しました。最終的には，内部で行われる集会のためのかなり慣習的な配置を採用したのです。空間構成は，そこで行われる儀式と大きく関わっています。この儀式にはいくつかの異なったクライマックスがあって，そのすべてが重要なのです。司祭が会衆に向かって説くとき行われるスピーチは，アンボ（説教壇）と呼ばれる特別な場所で行われます。祭壇そのものは内陣のなかにあり，典礼の間，司祭が座るベンチがあります。聖具は小さな戸棚の中に収めなければならず，そしてオルガンがあります。この儀式には多くの要素が含まれており，そしてそのそれぞれに適切な場所を見つけなければならないのです。これらすべての要素の分節には，儀式の進

Overall view from south　南側全景

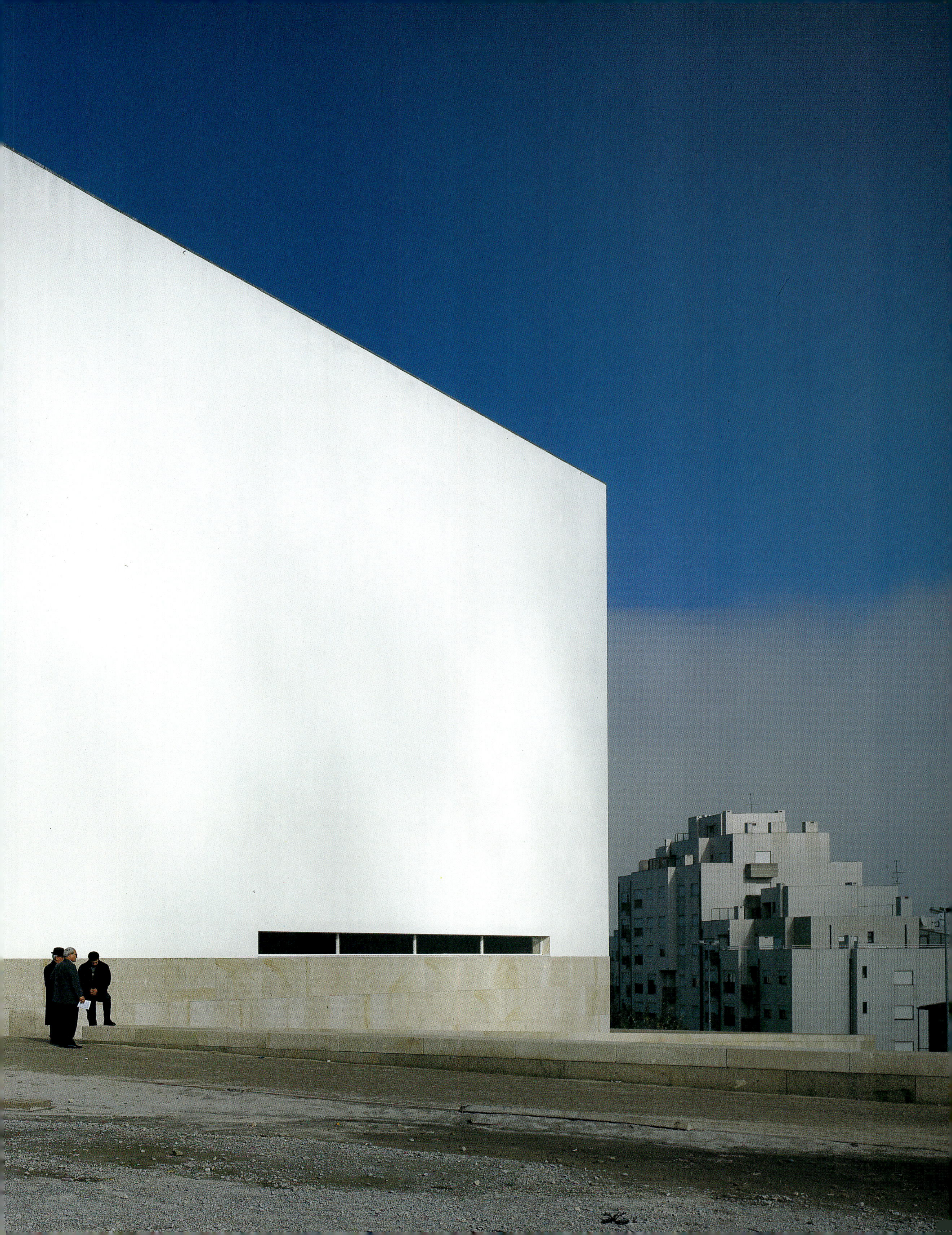

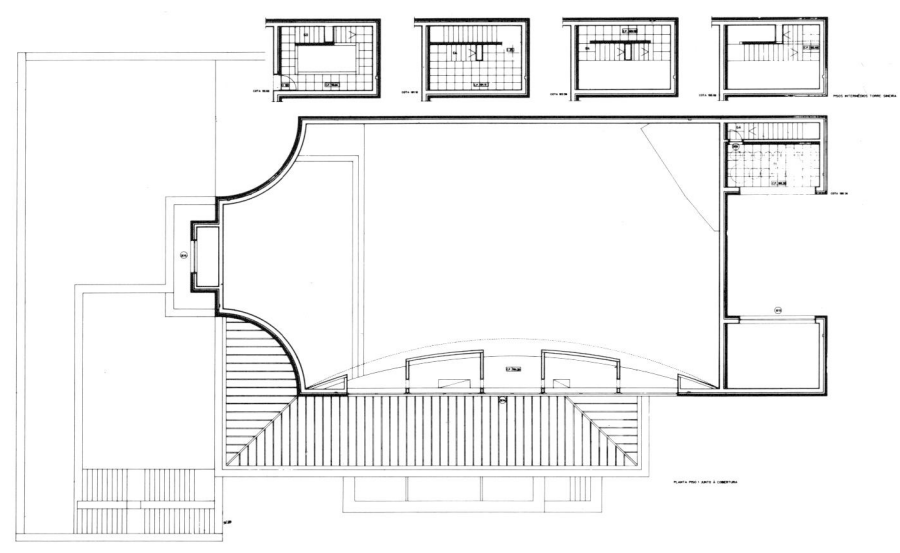

Upper levels

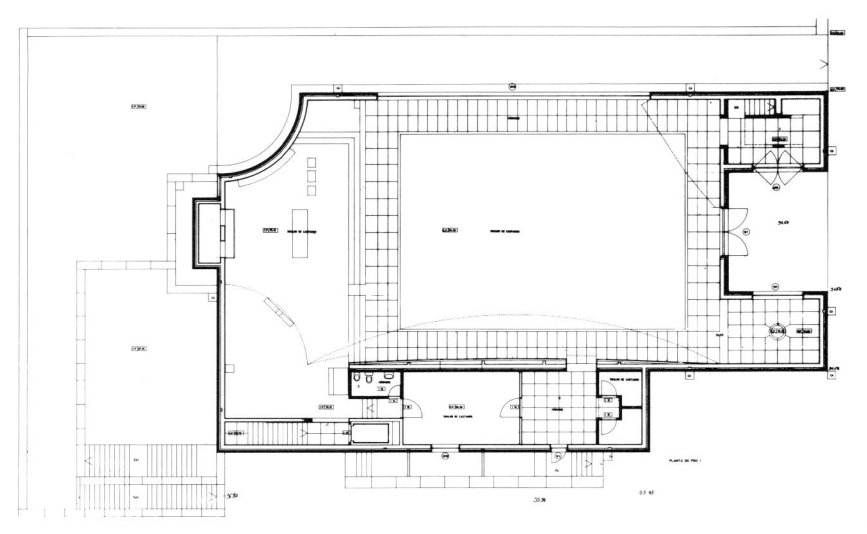

Ground level

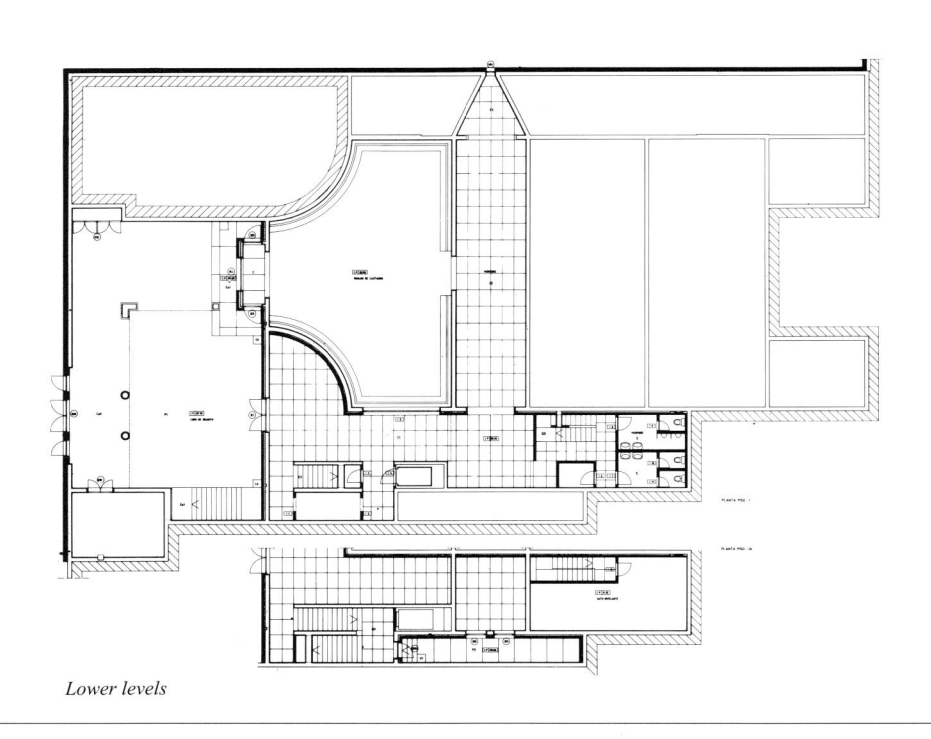

Lower levels

that enters through a kind of chute at the back. It's not direct, and gives a very soft light without much contrast. It creates a kind of aura around the space of the alter. Anyway there are also horizontal windows which allow the possibility of a view to the landscape since the church is on a small hill before a valley with some houses around it. It's a very rich and beautiful landscape. Actually when I arrived to the project I first chose a site near the center of town. It was a beautiful little square. But in the end the site wasn't good because it was at the border between two parishes. It should have been more central to the parish it was to serve so we found a new site.

GA: Was there already a building they were using for services?

Siza: There's a small chapel on the eventual site. The small chapel they were using was actually an old house from the 18th century that had been relocated. When I was there I was in panic because it was not a great site. It was very very difficult. When you are not familiar with an area and don't yet understand the history of an area it becomes hard to see the potential of how it can develop and it becomes hard to design the building. So it was very very hard for me in the beginning. We worked with many models and visited the site

行のなかで，各々に相対的な重要性を考慮しなければならない。そしてもちろん，ミサを執行する司祭の動きにも関わる必要があります。空間全体のなかでのさまざまに異なるミサの進行過程との関係についてです。それはとても難しく且つ面白いプロセスでした。礼拝式のこうした変化を考えるとき，教会は，新しいプログラムを喚起させ得る可能性を持っています。

GA：曲面の壁や内部のディメンションについてはいかがですか。

シザ：内陣の構成は，この伝統的な方式を採用しました。次に，動きの空間化と礼拝の形式の点で重要な要素があります。そしてまた，ある程度の非対称性も導入したいと思いました。建物は，ほとんどが対称性を備えたものであるわけなのですが，窓に，ある深度を与えるような角度もつけてあります。光が入って来るのは見えるのですが，実際の開口そのものは見えないのです。古い教会では，これは，厚みのある構築によって自然に備わっているのですが，今日では，約40センチ厚の壁をつくるのが普通です。そこで，私は厚みと密度というこの性質を再導入するようにしました。

曲面の帰結から生まれたこの空間では，ガラスを磨くために上階にも上れます。古い教会の多くにはこの種のヴェランダが付いていました。子供のとき，こうしたヴェランダの神秘性

Front facade 正面▷

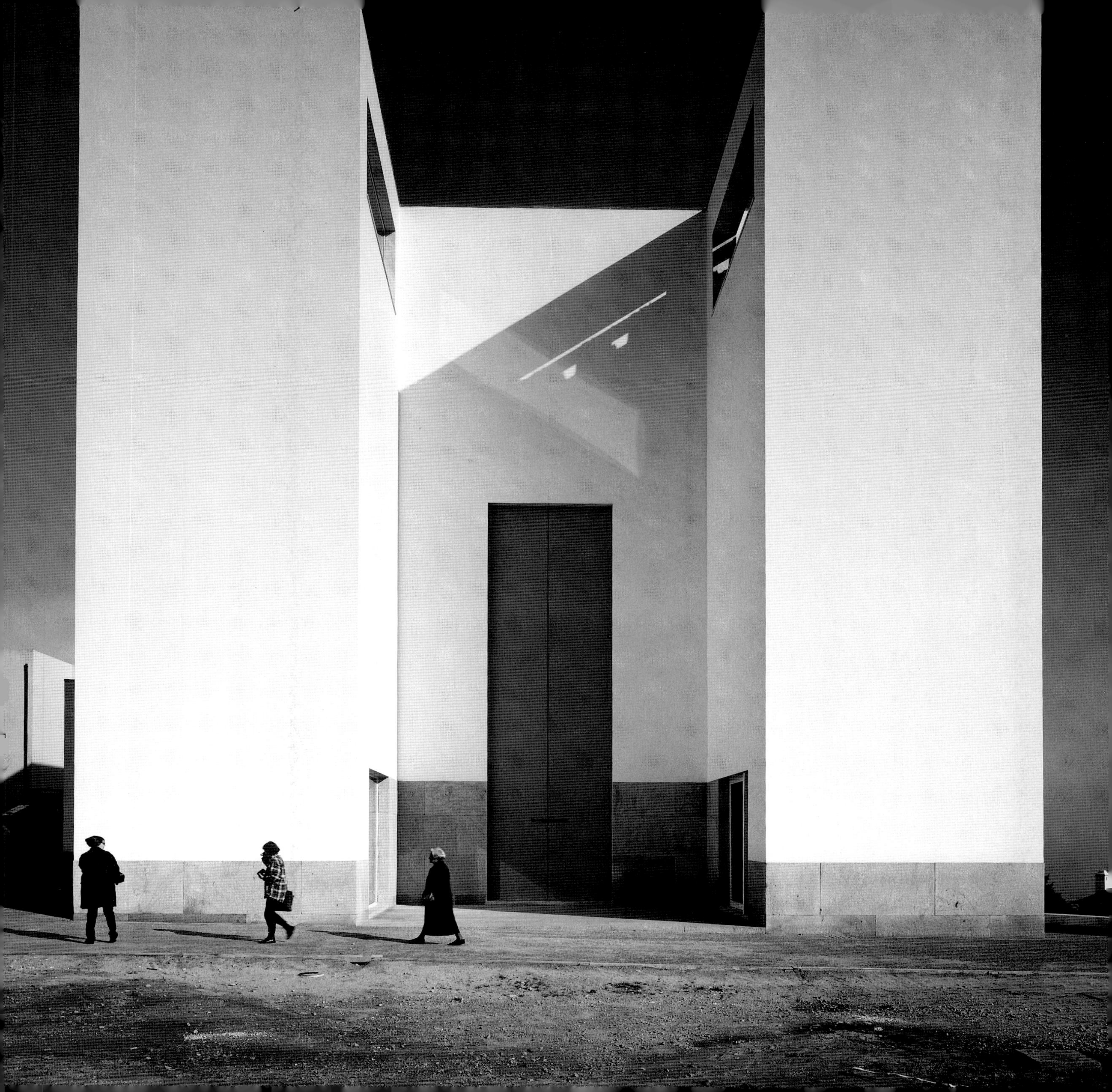

View from east　東より見る

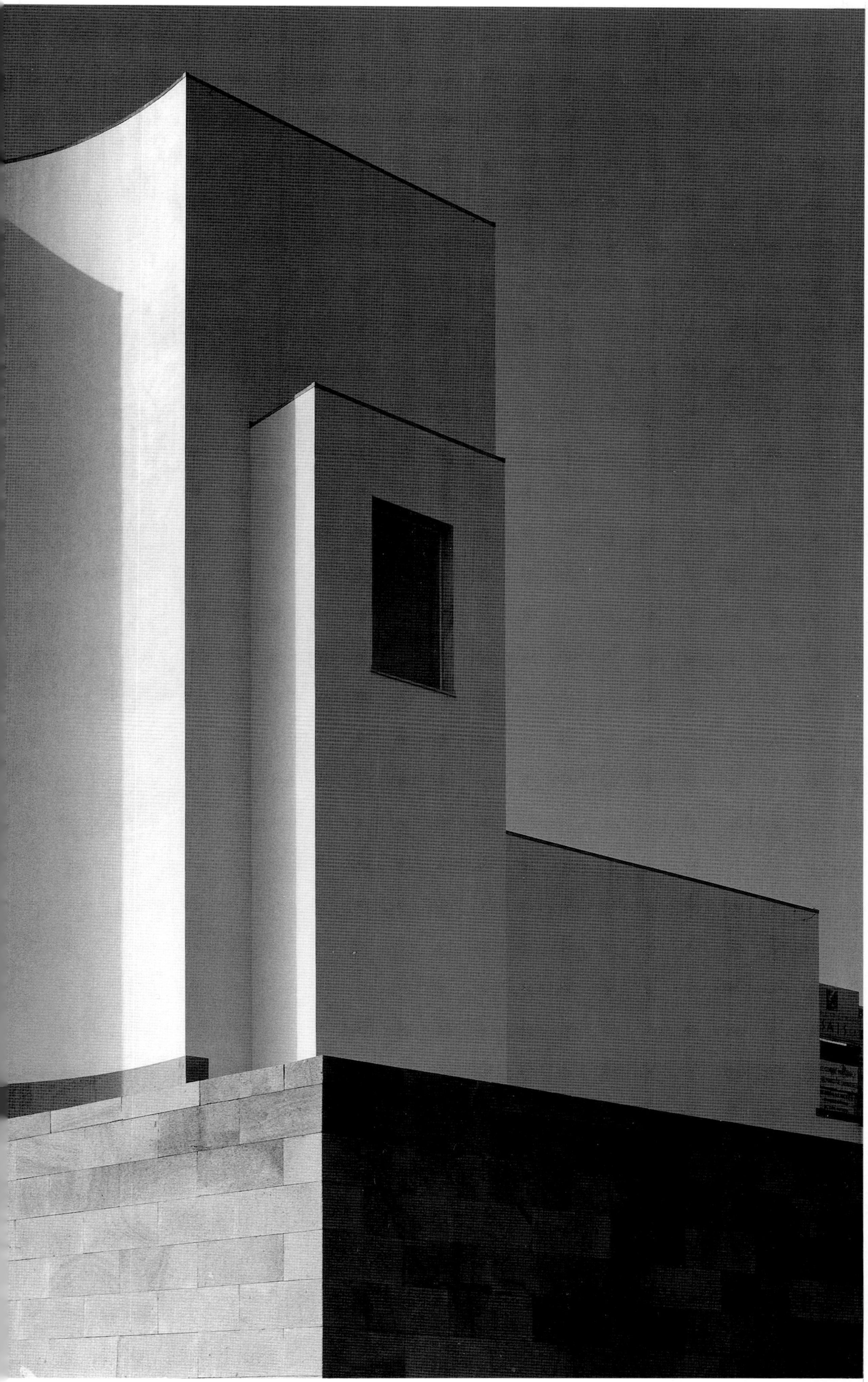

Plan: exterior stairs

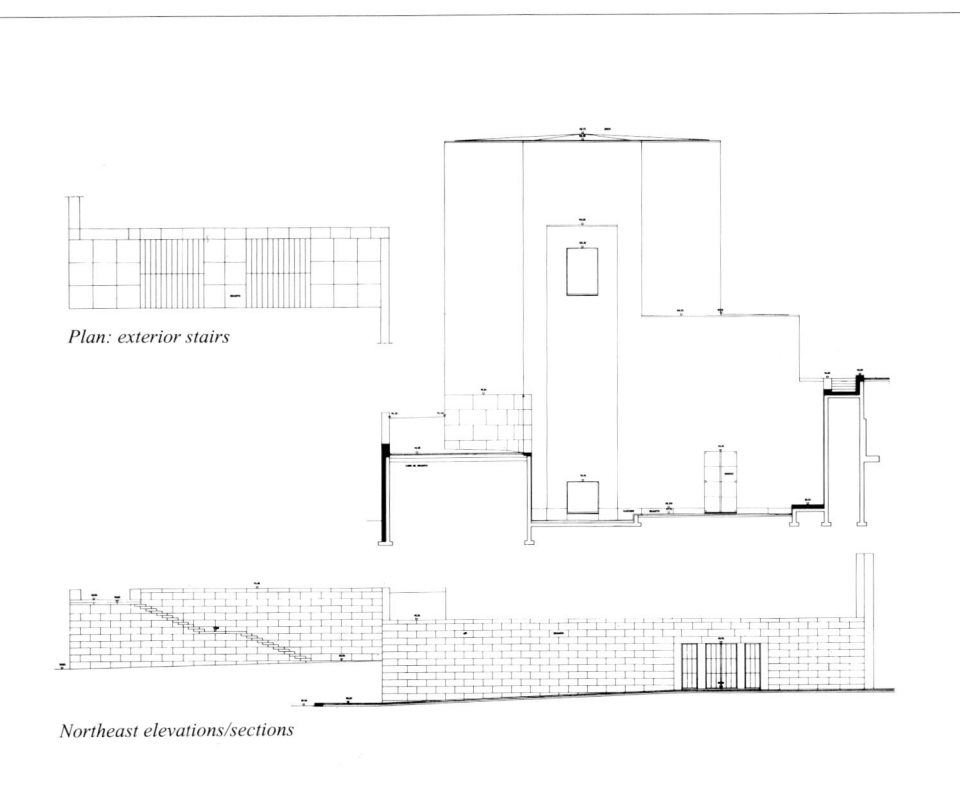

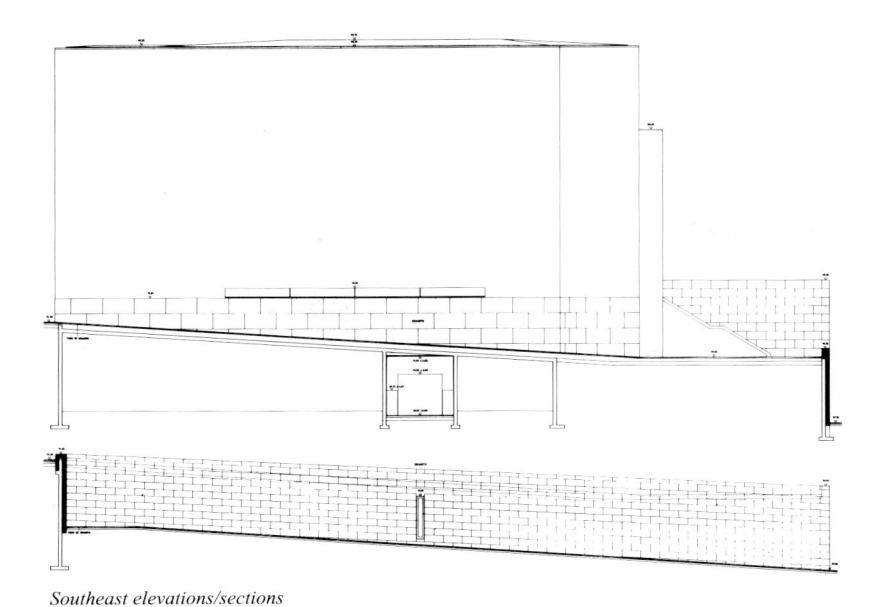

Northeast elevations/sections

Southeast elevations/sections

Longitudinal section

often. We decided to use this long building, and I put the church perpendicular to this. With this articulation I could combine stair access from the road and ramp access from the other side. So I could use these smaller volumes to transform the limitations of the topography. I used the level change to put the funerary chapel under the first floor with rear access. Then I had to deal with all the problems like the bell tower. In the end, I adopted a very conventional distribution for the assembly on the inside. The organization of the spaces had much to do with the ceremony there. There are different high points in this ceremony and all of them are important. The speech that the priest makes when he addresses the assembly is made at a special place called the ambo. The alter itself is in the sanctuary and then during the part of the ritual when the priests sit there are benches. The sacrary must be in a small armoire, and then there is the organ. The ceremony includes many elements and you must find the proper place for all of them. The articulation of all of these elements must consider the relative importance among them in the course of the ceremony. And of course you also have to deal with the movements of the celebrants. It is about the relationship between the different points within the whole of the space. It

に当惑したものです。見上げても，誰もそこにいたことがない。どうやってそこに出るのか，誰が行くのかが不思議でした。この謎めいた通路がこの教会にもあります。谷に向かって開く大きな扉があり，これはシチリアのパレルモにある教会を訪ねたときの強い印象からきています。そこには，祭壇と後陣に面した正面に，巨大な扉が付いていました。この印象的なビザンチンのモザイクのなかに入って行くのです。ビザンチン教会のオリエンタルな装飾様式の影響が分かると思います。アジアの仏像に見られるような巨大な金色のイメージがあります。床から天井まで広がっている。ですから，新しいオーダーによって解釈し直してはいますが，残そうとした歴史的痕跡がたくさん含まれているのです。

GA：第二期工事はいつになりますか。
シザ：まだその費用が工面されていないのです。しかし将来実現できるだろうことを期待しています。計画案全体が非常に重要なのですから。教会の外観はまだ密接に一体化したものではありません。古い建物とのつながりはあるのですが，私たちはまだ，教会風景との関係を完全には理解していません。それは道路から見えますが，もう一方の側からは見えません。何かが，まだ欠けているのです。いつか，それを完結させることが出来ればいいと願っています。

was a very difficult and interesting process. The church is something you might call a new program when you consider this change in the liturgy.

GA: Could you talk about the curved walls and the dimensions of the interior?

Siza: I used this traditional sanctuary organization. Then there are these elements that are important in terms of the spatialization of the movements and rituals of the ceremonies. And also I wanted to introduce some asymmetry, although it is mostly symmetrical. You have this angle that gives some depth to the windows. You can see the light comes in but you don't see the actual windows in perspective. This was obtained in old churches naturally with the thickness of the construction, but today we make walls about 40 cm so I tried to reintroduce this quality of thickness and density.

This space resulting from the curve is also accessible upstairs to clean the glass. A lot of old churches have this kind of veranda, and I remember when I was a child I was baffled by the mystery of this veranda. I would look up at it, and there would never be anyone there, and I would wonder how it was accessed and who goes there. I projected that sense of wonder here. There's this mysterious access here. The big door opens to the valley and came

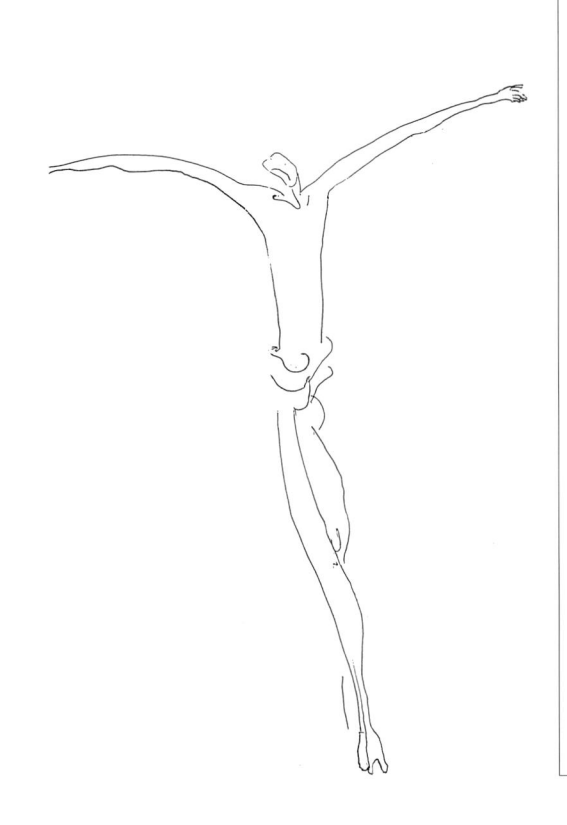

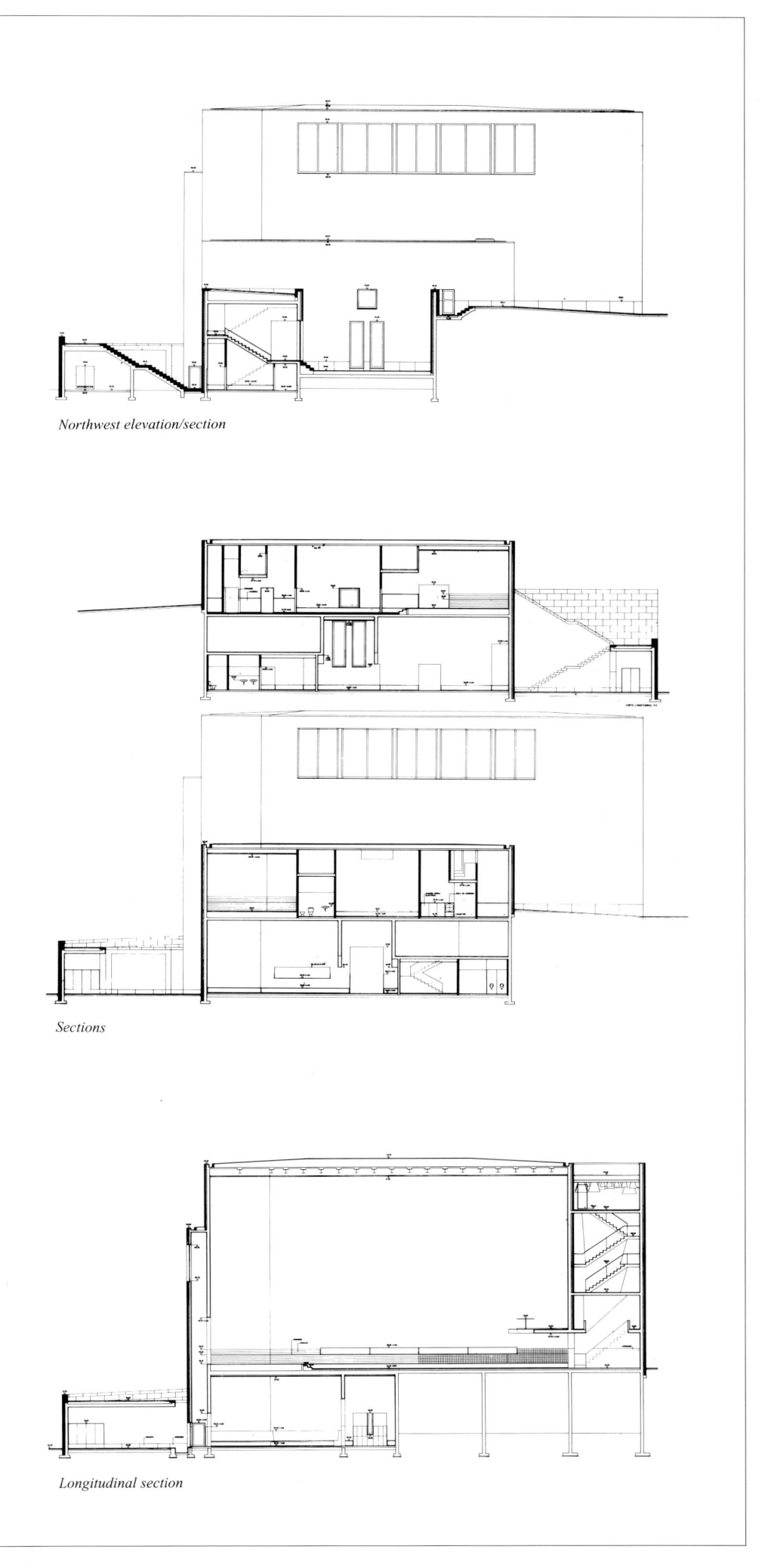

Northwest elevation/section

Sections

Longitudinal section

Southwest elevations

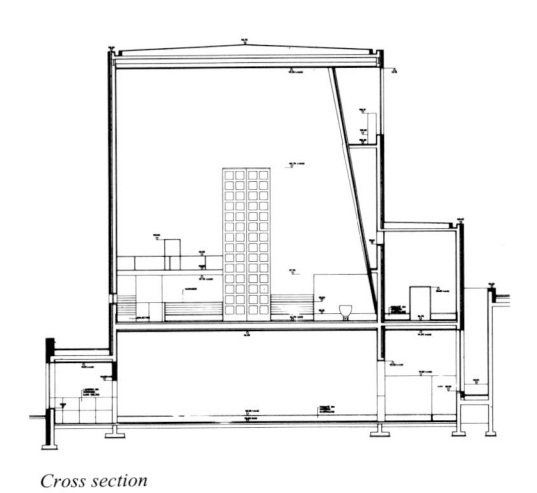

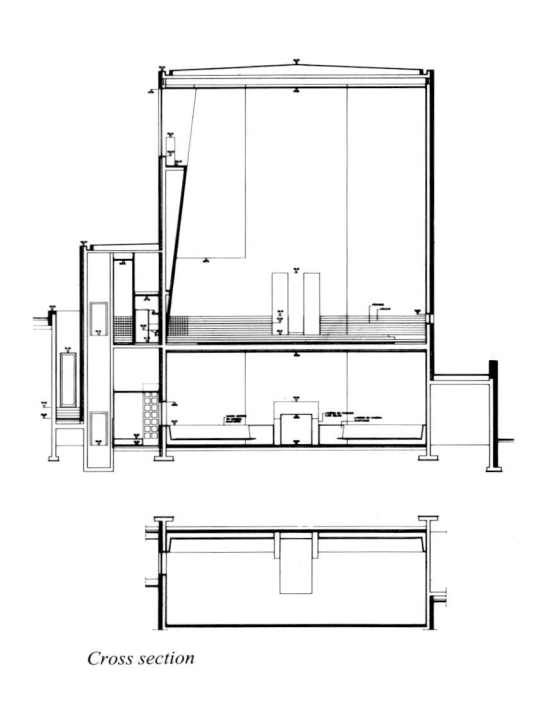

Cross section

Cross section

from a very strong impression when I visited a church in Palermo in Sicily. There was an enormous door at front that faced the alter and the apse. It opened onto this impressive Byzantine mosaic. You can see the oriental influence in the style of decoration of a Byzantine church. You see these enormous golden images like those of Buddha you find in Asia. They go from floor to ceiling. So there are many historic traces that I tried to keep although I reinterpreted them through a new order.

GA: When is the second phase?

Siza: There is no money for that yet. But I hope that there will be in the future because it is very important for the whole project. The exterior of the church is not yet coherent. There is the anchor with the old building, but we don't yet understand the relationship with the landscape of the church completely. You can see it from the road but not from the other side. Something is still missing. I hope that someday we can finish it.

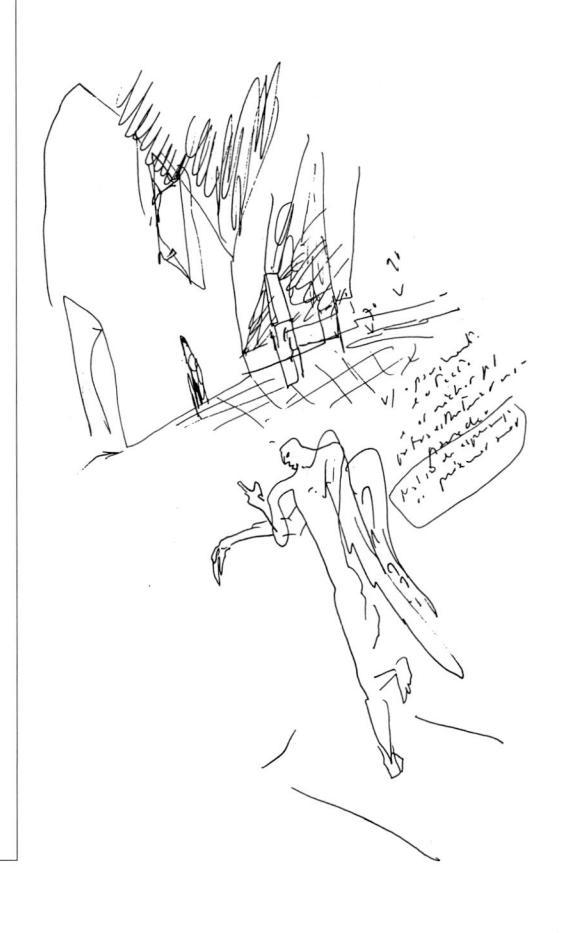

47

Nave 身廊

Nave 身廊

Galician Center for Contemporary Art
ガリシア現代美術センター

Santiago de Compostela, Spain

Client: Municipality of Galicia   Design and construction period: 1988–93
Architects: Álvaro Siza Arquitecto, Lda   Collaborators: [Design phase] Joan Falgueras, project architect; Mona Trautman, assistant; [Phase I] Yves Stump, project architect; [Phase II] João Sabugueiro, project architect; Jane Considine, Tiago Faria, Anton Graf, Cecilia Lau, Elisário Miranda, Luís Cardoso, Miguel Nery, Jorge Nuno Monteiro, João Pedro Xavier, José Luís Carvalho Gomes, assistants   Structural engineer: Euroconsult   Structural system: reinforced concrete structure

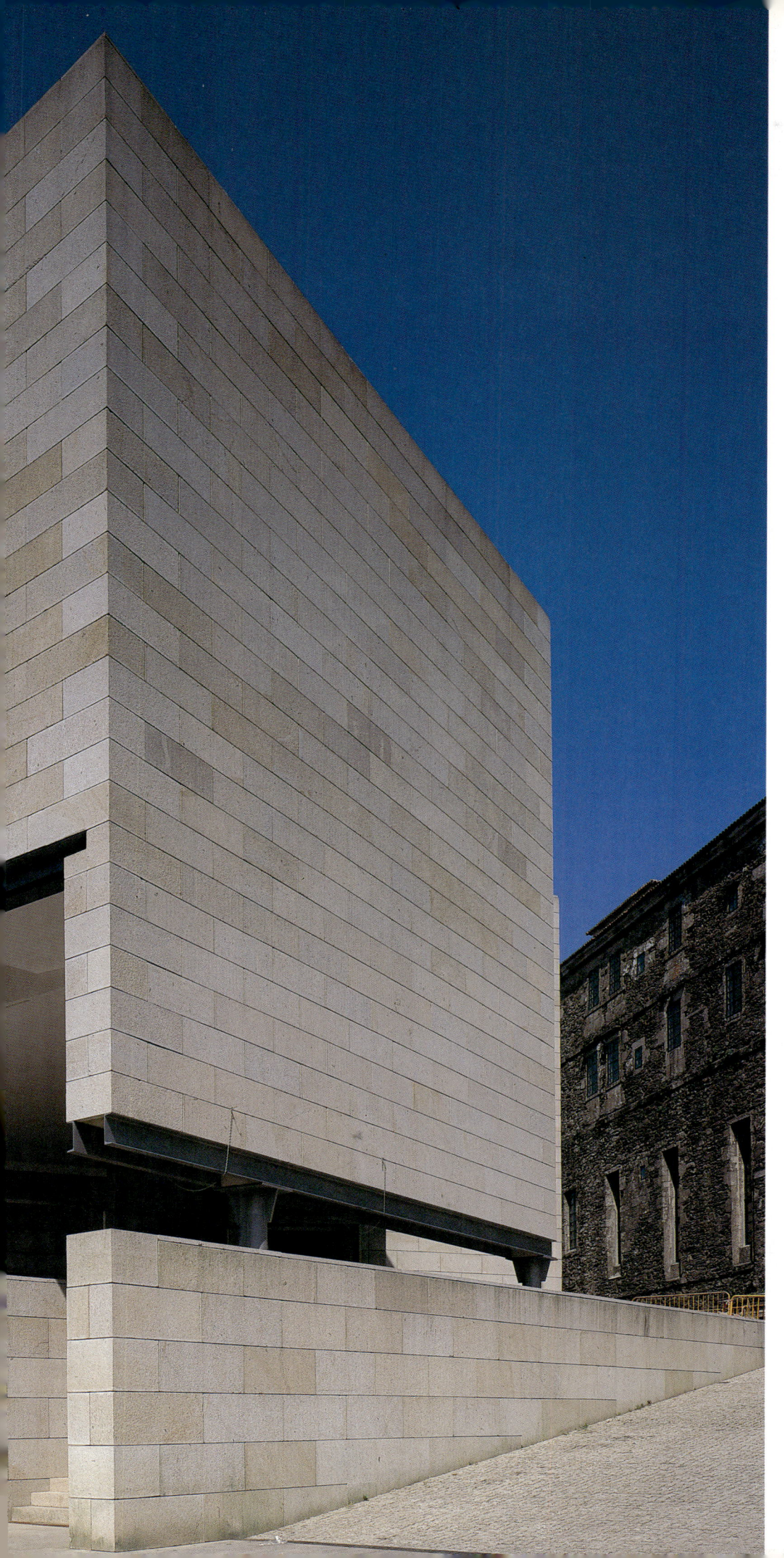

GA: You've done several museum projects. How would you characterize your approach to museum design versus the work of other architects?
Álvaro Siza: That's difficult to say since there are many kinds of museums. For instance here in Oporto they are making museums for trains or for cars or for airplanes. What I've done mostly is contemporary art museums. I've never done a museum for old paintings and sculpture. Those museums have fantastic collections like the Louvre. I make buildings for contemporary art, and oftentimes contemporary art museums rely on rotating exhibits. Of course this is not any kind of choice on my part. This just happens to be the case. Circumstances lead me to work on museums for towns where there didn't have great collections of art.

I worked in Galicia, Compostela. I'm building one here in Oporto. I did a competition for a museum in Helsinki. And I did a museum in Lisbon for a painter which was also partly a school for arts. Of course this did not have a big collection either.

What I noticed is that there is a tendency that these museums are all basically buildings for temporary exhibition. They sometimes have their own collection but these could be better. Even in those cases, the

GA：シザさんは，いくつかの美術館を設計されています。他の建築家の作品と比較して，美術館のデザインに対するご自分の方法にはどのような特徴があると思いますか。
アルヴァロ・シザ：いろいろな種類の美術館がありますから，答えるのが難しいですね。たとえば，ポルトでは，美術館を列車や車や飛行機であるかのようにつくっています。私が設計してきたのは，ほとんどが現代美術館です。古い絵画や彫刻を展示する美術館の仕事をしたことはありません。こうした美術館はルーヴルのように，素晴らしいコレクションを持っています。私は現代美術のための建物を設計していますが，現代美術館は多くの場合，巡回展に依存しています。もちろんこれは，私が選択するわけではありません。たまたまそうなるだけです。何らかの状況が，素晴らしいコレクションは持っていない，この街の美術館の仕事へと私を連れてきたのです。

ガリシアのコンポステラに美術館を設計しましたし，このポルトの街でも今，一つ建てているところです。ヘルシンキの美術館のコンペにも参加しました。ある画家のために，リスボンに美術館を建てましたが，これは一部が美術学校にもなっています。もちろん，ここも大きなコレクションは持っていませんでした。

気づいたのですが，これらの美術館はすべて，

Overall view　全景

Site plan

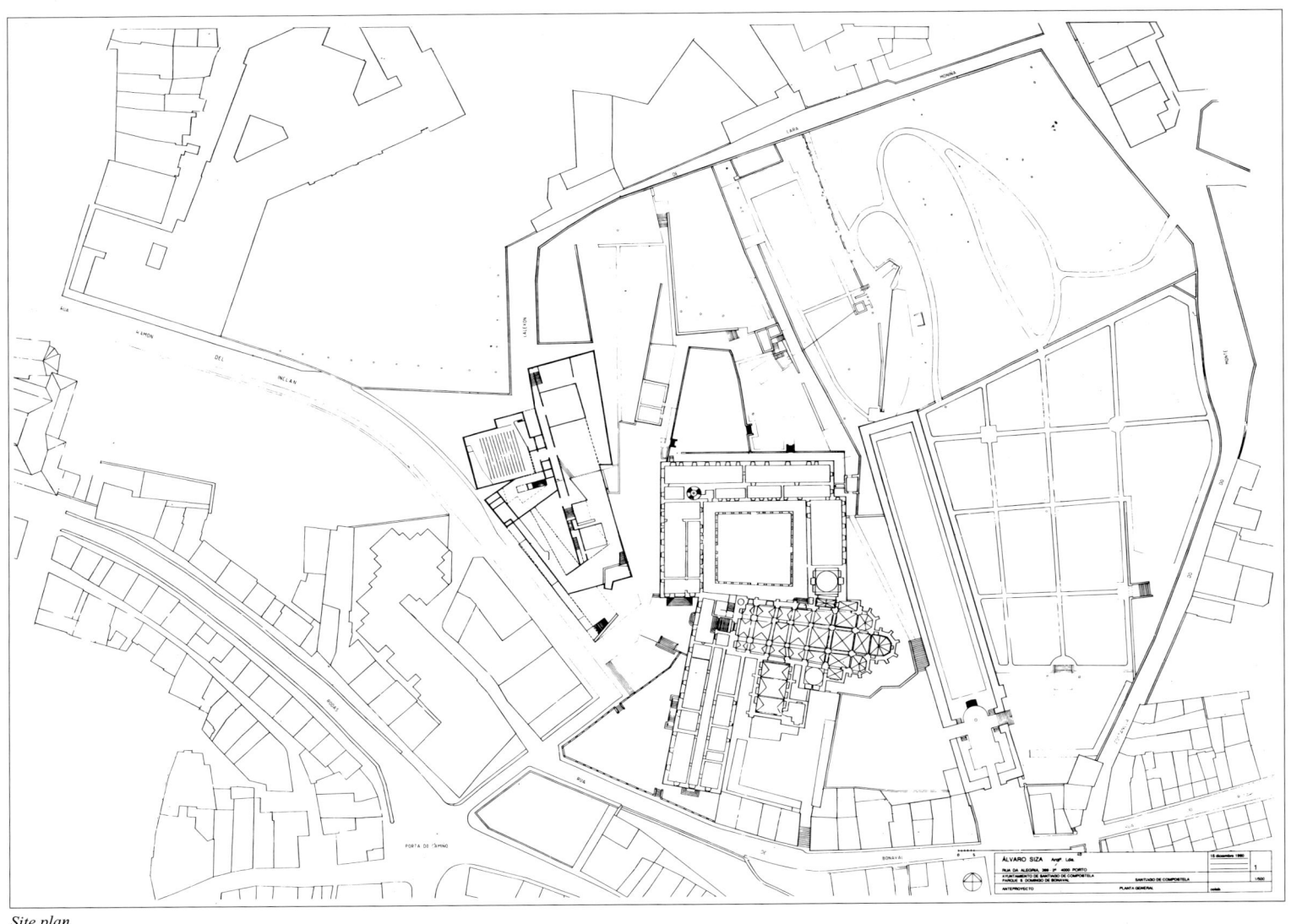

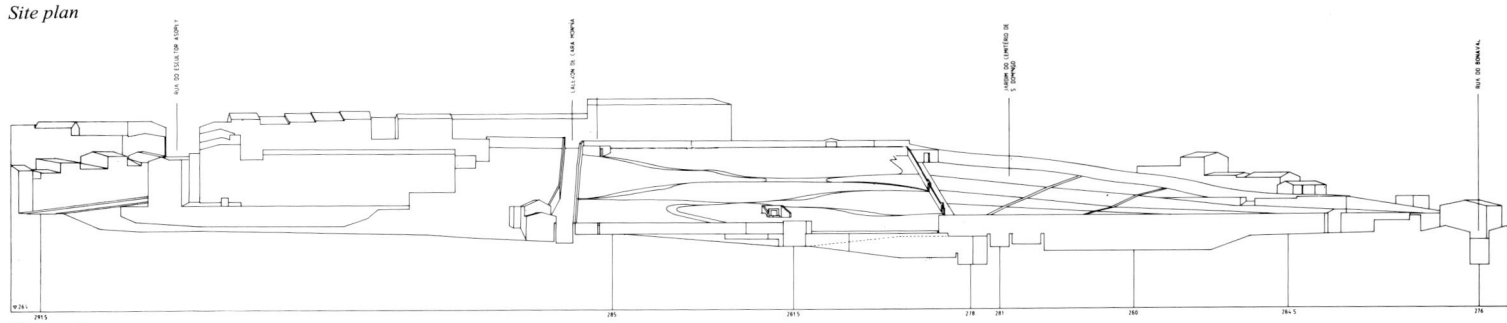

Site section

基本的にテンポラリーな展覧会のために建てられる傾向がありますね。時に、これらの美術館は自分のコレクションを持っていますが、それはよい方です。しかもその場合でさえ、所蔵作品は巡回しますから、展示作品は常に変わります。そして展示作品のほとんどは、世界を巡回する一定期間だけの展示となります。結果として、フレキシブルな部屋、つまり、様々な種類の展示に対応し得る部屋が必要になります。極端に異なる作品を受け入れることが出来るように、スペースは非常に柔軟なものでなければならないのです。今、アムステルダムの市立美術館の増築の仕事を進めています。たまたまこの美術館には素晴らしいコレクションがあるわけですが、会期の限定された、様々な展覧会のための施設も必要なのです。

GA：尊重する必要のある、柔軟性に対する規準を美術館側は通常、持っているものですか。

シザ：場合によります。現代美術においては、アーティストがギャラリー・スペースや美術館に来て、その空間で作業をするインスタレーションがよくあります。ですから、館長の多くが、無性格な建物を望みます。間仕切りの無い、フレキシブルな照明設備を持つ大きなスペースが良いと考えています。このモデルとなっているのはパリのボブール（ポンピドゥ・センター）かもしれません。多様な柔軟性を備えた大きな機械のようなものになる。つまり、アーティストやディレクターがやってきて、可能な面積のなかにどのように作品を創造し得るか自分で決めることが出来るのです。

私は別な展開の仕方を提案しました。インスタレーションがあるとしても、固有なスペースとの対話がある方が素晴らしくはないかということです。それは、芸術作品にとっても歓迎すべきことだと思うのです。固有の空間にインスタレーションを制作するという方法は、非常に独特なプロセスになります。そこには、一つの関係性が生まれるのです。ある館長はこれが気に入りませんし、そうした関係性も望まない。完全な自由、ついには存在し得ない何かを望みます。結局、ボブールでさえ、展覧会の会場構成は簡単ではないと言わざるを得ないでしょう。それはフレキシブルにみえます。しかし、実際には非常に難しいところがあります。つまり、私の意見では、美術館は自身の性格を持たねばならず、それによって、芸術作品と展示とのあいだに対話が生まれるのです。今、アムステルダムで仕事をしていますが、市立美術館の館長は私の見方に賛成です。最初の模型によって作業を進めていましたが、そのうちに、美術

permanent collections rotate so the exhibits are always changing. And most of the exhibits are temporary exhibitions that travel around the world. As a consequence, the museums have to have rooms that are flexible and that accommodate different kinds of exhibits. The spaces must be extremely flexible so that they can receive extremely different kinds of things. Now I'm also designing the addition to Stedelijk Museum in Amsterdam. They happen to have a fantastic collection but they also have to have facilities for these different exhibitions.

GA: Do the museums have given parameters for flexibility that you abide by?

Siza: It depends. Oftentimes, contemporary art entails an installation where an artist comes to the gallery space or museum and works on the space. Many directors want the buildings to have no character. They think that it's better to have big spaces without partitions and with flexible lighting. The model for this might be Beaubourg (Pompidou Center) in Paris. You have a big machine supposedly with a lot of flexibility so that artists and directors can come and make their own decisions of how exhibits can be created within the available square meters.

I offer another perspective. That's that even with an installation, it's nicer to have a dialogue with a particular space. I think that is good for the work of the artist. This way, creating an installation in a particular space is a very specific process. There are these relations. Some directors don't think like this and they don't want relations. They want complete freedom, something that in the end doesn't exist. In the end, I would argue that even Beaubourg is not so easy to organize for exhibitions. It seems to be flexible. But in the end there are extreme difficulties. So in my opinion a museum must have it's own character so that it can have a dialogue with the art and the exhibitions. It must have it's own character. I'm now working in Amsterdam and the director of the Stedelijk Museum agrees with my view. I was working within the first model and then they told me: no, this building must have it's own character. This is in no way an obstacle for the artists. On the contrary, it is a stimulus for the creation of the kinds of relationships I'm talking about. So I'm very happy with this project at Amsterdam because it is exactly what I believe what a museum should be.

GA: Can you give me a specific example of where this might make a difference within the spaces?

Siza: If you make a four-meter high room it is considered small. But if you make a six-meter high room someone might still consider it too small because complete freedom still doesn't exist. So if you give this vertical dimension over strictly to the idea of freedom and possibility, there is no limit. People can always want more and more. If you decide to design particular spaces, and an artist comes to create an installation, space may not be appropriate for a four-meter tall sculpture. But he can always make a two-meter high sculpture. Some rooms are appropriate for some things and some others for other things. And that difference is a point of richness and not an obstacle. That is the concept. Of course there are always reactions against this. But this is the attitude I agree with.

GA: And so you used this concept at Compostela?

Siza: Yes. And in this case, I'm also relating the museum design with my interest in the town, the places around my building. So I'm not working only for the users of the interior space, but also for the day to day life within the surroundings. All of this gives life and character to the building and this is good. There is a relationship with the life of the town, and with society. Let me be clear that I'm not proposing a kind of local or contextual thing. It must be open and universal, but not something

館側は，これでは駄目だ，この建物には個性を持たせねばならないと言ってきました。これはアーティストにとっては，疑いもなく障害です。反対に，私が先ほど話したような一種の関係性の創造にとっては刺激となります。ですから，アムステルダムのプロジェクトを進めるのは，とても嬉しいのです。美術館はこうあるべきだと信じているまさにそのままを行えるわけですから。

GA：その考え方によって空間のどこが変わるのか，実例をあげて説明して下さいませんか。

シザ：4メートルの天井高の部屋をつくったとすると，それは一般に小さいと見なされるでしょう。しかし，6メートルの高さの部屋をつくったとしても，ある人は，まだ小さすぎると考えるかもしれません。完全な自由は依然として存在しないからです。ですから，自由と可能性という考え方に，この垂直方向へのディメンションを厳密に与えていっても，限りが無いのです。人は常に，さらに多くを望んで行くものです。特別な空間をデザインすることに決め，そしてアーティストがインスタレーションをつくりにやって来たとする。空間は4メートルの高さの彫刻には適切ではないかもしれない。しかし，彼はいつでも，2メートルの高さの彫刻がつくれるのです。ある部屋はある作品に相応しく，別の部屋はまた別の作品に相応しい。そしてこの違いこそ，豊かな点なのであり，障害ではないのです。それこそがコンセプトです。もちろん，常にこれに対する反動はあります。しかし，これが彼らと合意した対し方なのです。

GA：そして，このコンセプトをコンポステラでも使われたのですね。

シザ：そうです。そしてこの場合，美術館のデザインを，私の，街に対する，つまり建物周囲の場所に対する関心とも結びつけています。ですから，内部空間を使う人々のためのみでなく，周辺で起こる日常生活のためにもデザインしているわけです。こうしたことすべてが，建物に生命力と性格を与えるのであり，そしてそれは良いことです。街や社会の生命力との関係があります。はっきりさせておきたいのは，一種の地方性やコンテクスチャルな事柄を提起しているのではないことです。開かれ，普遍性を備えたものには違いありませんが，タブラ・ラサのようなものではない。それ以上に関わりを持たせねばならないと思います。前に言ったように，私が関わったほとんどの美術館は，周期的に展覧会が交替して行われる種類のものでした。特定の画家や，特定の分野や時代の作品のための美術館があります。そこでは，その特定の種類の芸術作品のための空間をつくらなければなりません。それはまったく別なことなのです。現代美術館に対しては，人々の間に両方の考えが混在しているようにみえます。完全なニュートラリティ，つまり，最終的に何も存在しないと主張することになるであろう何かを望む人と，建物に性格を望む人たちです。

GA：しかし，シザさんは現代美術とは何か，について何らかの考えをお持ちであるにちがいないと思いますが。

シザ：もちろんです。

GA：そのことは，あなたの美術館空間のデザインにも影響するのではないでしょうか。たとえば，磯崎新や，フランク・ゲーリーやジャン・ヌヴェルの設計した美術館は皆，独特の性格を持っています。また，フランク・ステラの作品は，ある美術館にはふさわしくても，別な美術館には似合いません。つまり，建築家は創造する空間の内部に置かれる展示作品をあらかじめ想定しているように思えるのです。シザさんは，展示空間のなかに最終的に何が置かれるかを，予想されているのか，どうだろうかと考えているのですが。

シザ：おっしゃることは解ります。たとえば，フランク・ゲーリーが，独自のアイディアを持っていることも，美術館委員会との関係に同じ難しさをかかえていることも確かです。しかし私はこれまで，現代芸術に対する特定の考えを持って空間をデザインすることまではしていません。建築を，現代芸術のあれやこれやの傾向

that is a tabula rasa. It must relate to more than itself. As I said before most of my museum projects involve rotating exhibits. There are museums for the work of a special painter, or a specific genre or period. And there you have to work the spaces out for that particular kind of art. That's another thing altogether. As for contemporary museums there seems to be this mix between people who want complete neutrality, something that I would argue in the end does not exist, and people who want character for the buildings.

GA: But I think you must have some idea of what contemporary art is.

Siza: Of course.

GA: Doesn't this also affect the design of your museum spaces. For example, museums by Isozaki, Frank Gehry, or Jean Nouvel all have particular a character. And a Frank Stella piece might fit in one museum but not another. So it seems the architects already have an idea of the kinds of exhibits they envision inside the spaces they create. I'm wondering if you have any preconceptions of what will eventually inhabit the gallery spaces.

Siza: I understand what you are saying. And I'm sure that Frank Gehry, for instance, has his own ideas and that he has the same difficulties dealing with the museum committees. But I don't go so far as designing spaces with certain ideas of contemporary art in mind. I wouldn't try to use the architecture to dictate a relationship or support for this or that tendency in contemporary art. I try to create spaces that are open to everything. I don't think it's possible or responsible for an architect to control the content of a public building. What I look for is space that can be in balance with whatever artistic manifestations or social manifestations you can think of. It's not that different from when I design for other programs. For instance a restaurant. I have functional concerns that I have to solve. There are certain activities that will occur in this building so I must pay attention to them very carefully and very precisely. Even a restaurant can be many different things. If a client comes to me and says his restaurant has a certain character and a certain kind of service, I have to solve for those things very precisely. But at the same time I have to keep in mind the possibility that the program may change and building might be used for another kind of thing. That is the level of freedom I'm looking for. I have to give an answer to a particular problem, but my building and my architecture can not only be that. Everything can change in time. For example, convents were designed as precise and optimized solutions for the life of a very particular community. But now, centuries later, they are used for other things. They are well designed in that they are able to receive other activities. I guess I feel the same way about museums and spaces for art. I design for this reality of change. It must be able to receive any kind of activity, but at the same time it must have some limits within it so that there is a dialogue between the spaces and the activities that will happen within it. When I design museums I am never thinking about a particular trend or particular artist.

GA: You bring up an interesting point, and that is that a building has a life outside of its immediate time, and mere programmatic contents. Can you say more about this?

Siza: As I said, I always design spaces as precise solutions to a particular purpose. But I would never involve myself in an extensive study of the particular pieces that would go into that space. This is because the way we look at art is another thing that changes over time. The way 19th-century people looked at impressionism is different than how we look at it today. We have to maintain a kind of distance, which means a kind of openness, without limitations. This is a way of not letting the examination of the content limit the possibility of the architecture and also allow for a

---

の関係を支配したり支持したりすることに使おうとはしないでしょう。すべてに開かれた空間を創造しようとしているのです。公共建築の中身をコントロールすることが、建築家に可能であり、その責任であるとは考えていません。私が探し求めているのは、芸術的な表明であろうと、社会的な表明であろうと、何を思い浮かべようと、それと均衡を取りうるスペースなのです。それは、他のプログラムの建物を設計するときとそれほど違いがあるわけではありません。たとえばレストランでは、解決しなければならない機能面での配慮があります。建物のなかで発生するであろう特定の活動がありますから、それらに対し、非常に慎重に、非常に細かく注意を払う必要があります。レストランでさえ、多くの異なったことができるはずです。もしクライアントが私のところに来て、彼のレストランには一定の性格があり、一定の種類のサービスがあると言えば、私はこれらのことを非常に厳密に解決しなければなりません。しかし同時に、プログラムが変わるかもしれず、建物が別の種類のことに使われるかもしれない可能性を心にとめておく必要があります。それが、私の探している自由のレベルです。特定の問題に答えを与える必要がありますが、私の建物、私の建築はそれのみであり得るわけではありません。すべてを、将来、変えることが出来ます。たとえば、修道院は、非常に特殊な集団の生活のために、厳密かつ効率的な解として設計されたものです。しかし今、何世紀も後になって、それらは他のことに使われています。他の活動を受け入れることが出来るほど上手に設計されているのです。美術館や芸術のためのスペースについて、私は同じように感じているのだと思います。こうした、変化という現実のためにデザインしているのです。それは、どのような種類の活動も受け入れることが出来なければならない。しかし同時に、そのなかにはある限度が必要でもあります。それによって、そのなかで発生する活動とスペースの間に対話が存在することになるからです。美術館を設計するとき、特定の流行や特定の芸術家について考えることは決してありません。

GA：それは興味深い視点ですね。つまり建物は、その生命を時代の外に持つのであり、単なるプログラム上の内容を持つにすぎない。これについてもう少しお聞かせ下さいませんか。

シザ：言いましたように、私は、いつも、特定の目的に対する的確な解として空間をデザインしています。しかし、その空間のなかに収められる特定の作品について幅広く研究する方向には自分を持って行かないでしょう。これは、芸術は、時を越えて変わる、別のものとみているからです。19世紀の人の印象派の見方は、今日の私たちの見方とは違います。私たちは、一種の距離を保つ必要があります。これはある種、無限の開放性を意味します。これが、建築の可能性を狭めてしまうような展示作品の検討に進むことなく、状況の変化に応じて建築にさまざまな生命を与え得る方法なのです。

GA：では、このサンティアゴ・デ・コンポステラの美術館はどのようなものなのですか。

シザ：ある修道院の建つ公園の中にあります。修道院は既に文化センターとして使われています。建物とその周囲のレクリエーションのための公園の設計を依頼されることになってとても嬉しかったですね。私にとって、この2つのプロジェクトは一つのものになりました。互いに深く関わりを持つものとなったのです。公園を再構成することは建物の輪郭などを明確に決定するのにとても役立ちました。

最初、美術館を公園の内側に建てるように頼まれました。しかし、その代わりに、道路に面して、歴史的建造物と並べて配置することを提案しました。この建物は一種のアネックスとすべきではないと感じたからです。それは、この地域の生活のなかで一つの役割を持ち、地域全体の再活性化を主張すべきなかでの役割を持っています。私はこのアイディアを擁護し、現代建築を怖がるべきではないと彼らに話しました。そして、最終的に、この建物を道路に面し

Third floor

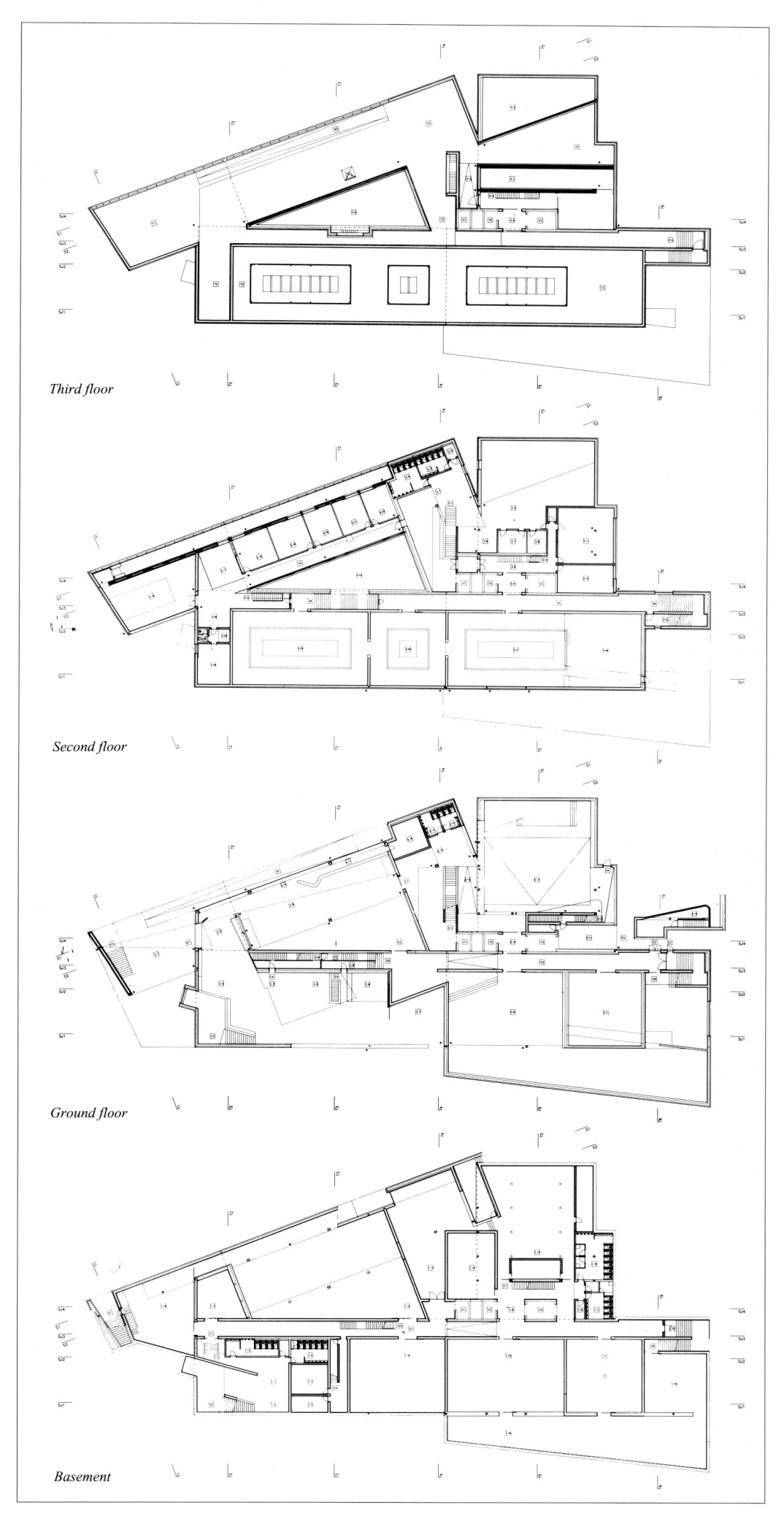

Second floor

Ground floor

Basement

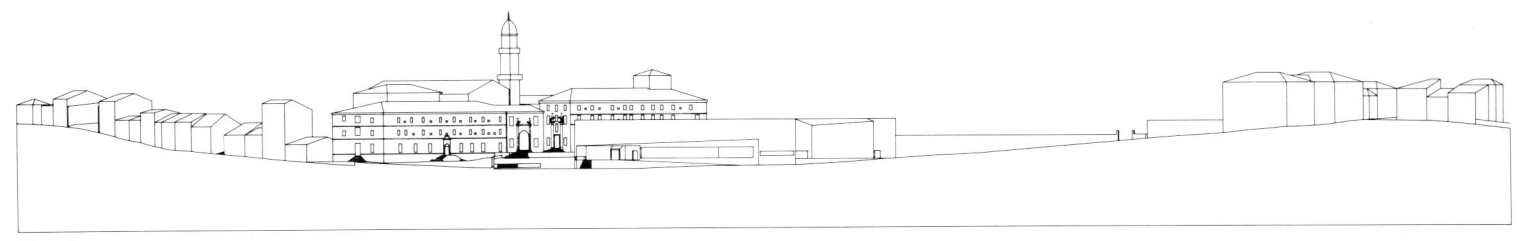

Elevation

different kind of life for the architecture as circumstances change.

GA: Can you tell me about this particular museum?

Siza: It is inside the park of a convent. The convent is already used as a cultural center. I was delighted to be invited to design both the building and the recreational park around it. For me, these two projects became one. They became very related. To reorganize the park was very good for the definition of the building.

In the beginning I was asked to build the museum inside the park. But instead, I proposed to put it on the street, side by side with the historical building, because I felt that this should not be a kind of annex. It had a role in the life of the area and a role in the rejuvenation of the whole complex which should be affirmed. I defended this idea and told them they should not be afraid of contemporary architecture. So finally I was allowed to build it on the street. And it was a way to reorganize the whole area or to create conditions to reorganize this whole area.

The whole tissue of the area had been cut in the 1960s by a street that created this rupture. What I tried to do was to create a step and repair the urban tissue of this area. The solution is different than the original but has a logic that worked with the old as well as new circumstances. You can see that the park goes up in stairs or ramps in a zigzag. You can also see that this same kind of language exists inside the building. This was based on old maps and things we found on the site like the old walls of basements. We were trying to discover the channels which were hidden. And all this could be the first step in organizing the exterior and interior of the building. If you look at the plans, you can see that this is the movement of the whole garden. These discoveries dictate not only the angles but also the circulation of the whole building. I believe they fit each other because they belong to the same logic.

GA: So the geometries of the building didn't extend into the garden.

Siza: No, it was the other way around. It comes from the garden. The open spaces are very important. There is another building nearby. And this facade had an angle so it results in a space that is a triangle. This triangle has a relation with other elements. And so the central hall became a triangle. Then the rooms were allowed to have geometrically simple shapes. I didn't want the architecture to be an imposition on the installations. Again in the plan you can see the triangle and you see that everything else is determined by this.

But it is extremely important that the interior organization doesn't come from this geometry, but from time and use, and that is all related to the garden. This strategy allows the project to make a whole between

て建てることを認められたのです。そしてそれは，地域全体を再構成する方法，つまり，この全地域を再構成するための状況をつくりだす方法でもありました。

この地域の町並みを構成するファブリックはすべて，この亀裂をつくりだすことになった道路によって，60年代に切り崩されてきました。私が試みたのは，階段をつくりだすこと，そしてこの地域の都市構成を修復することです。この解決案は，オリジナルとは違っていますが，古いものにも新しい状況にも有効に作用するロジックを備えています。公園が階段状にあるいは，ジグザグな斜路のかたちで上って行きます。また，この同じ種類のランゲージが建物内部にも存在するのが解ると思います。これは，地下室の古い壁のように，私たちが敷地に発見した，古い地図や事物に基づいていました。隠されていた道筋を発見しようとしたのです。こうしたことすべてが，建物の外部と内部を組み立てる最初のステップになっています。プランを見れば，これが庭園全体の動きを示していることが解ります。これらの発見は，建物全体の角度だけではなく動線も支配しているのです。私は，それらが同じロジックに属しているがゆえに，お互いに適合しているのだと信じています。

GA：では，建物のジオメトリーは庭園へと伸びて行くのではないのですね。

シザ：ええ，それは逆に，庭園から発生するのです。オープン・スペースはとても大切です。近くに別の建物があります。そしてそのファサードには角がついていて，この結果，三角形のスペースになっています。この三角形が他の要素との関係を持っている。つまり，中央ホールが三角形となりました。次に，部屋部屋は幾何学的に単純な形態を与えられる。この建築をインスタレーションの際に重荷になるようにしたくなかったのです。ここでもまた，プランには三角形が見られ，すべてが，これによって決められているのです。

しかし，内部構成がこのジオメトリーからではなく，時間と使い方から生まれていること，つまり，すべてが庭園と関わっていることがとても重要です。このストラテジーが，プロジェクトを，修道院と共にある総体，コミュニティのなかの総体という，二者の間の総体へとつくりあげることを許しているのです。もちろん，また，街の他の修道院とも関係がつけられています。ですから，この街にやって来た人は，こうした種類の豊かさを与えられます。無関係では全くないのです。別な存在であるが関係性がある。美術館自体の内部空間の性格は，柔軟性について，前にわれわれが論じたものと符合するものであるのはもちろんです。何でも受け入れられるようにデザインされていますが，同時に，互いに無関係なものではない。対話があります。もしこれを大規模なコンテクストとの関係のなかに置けば，他に開かれた状況をつくりだす助けとなります。というのは，建物は他の事物に向かって関係づけられ，試されるのですから。それは街のなかで，目的や目標を持ち始

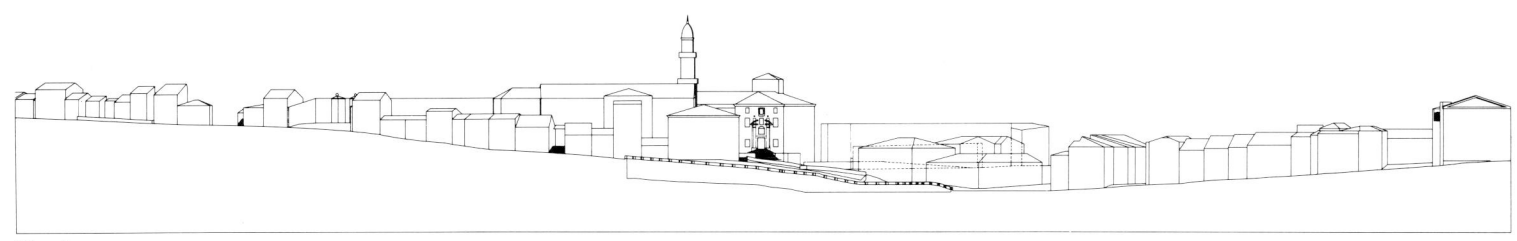

Elevation

Sections

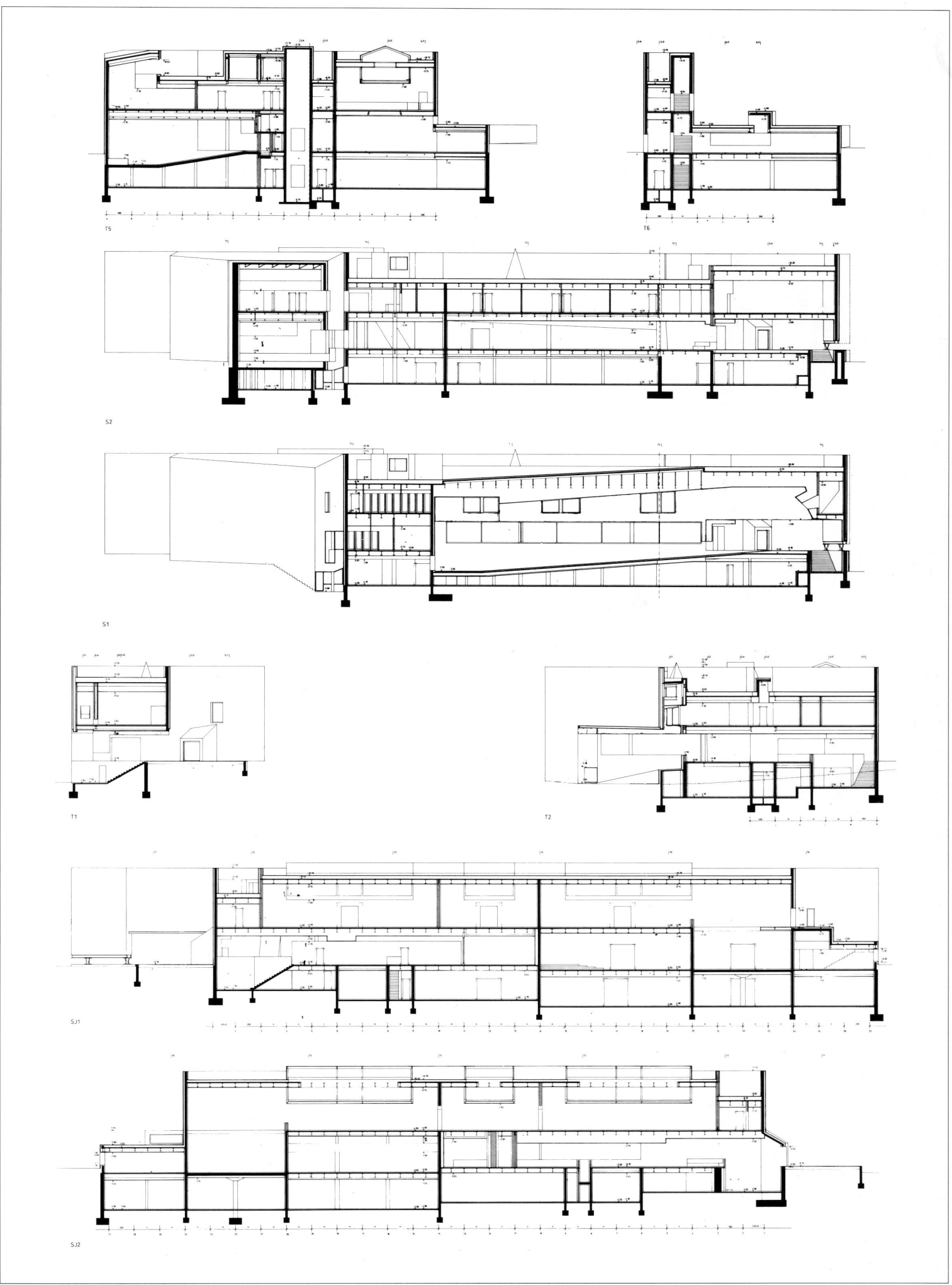

57

Reception レセプション

the two, a whole with the convent, a whole within the community. Of course this is then in relation to other convents in the town. And so someone coming to this town is offered richness in this kind of variety. It isn't at all indifferent. It is different, but it is related. The interior quality of the museum itself, of course, relates back to our earlier discussion of flexibility. It is designed so that it can receive anything but at the same time it is not be indifferent. There is a dialogue. If you put this in relation to a big context, it helps to get that atmosphere of openness, because the building is related and tested against other things. It begins to have a purpose and objective in the town.

GA: I haven't been there for two or three years. What stage is this in now?

Siza: It's finished. Well, of course, things are never finished. Some things are missing, like some benches. In my mind it is not yet finished, but the structure of it is finished. I think it is strong enough to support any sort of transformation.

GA: The other day. You complained about the way the museum used the space.

Siza: Yes. Exactly, because in my mind the museum is open to different uses. It shouldn't be necessary to alter the building. If you take a window out then something is missing. A window is placed because you need a balance of light and so that people can have a view. The spaces should be used with the window. You can design an installation considering that window also. But what they are doing is covering the window. One day I went there and the entire facade was covered with hanging pieces of steel. It was supposed to be a polemic intervention, but it is not at all polemic. It's funny. It's just consumerist extravagance. I'm not interested in these kinds of things.

Reception レセプション

める。

GA：ここ２，３年，見に行っていないのですが，今は，どんな状態にあるのですか。

シザ：完成しています。でも，もちろん，物事は決して終わることはないわけですが。いくつかのベンチのような物は欠けています。私のなかではそれは終わっていませんが，建物は完成しています。どのような変貌にも対応するに十分な強さがあると思っています。

GA：いつか，美術館側のスペースの使い方をこぼしておられましたね。

シザ：まさにそうなのです。といいますのは，私のなかでは，美術館はさまざまな使い方に対して開かれているからです。建物を改造すべき必要などないのです。もし窓を取り去ったりしたら，何かが失われます。窓は光のバランスが必要であるので配置されているのであり，それによって，観客は見晴らしを手にすることが出来る。空間は窓のあるままで使われるべきなのです。あの窓を考えに入れながら，展示計画が出来るのです。ところが彼らは窓をふさいでしまった。ある日，そこに行ってみると，ファサード全体がスティールの看板で覆われていたのです。ポレミックな一時的休止期間であるとも考えられましたが，それはまったくポレミックではなかった。おかしなことです。単なる消費主義者の浪費にすぎません。こうした類のことには，私にはまったく興味がありません。

View from staircase on second floor　階段室：2階より見る

Bookshop on ground floor　1階 ブックショップ

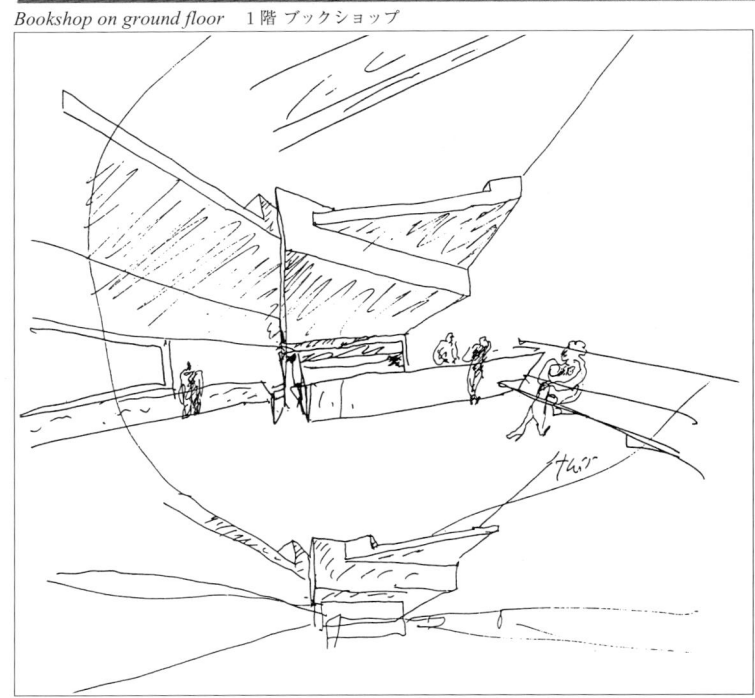

View toward main entrance　メイン・エントランスを見る

Exhibition space on ground floor　1階展示スペース

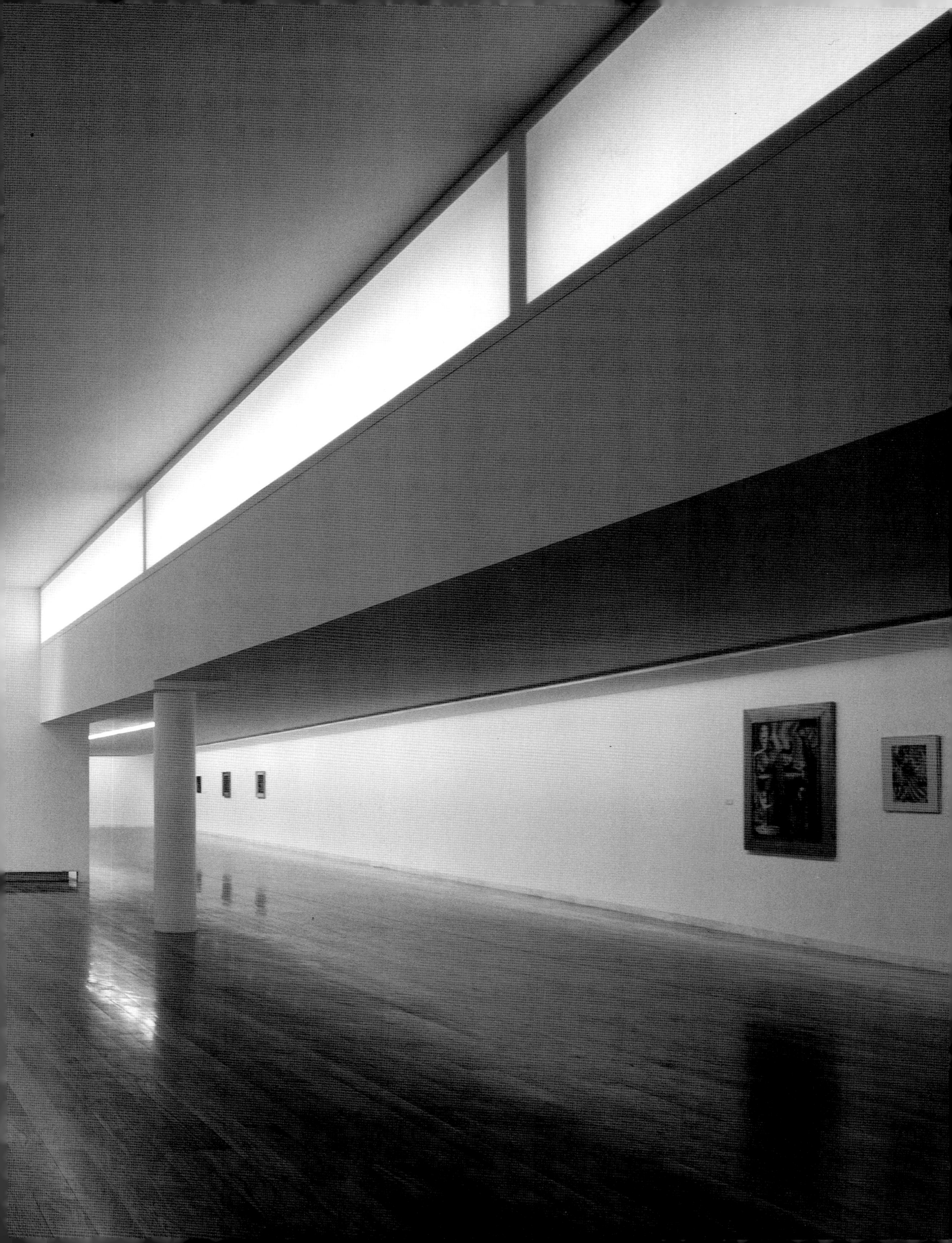

△▽ Exhibition space on ground floor　1階展示スペース

Exhibition space on second floor　2階展示スペース

Exhibition space on basement　地階展示スペース

Lecture hall レクチャー・ホール

Double-height exhibition space on second floor 2層分の高さの2階展示スペース ▷

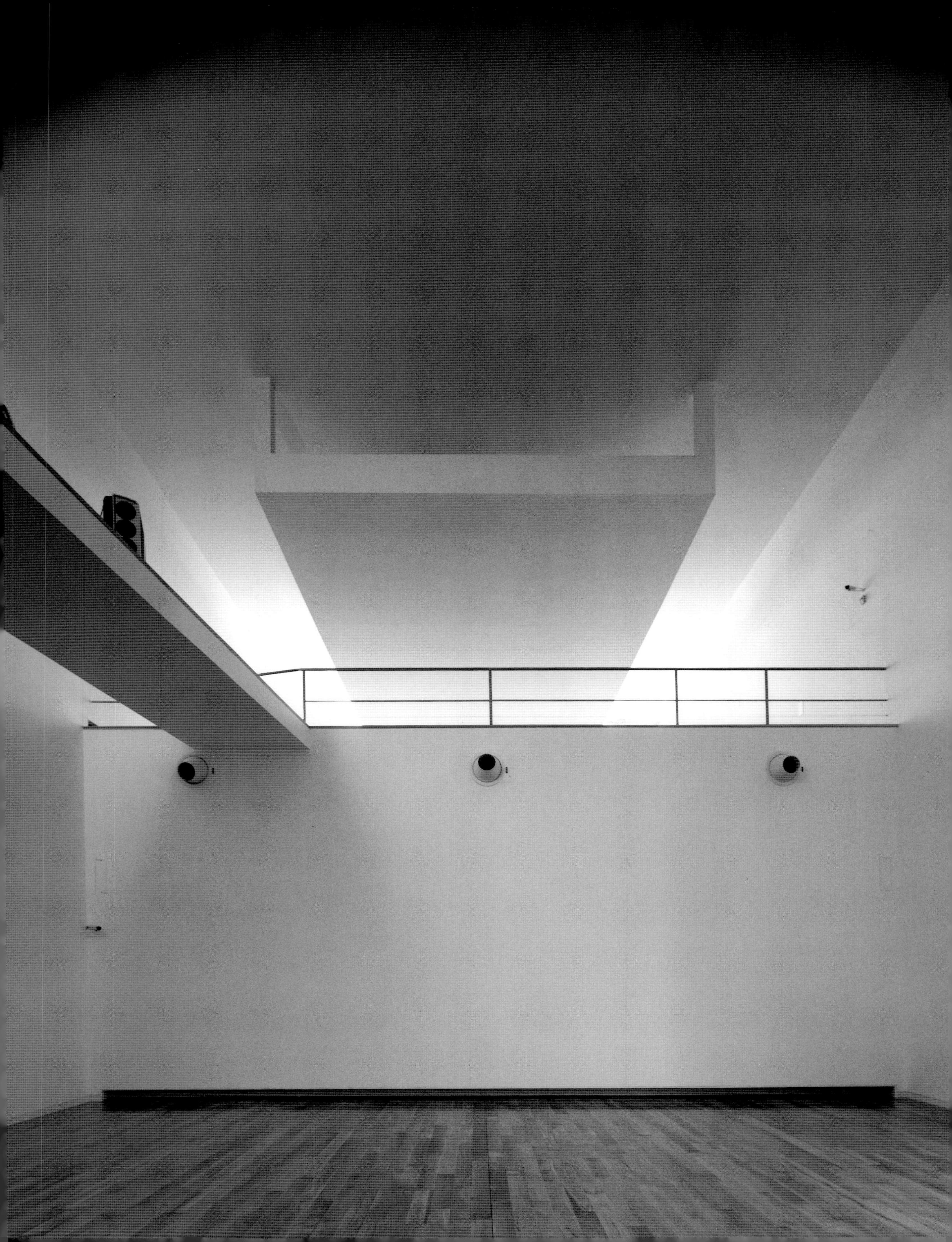

Main Library, University of Aveiro
アヴェイロ大学図書館

Aveiro, Portugal

Client: University of Aveiro Design period: 1988–95 Construction period: 1990–95 Architects: Álvaro Siza Arquitecto, Lda Collaborators: [Phase I] André Braga, Anton Graf, project architects for execution; Maria Clara Bastai, Cristina Ferreirinha, Ashton Richards, Chiara Porcu, Alessandro D'Amico, assistants; [Phase II] André Braga, Edite Rosa, project architects for execution; Clemente Menéres Semide, Matthew Becher, assistants; Matthew Becher, Peter Testa, Edite Rosa, Clemente Menéres Semide, project architects for exterior arrangements; Edite Rosa, Clemente Menéres Semide, project architects for furniture; [Exterior arrangements (1995)] Edite Rosa, Jorge Nuno Monteiro, project architects, Paul Scott, assistant Structural engineer, G.O.P. Mechanical engineer: Matos Campos Interior designer and landscape architect: Álvaro Siza Arquitecto, Lda General contractors: [Phase I] Obrecol; [Phase II] Campo Alegre Structural system: reinforced concrete structure

View from south 南より見る

Site plan

View from east 東より見る

Fourth floor

Third floor

Second floor

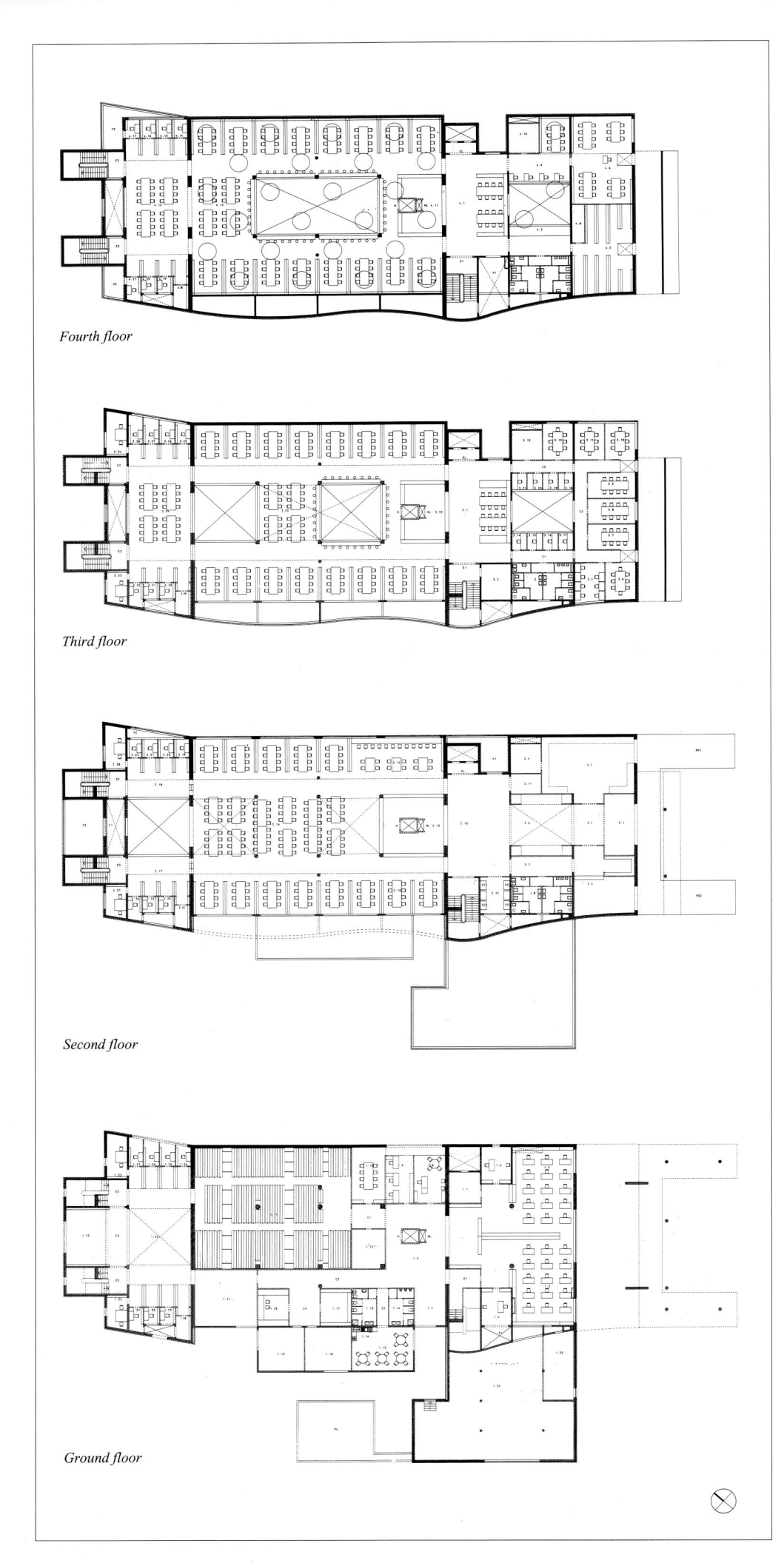

Ground floor

GA: This library is part of your own masterplan for the campus. Tell me how the project started.

Álvaro Siza: Actually, I didn't do the master plan, but that's another story. The University of Aveiro had a master plan before I came to the project. This existing building, a canteen and elevated square, were a part of a Unitarian building which was the campus. It was the concept of having a single structure with faculties and classrooms inside. Also, the water of the area is at a high elevation, and there are underground areas where water penetrated. The university was not happy with the plan and charged the faculty of architecture of Oporto to study a new one. At the same time I was called upon to do the library. There were no constraints. There were the beginnings of a new plan. And in fact, I was told that the library should be located in a free space in front of water. And there were discussions between the people involved in the new development. I presented a sketch where I indicated the library in the siting where it is now. The first floor at the same level of the existing elevated square related with a bridge platform and with another floor below. And I proposed these things to be in sequence with the line of the buildings according to the former plan. I also proposed to make a ramp on pillars crossing this free space. Services and administration would be in the first floor together with a reading room extended to a garden. The whole is finished with a platform, slightly elevated with grass. This hasn't been built yet. The ramp is currently under construction. When I proposed this, I said the new buildings should be put around a big space. The sketch showed the basic organization. The concept was adopted, and my buildings stayed as I had wanted. But the line of the buildings that I suggested was shifted, so in my opinion the resulting open space is not at the right scale. It's too small.

The other thing is that after the construction of the library was underway, they decided to make a new building which didn't work well in the overall composition. It was outside of the master plan. This is the story. I presented a sketch which gave an idea of what I thought the plan should be. I was allowed to do the library but the rest was more or less thrown out. So I don't recognize it as my own.

GA: Did you have a particular strategy for the library itself?

Siza: I've always thought of a library as being a special building. You think immediately of these large spaces, surrounded by books. It is about preserving knowledge in books and then being able to access them. But the tenets in the 1950s was to reduce the library spaces into a linear organization, instead of having a central space. Recently this is again changing with the development of open-stack libraries. The relationship of the stacks and the public has changed again, so once again you have the need for a central space. So here what I wanted to do was to connect the three floors by openings and thereby create the sense of a total space and also bring in natural light to the center of the building. I was able to create an atmosphere that wouldn't be possible within the systematically organized models.

GA: The first time I visited the building, I sensed the influence of Aalto.

Siza: This concept of using light is a solution Alvar Aalto used in his libraries. If there are good precedents, you learn from them and use them.

GA: You also designed all of the furniture?

Siza: Yes. I did. I always try to design all of the furniture. Sometimes I use past designs, sometimes I try to design new things. I think it's important in designing the atmosphere of a building to be able to choose from other designs or to design yourself. Sometimes of course a client doesn't let you choose. I wouldn't mind if a client was able to make good choices, but usually the choices are not so good and the results are bad.

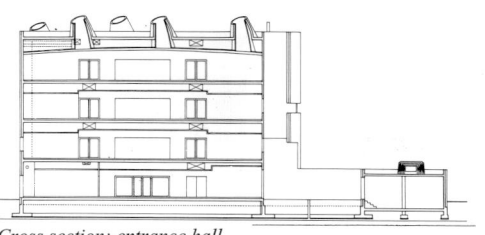

Cross section: entrance hall

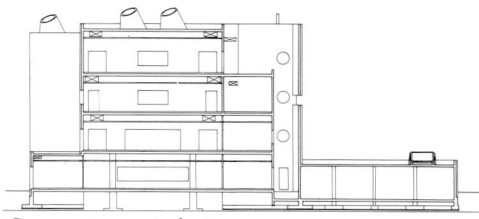

Cross section: central axis

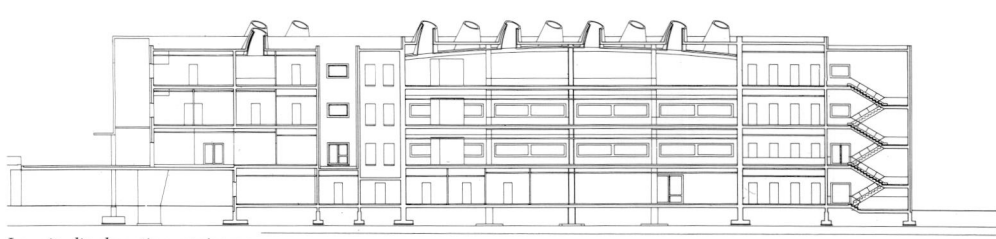

Longitudinal section: staircase

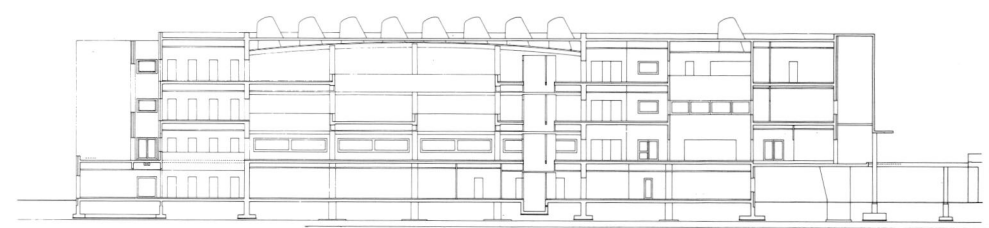

Longitudinal section: central axis

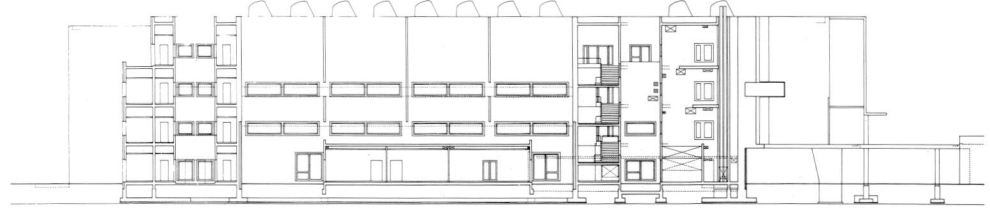

Longitudinal section: gap between facade

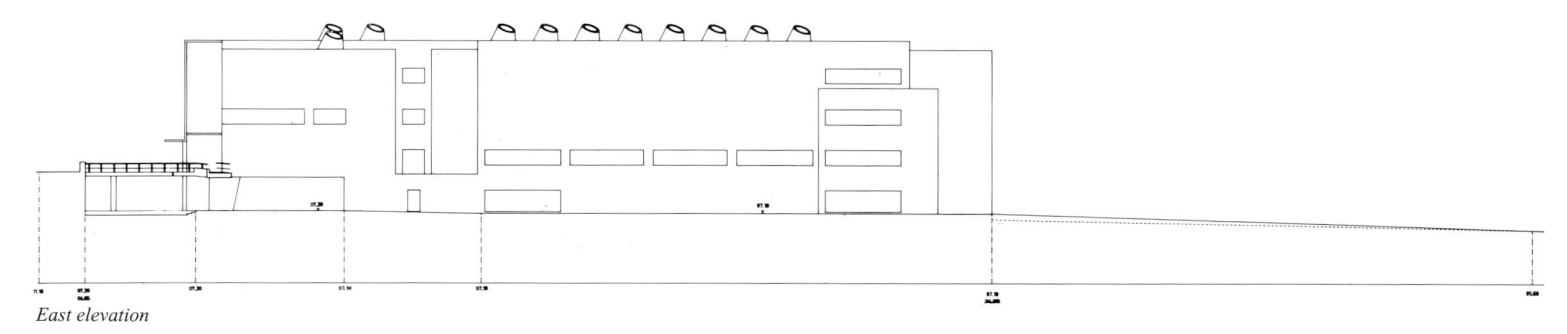

East elevation

West elevation

Reading room on second floor　2階閲覧室

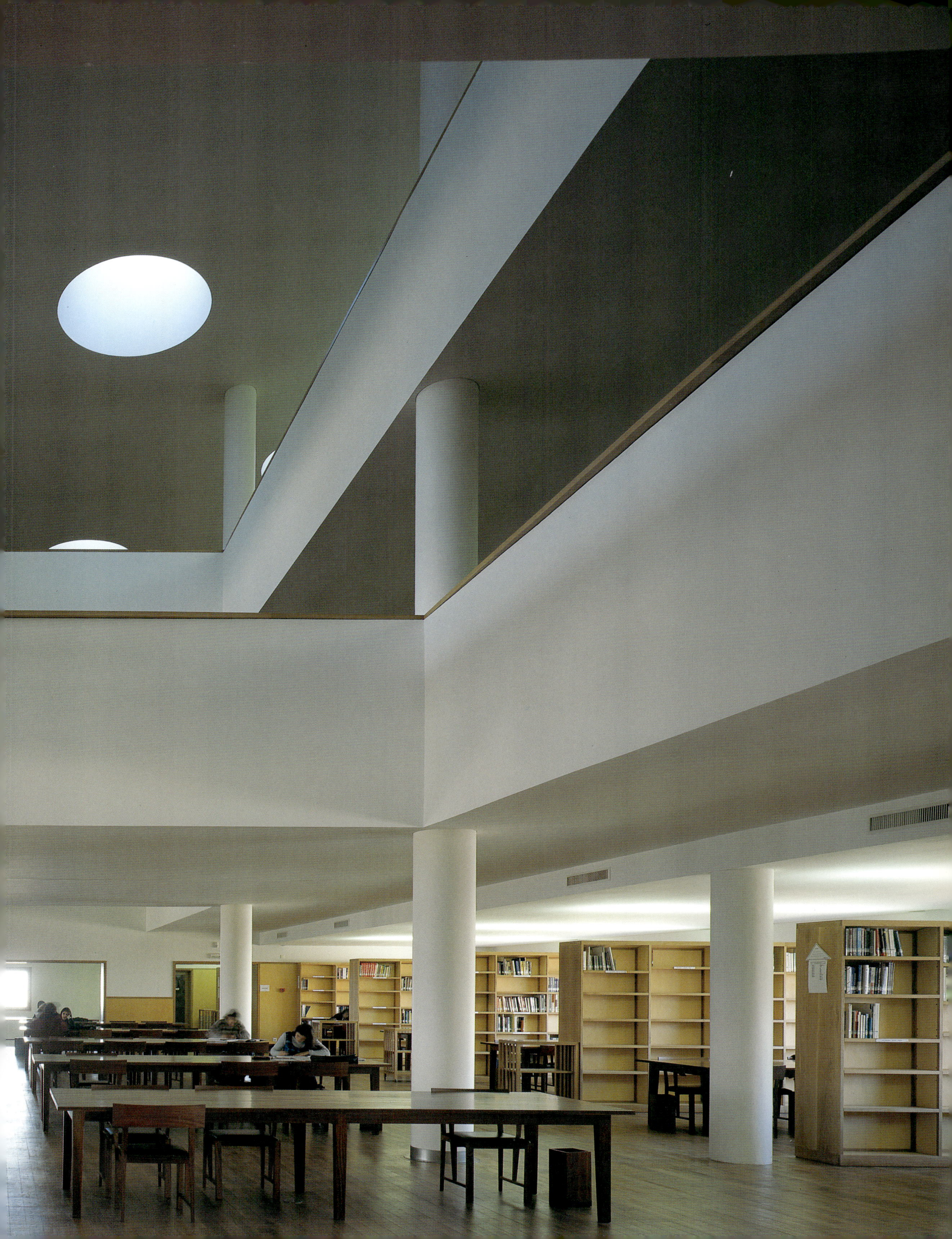

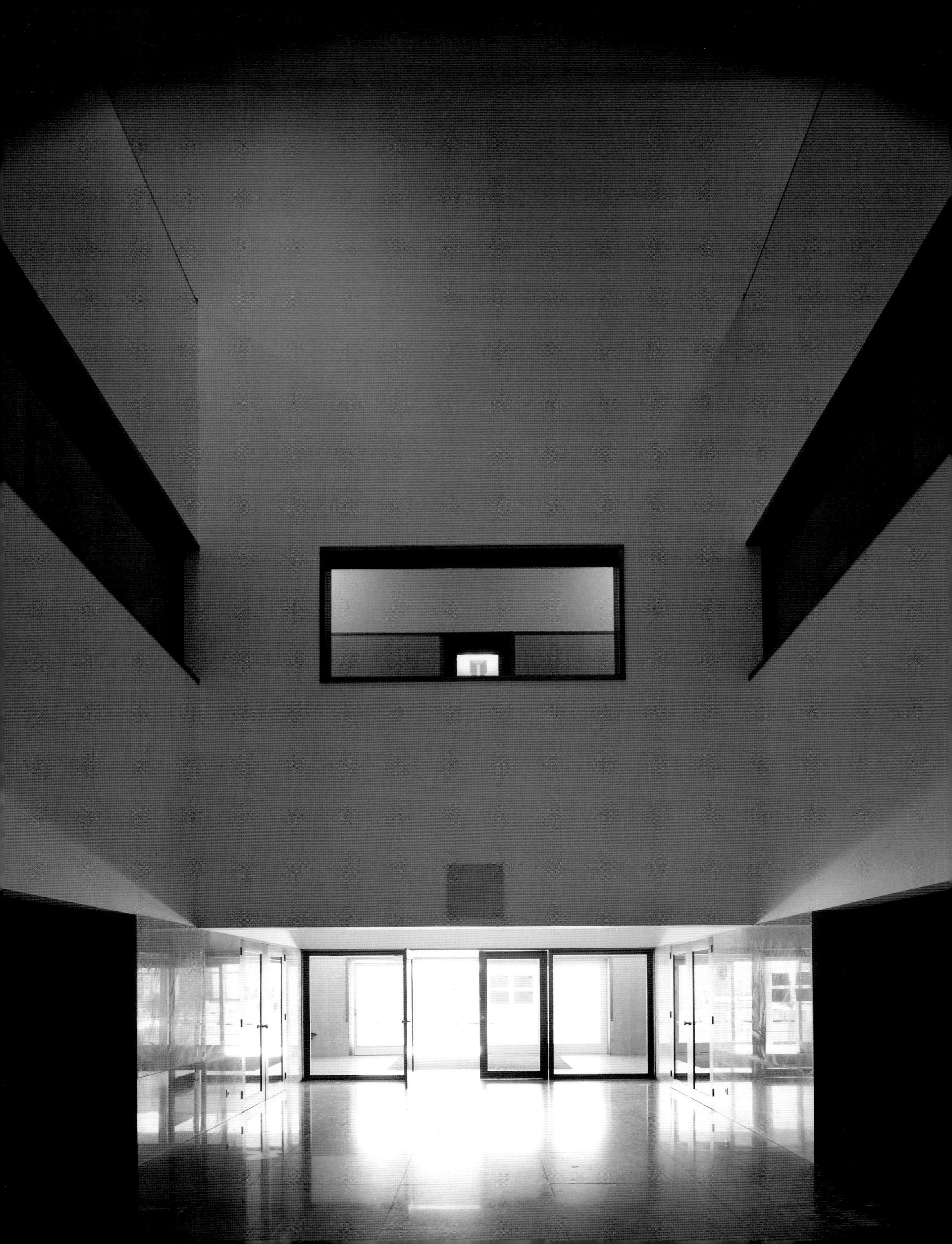

GA：この図書館はシザさんご自身でつくられたキャンパスの全体計画に組み込まれているものですね。

アルヴァロ・シザ：実際には，私は全体計画をつくっていないのですが，そこにはまた別なストーリーがあるのです。アヴェイロ大学には，私がこのプロジェクトに参加する前に既に全体計画があったのです。既にあったこの学生食堂と造成されて高く持ち上げられている広場(プラットフォーム)は，その全体計画の一部だったのです。ファカルティ・ルームと教室が内部に置かれた単一の建物にするというのがコンセプトでした。また，この地域の水位は高く，地下水が浸透しています。大学側はこのプランに不満で，ポルト大学建築学部に対し新しい案の作成を依頼したのです。同時に私は，図書館の設計も頼まれました。束縛は何もありません。新しい計画案の始まりです。そして実際に，図書館は水辺の前の何もない空間に配置すべきだと言われていたのです。そしてこの新たな開発計画に関わっている人たちの間での討議がありました。そこで，今の敷地にその図書館を配したスケッチを提示したのです。エントランス階は高く持ち上げられた既存の広場と同じ高さにあり，ブリッジで広場や下の別の階とつながっています。そして，これらのものが，以前の全体計画に従った建物の列につながるようにすることを提案しました。また，この何もない空間を横断する，支柱に乗せたスロープをつくることも提案しました。サービスと管理事務局は，庭へ伸びる図書室と共に同じ階に置かれることになるでしょう。全体が，芝生で少し高くなっているプラットフォームというかたちになります。これはまだ建設されていません。スロープが目下，工事に入っています。これを提案したとき，新しい建物は広い空間の周囲に配置すべきだと主張しました。このスケッチは基本的な構成を示しています。コンセプトは受け入れられましたし，建物の設計案は希望通り残りました。しかし，私が提示した建物のガイドラインは変えられてしまいましたから，私の意見では，結果として生まれた空間は正しいスケールではありません。小さすぎます。

それともう一つ，図書館の工事が始まった後で，全体構成とはうまくかみあわない新しい建物を建てることが決められました。それは全体計画から外れたものでした。これが顛末です。計画がどうあるべきと思うかというアイディアを説明するスケッチを提示しました。図書館は認められましたが，残る部分は多かれ少なかれ放棄されました。ですから，これが，私のものであるとは認めるわけには行きません。

GA：図書館そのものに対する特別なストラテジーはあったのでしょうか。

シザ：図書館のことを特別な建物としてずっと考えていました。書物に囲まれた，大きな空間

◁ *Entrance hall* エントランス・ホール

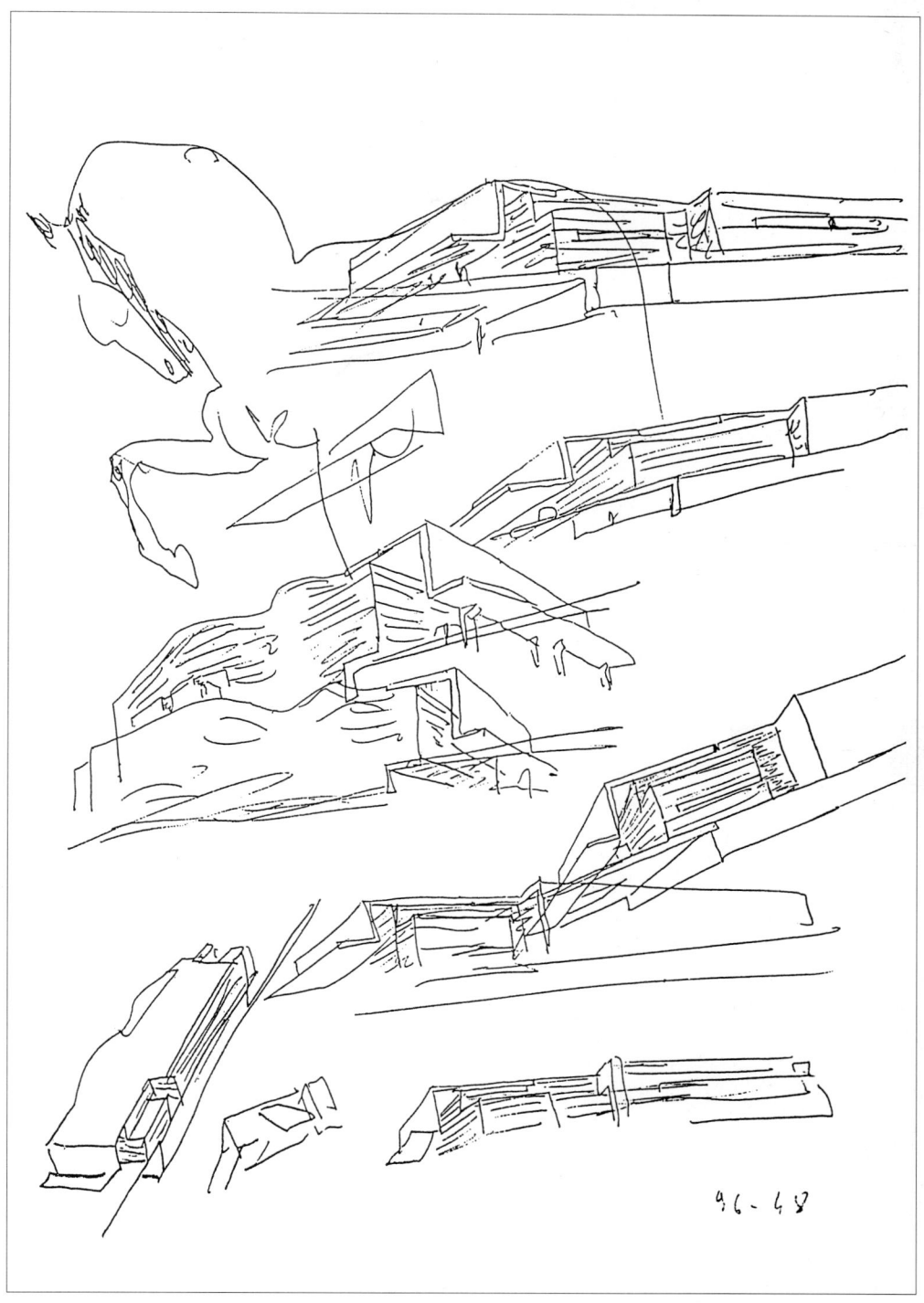

がまず頭に浮かぶ。それは本のかたちで知識を保存することであり，次にそれらにアクセスすることが出来るということがある。しかし，1950年代の見解は，中央空間をつくる代わりに，リニアーな編成へと図書館の中央空間を縮小するものでした。最近これが，開架式図書館の発展に伴って再び変化してきています。書庫と来館者との関係がまた変わったため，中央の空間が再び必要になったのです。そこで，ここで私がやりたかったのは，開口で3階分をつなぎ，それによって全体空間の感覚をつくりだすと共に，建物の中央部に自然の光を浸透させることでした。システマティックな編成モデルの範囲内では不可能と思われる，ある雰囲気をつくりだすことが出来ました。

GA：初めてこの建物を訪れたとき，アアルトの影響を感じました。

シザ：光の使い方についてのコンセプトは，アルヴァ・アアルトが彼の図書館で使っている方法なのです。良い前例があれば，そこから学び，それを使うことです。

GA：家具もすべてデザインされたのですね。

シザ：そうです。いつも家具をすべてデザインするようにつとめています。時には，前にデザインしたものを使い，時には新しくデザインするようにしています。家具を，他のデザインから選んだり，自分でデザインできるように建物の雰囲気を構成することは大切だと思います。もちろん，ときにはクライアントは選ばせてくれません。クライアントが良い選択を出来た場合は気になりませんが，たいていの場合，選択はあまり感心できないもので，その結果は良いものとはなりません。

Reading room on fourth floor 4階閲覧室

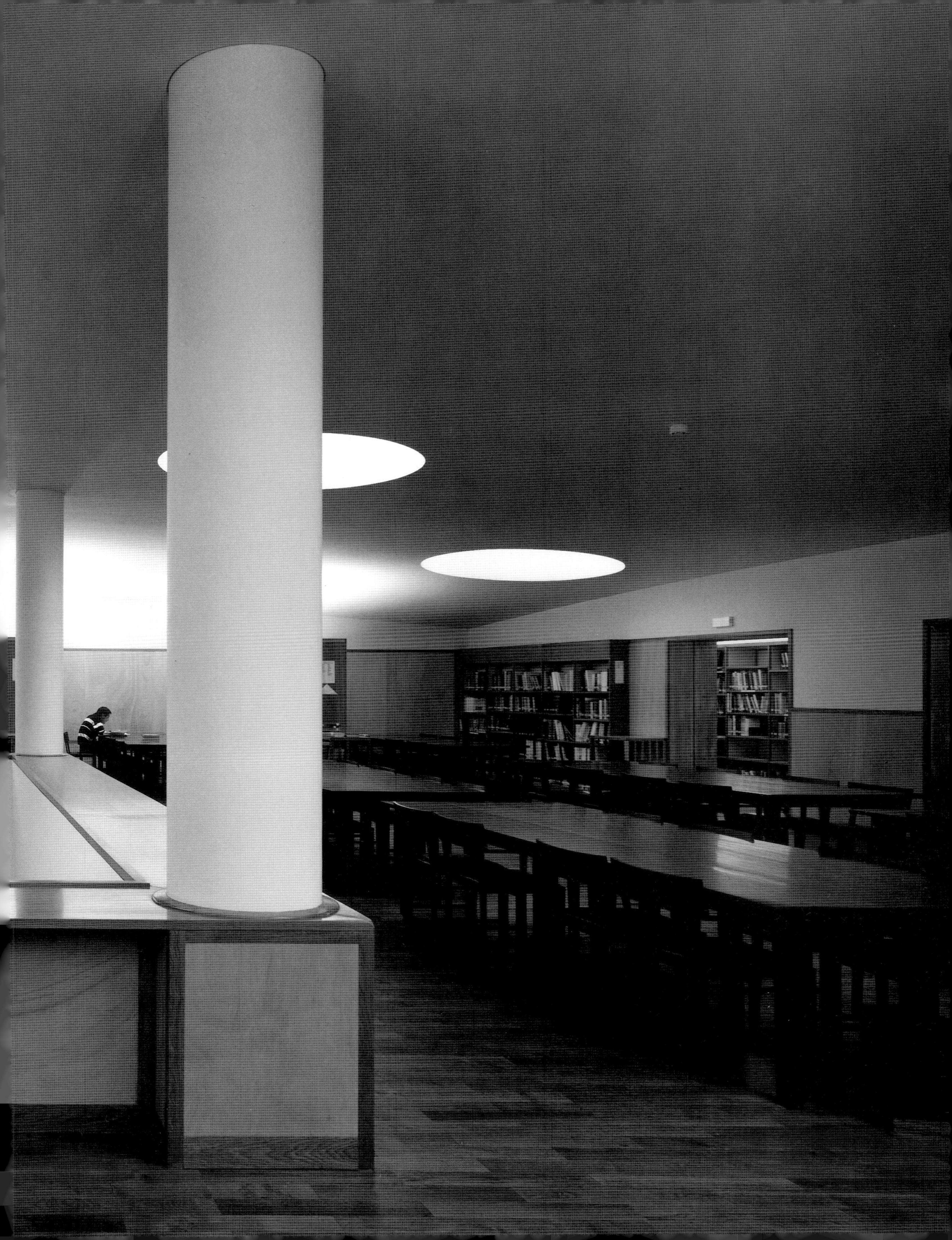

DESCRIPTION
Siting

The siting and volumetrics of the Library building, as well as its relation with the surrounding spaces (the areas of parking and exterior access) are integrated into the master plan of the University Campus. The study of the exterior arrangements, to be delivered opportunely, will be finalized, in terms of the execution project, with the above mentioned ideas.

Program

(1) The organization of the Library program rests in the definition of three types of zones:

a) zones of utilization—that include diverse types of spaces, either open, or in offices and study rooms.

b) zones for the storage of publications—that include air conditioned spaces and the storage of publications in use and in deposit.

c) zones of service—that include spaces for the maintenance and support of the Library's functioning.

(2) The depth of the questions raised in the analysis of the program determined the option of free access to the publications by the users. In terms of organization this signified an overlapping of spaces dedicated to the zones of utilization and the zones for the storage of publications, with the exception of the special resources, whose access is controlled, and the book deposit, whose demand for consultation is sporadic. In consequence of this option, the basic unit in the organization of the Library is constituted by a reading table surrounded by two or three divider/shelves, in a manner of defining a semi-autonomous space.

(3) The program of the Library is distributed into four floors, in accord with the following principles:

a) The ground floor is destined fundamentally to technical services, maintenance, and the staff installations, this includes the director, secretary, conference room, the divisions of information and library organization, conference room for librarians, the book deposit, administrative archive, lunch room for staff, bathrooms, offices of binding and printing, microfilm laboratory, material storage, air conditioning, heating and machines for the elevators. It also includes, at the northwest end, an area dedicated to the activities of the users accessible from the second floor and is understood as a reading room with a partial double height space and individual offices, these with the possibility of functioning autonomously.

b) The second, third, and fourth floors are destined to the activities of the users and are divided longitudinally in three parts (a central part and two ends) in the following manner:

—the central part, occupied by reading rooms and information and check-out, including on the second floor, areas for card catalogues and general works;

—the southeast end, occupied on the second floor by an access to the building from the central platform of the University, an exposition room, coat room, control point, photocopy room on the third floor are audio-visual rooms, study rooms, and a typing room; and on the fourth floor, special resource rooms. Included, as well, on these three floors are the vertical circulation, informal reading areas, storage and bathrooms;

—the northwest end is occupied by individual offices and reading rooms.

(4) The total area of the building is 6,242 square meters. The maximum number of occupants is envisioned to be 1,020 users with 300,000 volumes.

Illumination and Environment

Special attention was given to the problems of visual comfort in the reading areas. Although it was not possible to dispense with artificial lighting, it was opted, as much as possible for the utilization of natural light of a form indirect and diffuse, through the application of corrective elements of the sun angles in the openings of

＜解説＞

敷地

図書館の配置と大きさ，また周辺領域（パーキングと外部アクセス）との関係は，大学キャンパスの全体計画に統合されている。適切に配分されるべき外部構成のスタディは，実施される計画という点から，上述のアイディアによって最終的なかたちにまとめられることになる。

プログラム

1）図書館のプログラム構成は，3種類のゾーンを定義することに基づいている。

　a）利用されるゾーン：オープンなまたは内部のオフィスや学習室など多様なタイプの空間から成る。

　b）書庫ゾーン：空調された，内部利用，貸出用の書庫から成る。

　c）サービス・ゾーン：メンテナンス及び図書館機能をサポートする空間から成る。

2）プログラム分析から提起された問題の複雑さから，利用者が書庫に自由に入れる方式の選択を決定した。組織化ということにおいて，これは，利用者のためのゾーンと書庫ゾーンとが重なり合うことを意味する。しかし出入りが制限され，保管されている本の閲覧相談が散発的に行われる特別資料部分は除かれる。この選択の結果，図書館の基本的なユニットは，2つか3つの間仕切り兼書棚が，一台の読書テーブルを囲み，半ば独立したスペースを構成するものとなった。

3）図書館のプログラムは，以下の原則に従って4階にわたって配分する。

　a）1階には基本的に，テクニカル・サービス，メンテナンス，スタッフ関係の諸室を配置する。これには館長室，秘書室，会議室，情報及び図書館組織部門，司書会議室，図書貸し出し，管理部門資料室，職員食堂，バスルーム，装丁・印刷室，マイクロフィルム・ライブラリー，材料収納，空調暖房設備，エレベータ機械室が含まれる。また，北西端には，2階から行ける，来館者の諸活動に使えるエリアがあり，ここは，部分的に2層吹抜けになり個室オフィスの付いた読書室と解釈されるが，これらは自律的に機能する可能性を備えている。

　b）2，3，4階は，図書館利用者のためのスペースであり，長手方向に沿って3つの部分（中央と2つの端部）に，以下のように分割されている。

——中央部：閲覧室，インフォメーション及びチェックアウト。2階を含め，蔵書カード及び一般事務。

——南東端：2階は，大学の中央プラットフォームからこの図書館への進入路，展示室，クローク，コントロール・ポイント，コピー室。3階はオーディオ・ヴィジュアル室，スタディ・ルーム，タイプ室。4階は特別文献室。また，3層は垂直動線でつながれ，それぞれの階にインフォーマルな閲覧エリア，収納，洗面所が付いている。

——北西端：個室オフィスと閲覧室。

4）延べ床面積は6,242㎡。利用可能な人数は最大1,020人。収蔵図書は最大300,000冊を想定している。

照明と環境

閲覧エリアの光の制御の問題については，特別の注意が払われている。人工照明なしで済ますことは不可能だが，壁の開口部や屋根のスカイライトに太陽光線の角度を調節する装置をつけることによって，できるだけ，直接光や拡散光というかたちで自然光を利用している。床にとった開口（2層吹抜け空間）の存在が光の拡散を調節し，各階を視覚的に連続させ，全体を大きくまとめている。

　建物の環境制御は，外壁と屋根に充填した密な断熱材，二重ガラス，空調によって行う。

建設

鉄筋コンクリート及び金属部材からなる躯体は，建物の仕上げなしの構造体のほぼ全部を構成しており，図書館の基本的な区画のディメンションの機能のなかで調節されている。構造グリッドは，中央部では，8ｍ（幅）×8.2ｍ（長さ）の構造部材によるスペーシングとなり，両

the walls and in the skylights of the roof. The existence of openings in the floors (double height spaces) adjusts the diffusion of light and the visual continuity between the various floors, bringing all into a greater unity.

The environmental control of the building is comprised of a system of compact thermal insulation in the exterior walls and roofs, double pane glass and a mechanical system of air conditioning.

Construction

The structure, composed of reinforced concrete and metal elements, comprises almost all of the rough structure of the building and is modulated in function of the dimensioning of the principle compartments of the library. The structural grid obtained like this results in a spacing of structural elements of 8 meters (width) by 8.2 meters (length) in the central part, varying in the ends to smaller measures. The non-structural partition walls are in hollow brick.

The interior finishes do not present a great variety, and in general finishes in wood were chosen for the reading areas, marble in the access areas and bathrooms, and ceramic tile and finished concrete in the offices and technical areas, with the majority of the ceilings in gypsum wall board in a manner to allow piping, all the interior doors and windows are painted wood, while some exterior doors have complementary metallic elements.

The exterior was defined by four types of materials—brick, limestone and dryvit on the walls, and limestone and gravel on the roofs.

端部ではそれより小さな寸法へと多様に変化する。構造体ではない間仕切壁には中空のレンガを使っている。

　内部の仕上げは多彩なものではない。全般的に閲覧室には木材が、アクセスや洗面所には大理石、オフィス及び機械室にはセラミック・タイルと上塗りしたコンクリートが使われている。天井は大部分が石膏ボードで配管が可能なように処理している。内部のドアと窓はすべて塗装した木材、外側のドアのいくつかには金属部材を補足している。

　外観の仕上げには4種類の材料を用いている。レンガ、ライムストーン、乾式壁を外壁に、屋根にはライムストーンと砂利。

Faculty of Architecture, University of Oporto
ポルト大学建築学部

Oporto, Portugal

Client: University of Oporto   Design and construction period: 1987–93   Architects: Álvaro Siza Arquitecto, Lda   Collaborators: [Preliminary design phase] Peter Testa, project architect; [Phase I (execution and construction)] Adalberto Dias, associate; J. M. Resende, E.M. da Cruz, A. Silva, L. Mendes, assistants; [Phase II (execution and construction)] A. Dias, associate; J.M. Resende, C. Porcu, A. Williamson, J. Carvalho, assistants; [Phase III (execution)] A. Dias, João Pedro Xavier, project architects; C. Porcu, C.M. Semide, J. Eusébio, U. Machold, G.P. Couto, J.E. Rebelo, S. Coelho, J.L.C. Gomes, P. Dominges, Ch. Gaenshirt, D. Laurentini; assistants; [Phase III (construction)] Chiara Porcu, project architect; [Phase IV (design)] Matthew Becker, project architect; [Phase IV (execution)] C. Porcu, project architect; M. Nery, C. Ferreirinha, E. Miranda, P. Cody, assistants; [Exterior arrangements (1987–)] C. Porcu, J. L. C. Gomes   Structural system: reinforced concrete structure

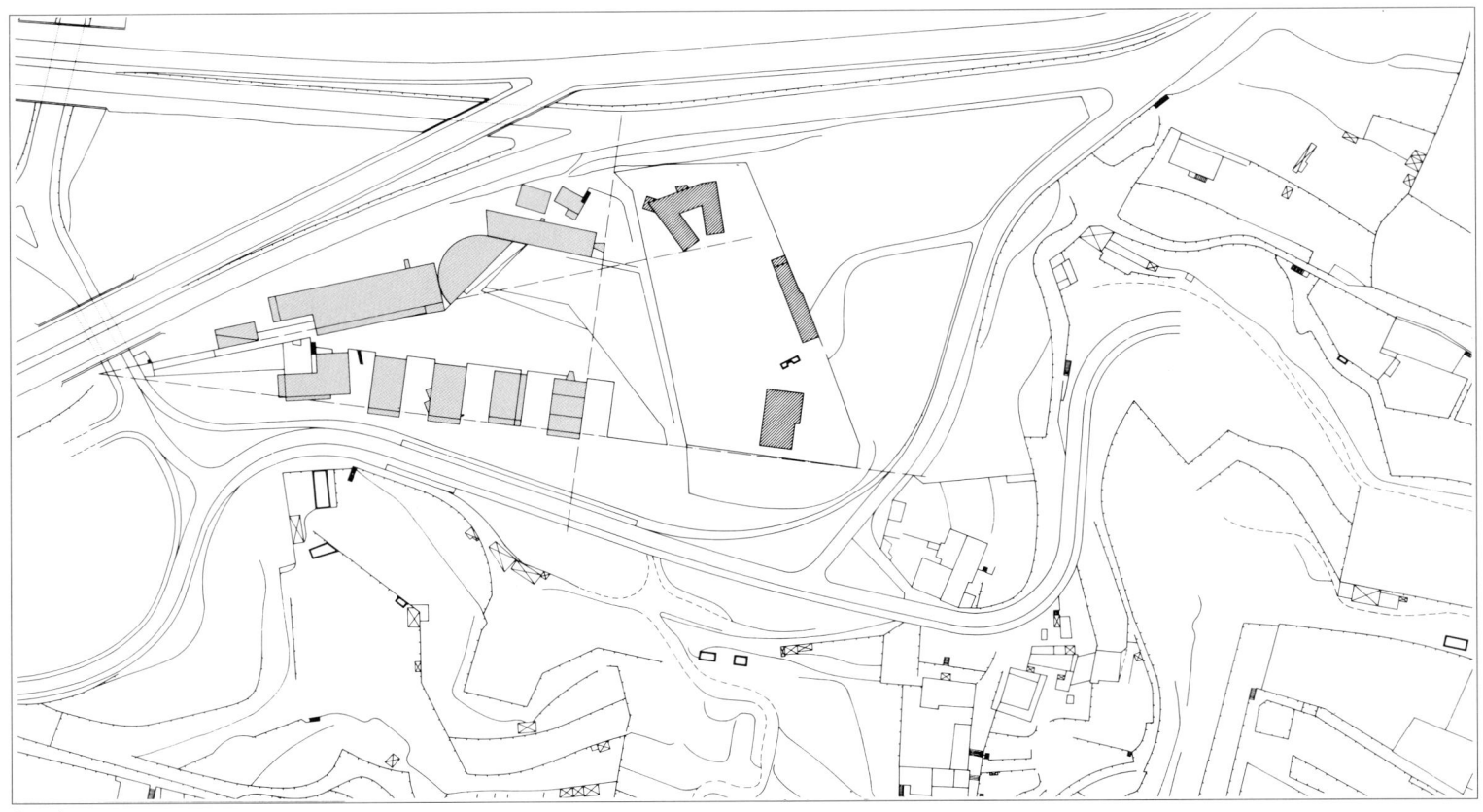

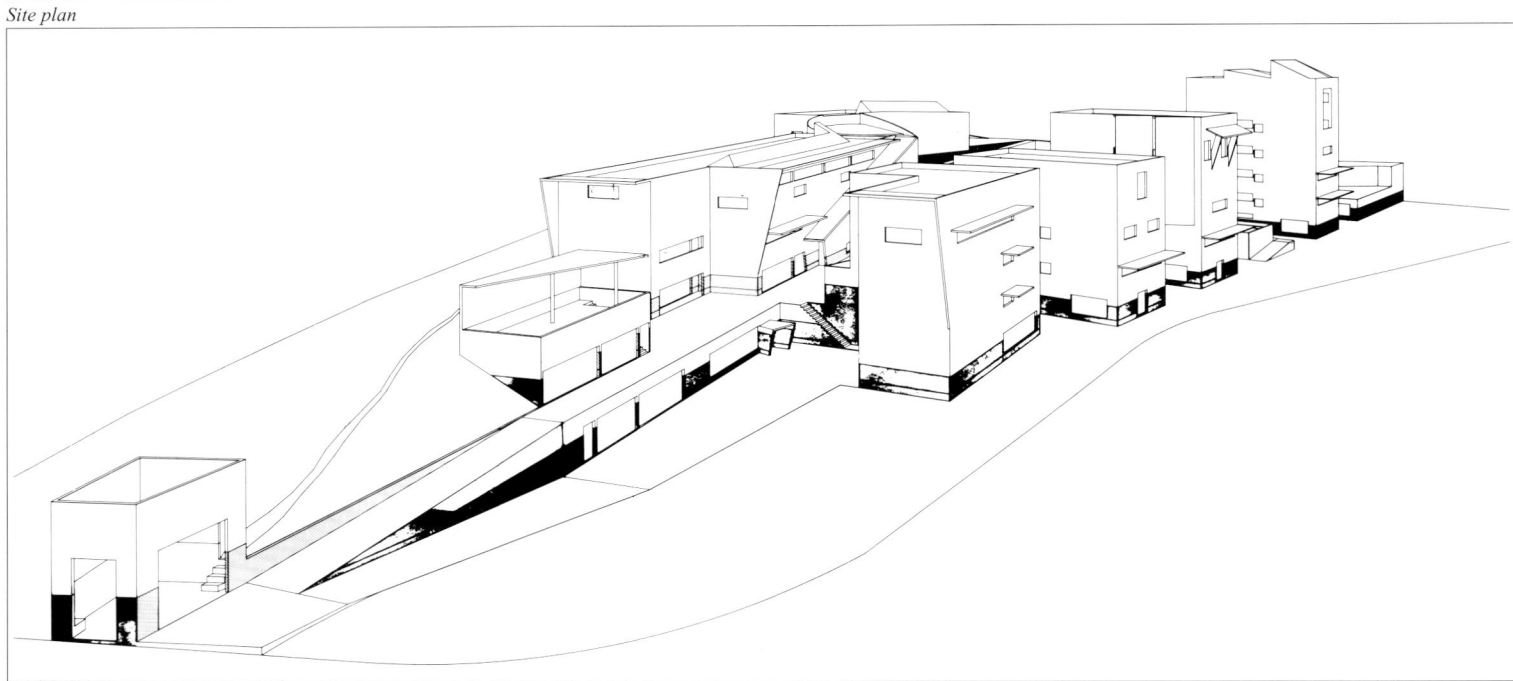

Site plan

Perspective

GA：このプロジェクトはサンティアゴ・デ・コンポステラの美術館と共に，あなたの作品のなかで一種の転換点を標すものだと思いますが。これ以降，建物の性格が少し変化したように見えます。

アルヴァロ・シザ：これは，いくつかの理由から，重要なきっかけになったものでした。第一に，私はこの学校で長い間，建築を教えていました。学校の仲間から，選ばれたわけですから，この建物を設計することになって，とても心がはずみました。第二に，これは，自分の町に設計した，私の最初の公共建築でした。今，また美術館の仕事もしていますが。二つとも，町からではなく，仲間か行政府から指名されたものです。町は私の設計する建物を望んでいないよ

GA: I think this project, along with the Museum at Santiago de Compostela, marks a kind of turning point in your career. It seems that the nature of your work has changed a bit since this project.

Álvaro Siza: This project was a big opportunity for several reasons. First, I was teaching architecture in this school for a long time. For me it was very exciting to design the building because I was chosen by my colleagues in the school. Second, it was my first public building in my town. Now I also have the museum as well. In either case, I was chosen by my colleagues or by the government ministry and not by the town. This town it seems doesn't want my buildings. But I was excited to built in Oporto. It's a wonderful site, along the river in the middle of this marvelous landscape of terraces and gardens. The area has these beautiful 19th-century houses with big gardens, some of them belonging to English families. The garden of the faculty building is also like an English garden. However, during the project there were many problems and conflicts. The master plan is not very good. There is no real comprehensive traffic planning since over time it has been altered piece by piece. My project was among the first to begin construction and my design respected the plan even though I didn't like it. I did my best. The important thing for me was to make it according to the plan and to maintain the terraces which were made all along the river for vineyards. I felt it was important to reinforce this as the landscape for the whole border of the river. Some of this was cut by streets in the 50s, but I was able to change the curve of the street a bit, and create a ramp to reconnect the system of walls. And then I remade the last terrace to define the limits of a triangular patio. It was important to reestablish this system of terraces. I also tried to work with the streets and to protect from the parkway that passed here. I wanted the platform to open to the river and remain closed along the street. I put towers here with lights on the four sides. So even inside this patio you have openness to the landscape. It completes the connection of the movement of the terraces, inside the logic of the topography, a topography worked by man.

I aligned the towers with the existing house which already belonged to the university. This kind of solution fit in well with the surrounding context. In the back, you can see the terraces and the houses on the river. It also would work together with the new elements in the landscape like the towers that were made in the 1960s. But then my relationship with the university began to deteriorate because I criticized some of the changes they made in the master plan and the way things were being handled. The newly proposed insertion of volumes in the landscape was completely indifferent to the context. And also there were intentions to change the street completely and to go on the terraces. So I became increasingly unhappy with the proceedings of the project. I told them that the university has a big cultural responsibility in terms of its building, but they never listened to me. I had a lot of problems with them, and now the works are still not finished.

GA: Construction stopped?

Siza: The main construction is done but the landscaping is not done and apparently there is no money for this. I was isolated and I didn't even have the support of my school. The building was occupied before finished. Today I get news of another change, yet this building remains unfinished.

GA: Can you tell me about the interior organization?

Siza: Basically you have the classrooms and space for group work in the four towers. It is essentially the same in each building, but the orientation of the rooms change, so that people can have different views, facing the river, or the courtyards.

Fourth floor

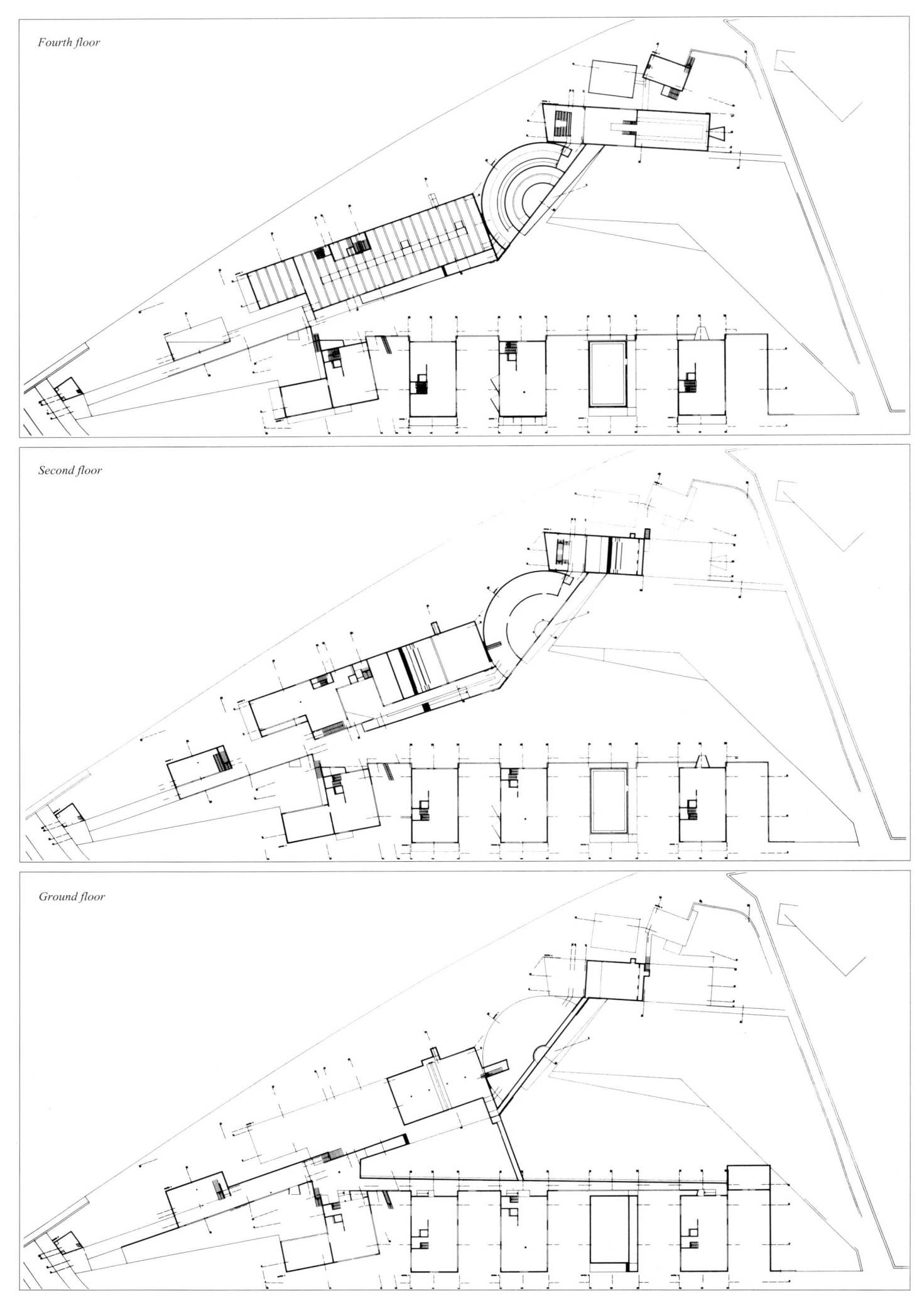

Second floor

Ground floor

Then according to the orientation comes the variety in the size and shapes of the openings, windows, and sun protection devices if needed. There is also some variations in the building profiles although they are all more or less the same dimensions as the houses on the terrace. There are lot of indications for the design decisions in the project came from both inside and outside.

GA: Did you have to consider the issue of style? In other words, was it a particular concern in light of this being a school for architecture? Some may say that a school of architecture should be as neutral as possible to allow for other voices.

Siza: In terms of program I had no options. I had a very precise program made by a commission of teachers at the school and the people at the university. It used to be a beaux-arts school and when it changed to a university the leaders of the school prescribed a very specific set of rules. For instance the school was to be for exactly 500 students. Today the school has 700 students. All of the dimensions of the different parts of the building were fixed. Students are organized in groups of fifteen so all of the rooms are designed for this many students in mind. All of these things were determined by the commission and I could not change that. I might have thought that this was not flexible enough but I could not do anything about it.

Another condition imposed by the ministry is that not more than 30% of the total square footage could be used for circulation. In my opinion, this is not enough because so much of the interaction between students and faculty occur in these kinds of spaces. It is silly. Especially when you realize that so many facilities are still missing. The auditorium is not big enough. There is no canteen, because the idea was to have canteens on the campus where all the students of the school could meet each other. And after years there are still no canteens. These are examples of disastrous planning and execution by the planning committees. In fact, in my opinion this is not a university campus at all and the mistake began with the choice of the area surrounded by big streets with access to the bridge and parkway. But even then, a good plan could have made up for the difficult location. Of course, this didn't happen.

In terms of architectural expression, I don't think anything can be completely neutral. It's an illusion to speak about neutrality. I find that the most successfully designed neutral buildings are in modern architecture. They are also the strongest and most restrained in character and effect. So it is an illusion. I don't think I have a personal style. I work according to the atmosphere of the context of where I work. The architecture of this school are related to the main lines of the landscape as I discussed before. It's the new architecture that is appearing now, that is changing and destroying this consolidated piece of landscape. It will make this building stand out as acontextual but that was not the intent. Whenever you make a building in a town or anywhere, you are a part of the town and you are a part of the landscape. And this is what an architect should always strive for. Unfortunately, very few architects work like this. When I speak of an architecture related to the landscape or the town, I'm not talking about repeating things to make the same thing. I'm not talking about a conservative contextual solution. It can be outside of the context but there must be a reason for this. The faculty building is both public and private. It is where people meet and learn. It is not the palace of the Bishop. It should be part of the tissue of the area.

受けています。

GA：スタイルの問題について考慮される必要がありましたか。つまり，建築のための学校であるということから，特に配慮されたことがありますか。建築学部の建物は，他の表現を受け入れるために，出来る限りニュートラルであるべきだと言う人もいるかもしれません。

シザ：プログラムの点では，私に選択の余地はありませんでした。学部教師と大学関係者による委員会が非常に緻密なプログラムをつくっていました。それははじめ，美術学校として計画されていたもので，それが大学に変更されたとき，学校の指導者は非常に細かな規則一式を決めていました。たとえば，学生数は正確に500人であるとか。現在，この学校には700人の学生がいます。建物のそれぞれの部分は寸法がすべて固定されている。学生は15人のグループで構成されているので，部屋はすべてこの数の学生を頭において設計されています。こうしたことはすべて委員会が決定し，私にはそれを変更出来ません。これはかなり柔軟性に欠けていると思いましたが，それについては何をなす余地もありませんでした。

政府から課せられたもう一つの条件は，延べ床面積の30％以上を動線に使用してはならないというものでした。私の意見では，これでは不十分です。学生と教師の交流のほとんどがこうしたスペースで発生するのですから。馬鹿げています。特に，かなり多くの施設が欠けていることに気づけば尚更です。オーディトリアムは十分な大きさがありません。学生食堂もありません。キャンパスにこれがあれば，学生全員がここでお互いに会えるという考えでした。数年が経ちましたが，依然として学生食堂はありません。これらは，計画委員会のひどい計画案とその強制執行の実例なのです。実際，私の考えではこれではまったくのところ大学キャンパスとはいえませんし，間違いは，橋やパークウェイへのアクセスのある大きな道路に囲まれた地域を選択したところから始まったのです。しかし，それでも，良い計画案は困難なロケーションにもつくり得るはずです。もちろん，そうはなりませんでした。

建築表現の点ですが，どんなものでも完全にニュートラルにできるとは思いません。ニュートラリティについて語ることは幻想です。最も成功したニュートラルな建物は近代建築のなかにあります。そうしたものは，その性格と効果の点で最も強く，しかも最も抑制されたものでもあるのです。つまり，一つの幻想です。私は自分がパーソナルなスタイルを持っているとは思っていません。仕事をする場所のコンテクストの持つ雰囲気に従って仕事をします。この学校の建物は，前にお話ししたように，風景の備えている主要な複数の線に関係を持たせています。それは，今，現れ始めている新しい建築であり，つまり，固められた風景のこの断片を変化させ打ち壊しているのです。それはこの建物を非文脈的なものとして際だたせるでしょうが，それは意図したものではなかったのです。街中やどこかに建物をつくるときは常に，つくり手は街の一部であり，風景の一部なのです。そうあることを，建築家が常に懸命に努力すべきなのです。残念ながら，こうした仕事の仕方をする建築家はとても少ない。風景や街に関わりを持つ建築についてお話しするとき，私は，同じものをつくるために物事を反復することについて言っているのではない。保守的な，コンテクスチュアルな解について言っているのでもありません。それはそうしたコンテクストの外にあるはずですが，そのための理由がなければならないのです。ファカルティ・ビルディングはパブリックでありプライベートなものです。人が会い，学ぶ場所です。それは司教の宮殿ではない。この地域をつくりあげて行く織物（ティッシュー）の一部であるべきなのです。

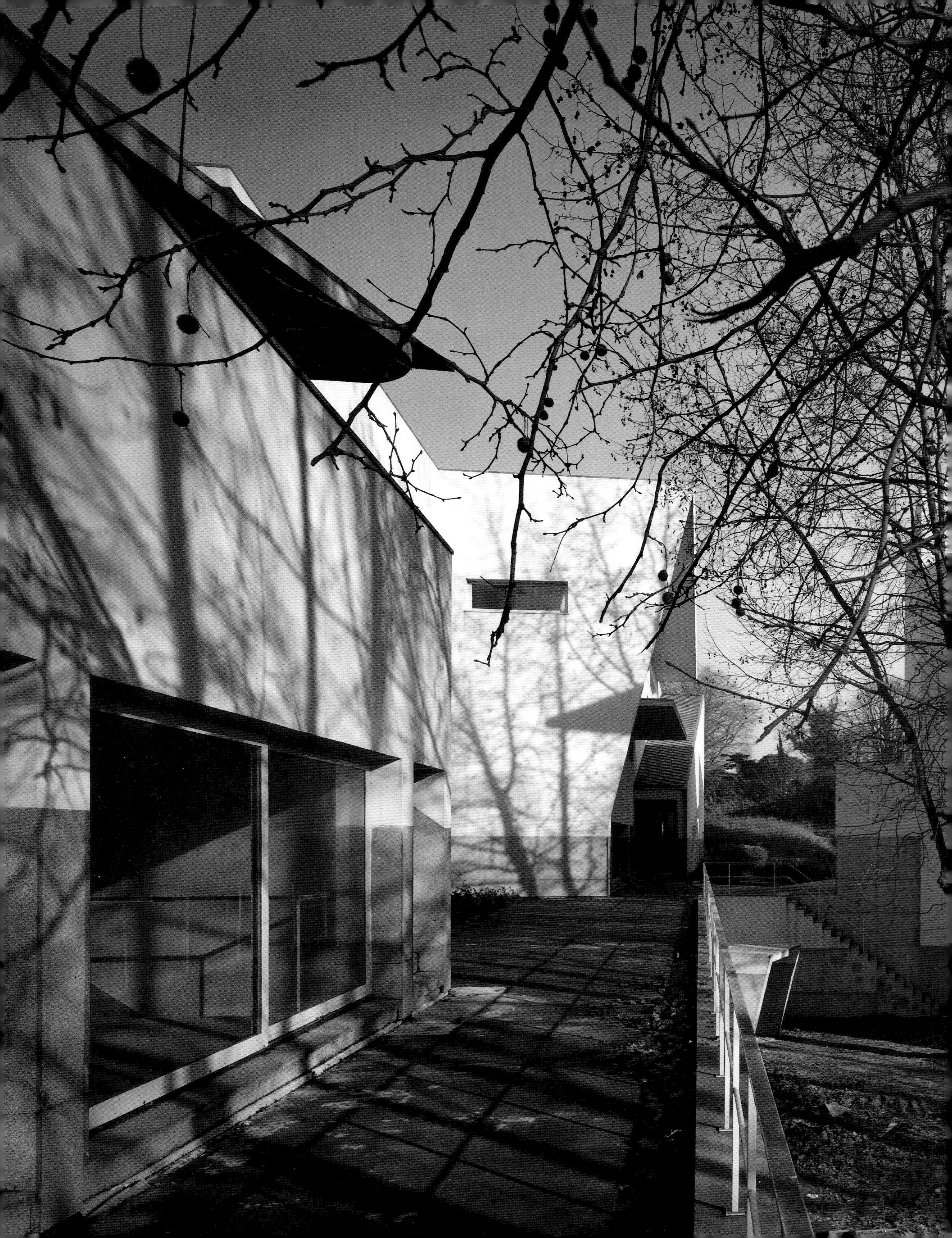

View from west: cafeteria on left 西より見る。左はカフェテリア

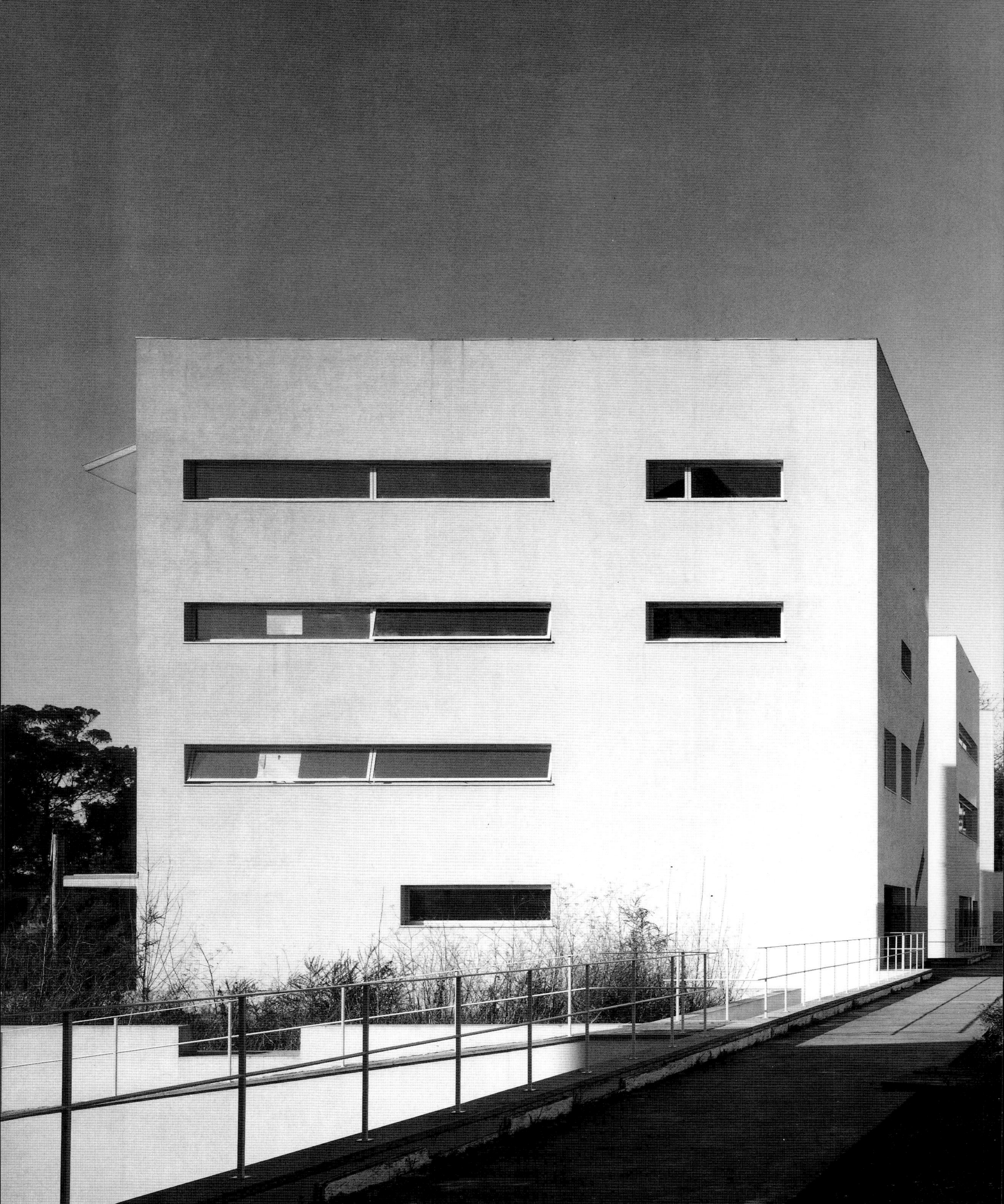

View from east 東より見る

South elevation

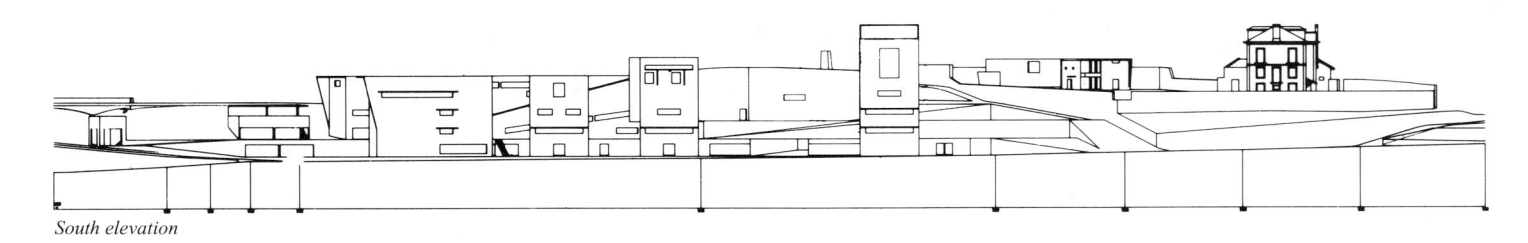

View toward cafeteria カフェテリアを見る △▷

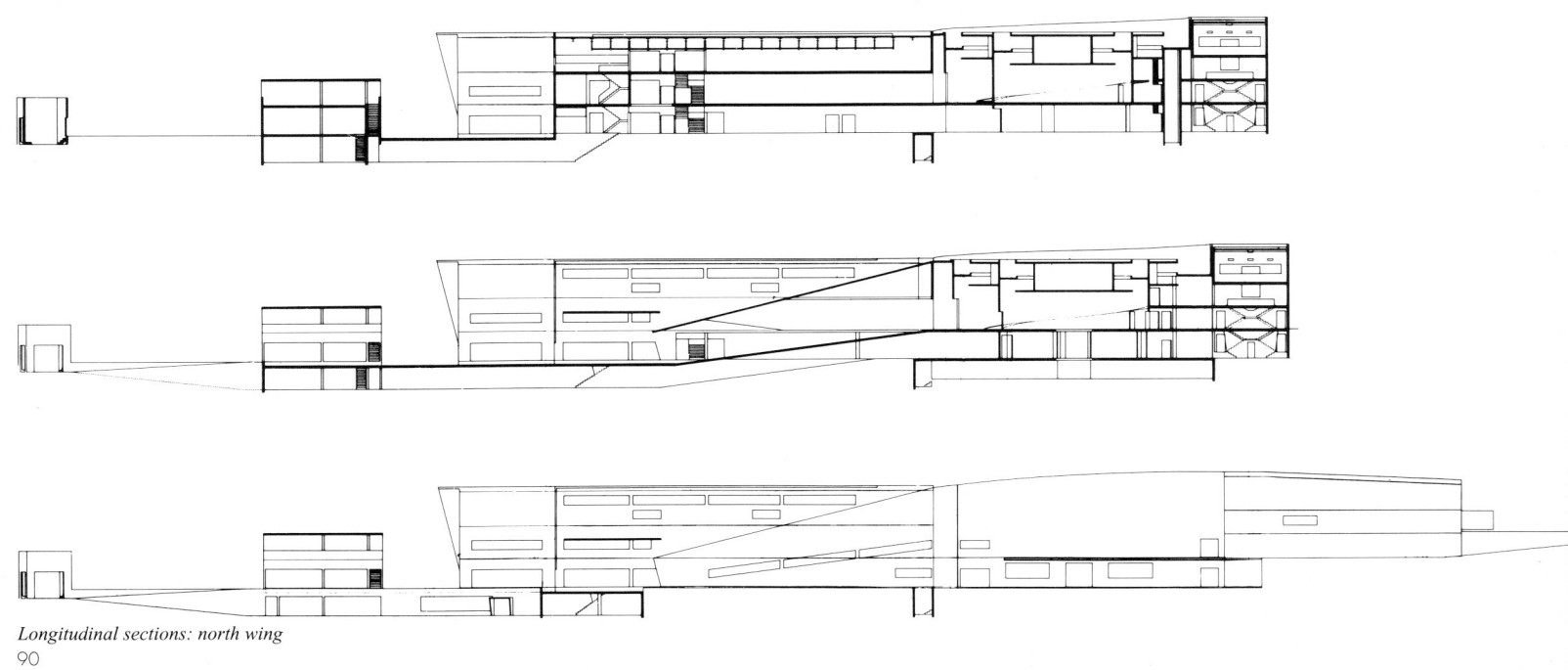

Longitudinal sections: north wing

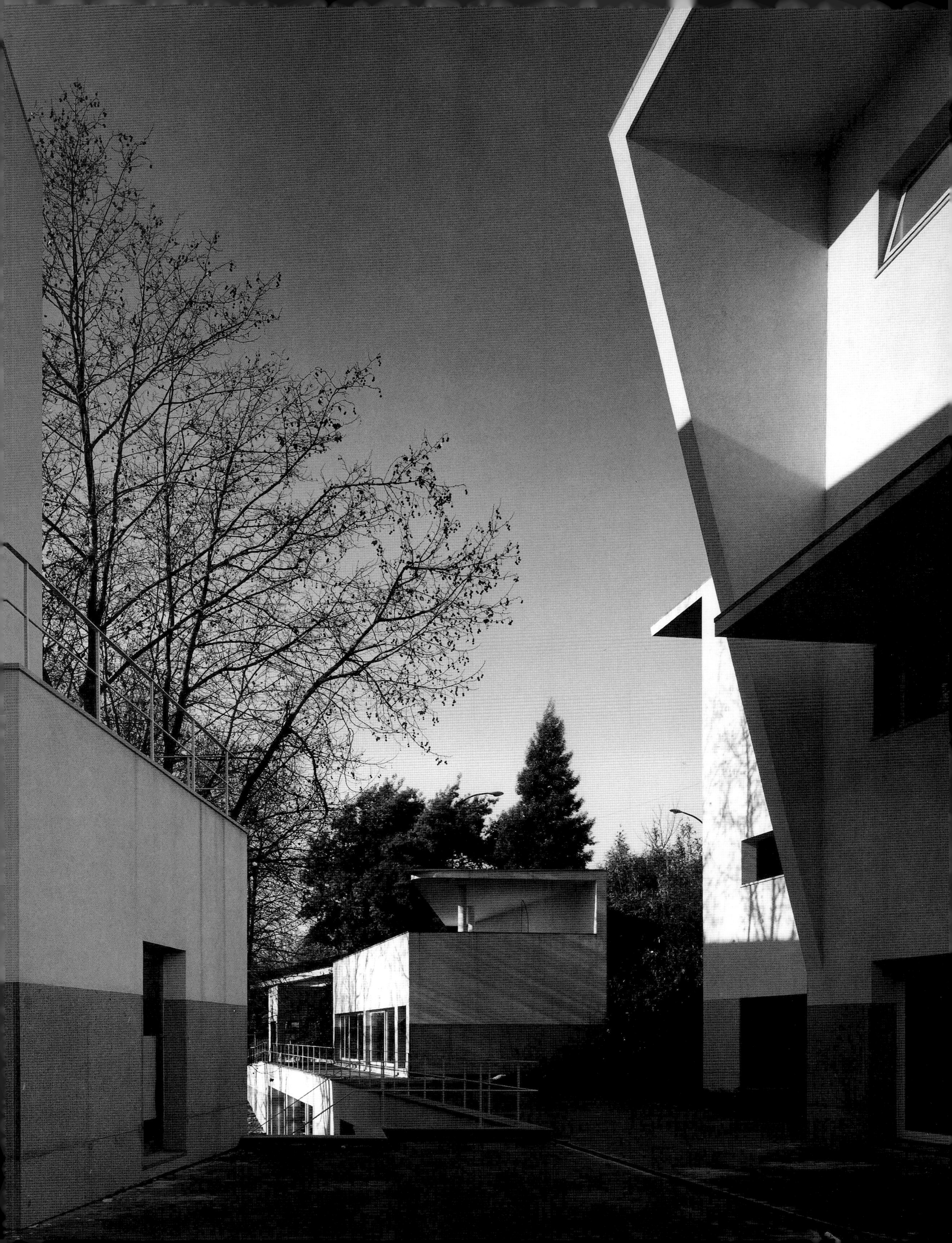

Sections

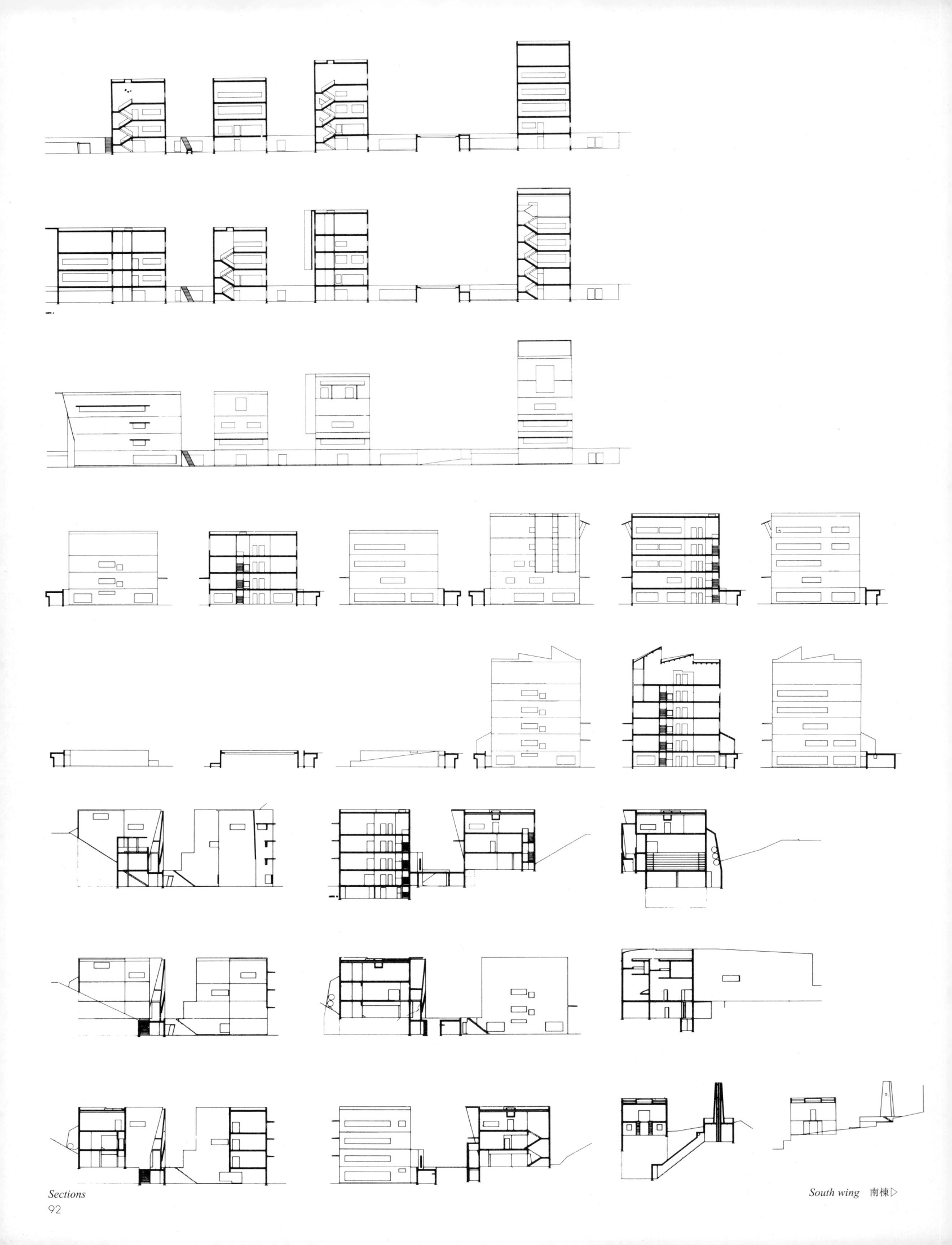

South wing 南棟▷

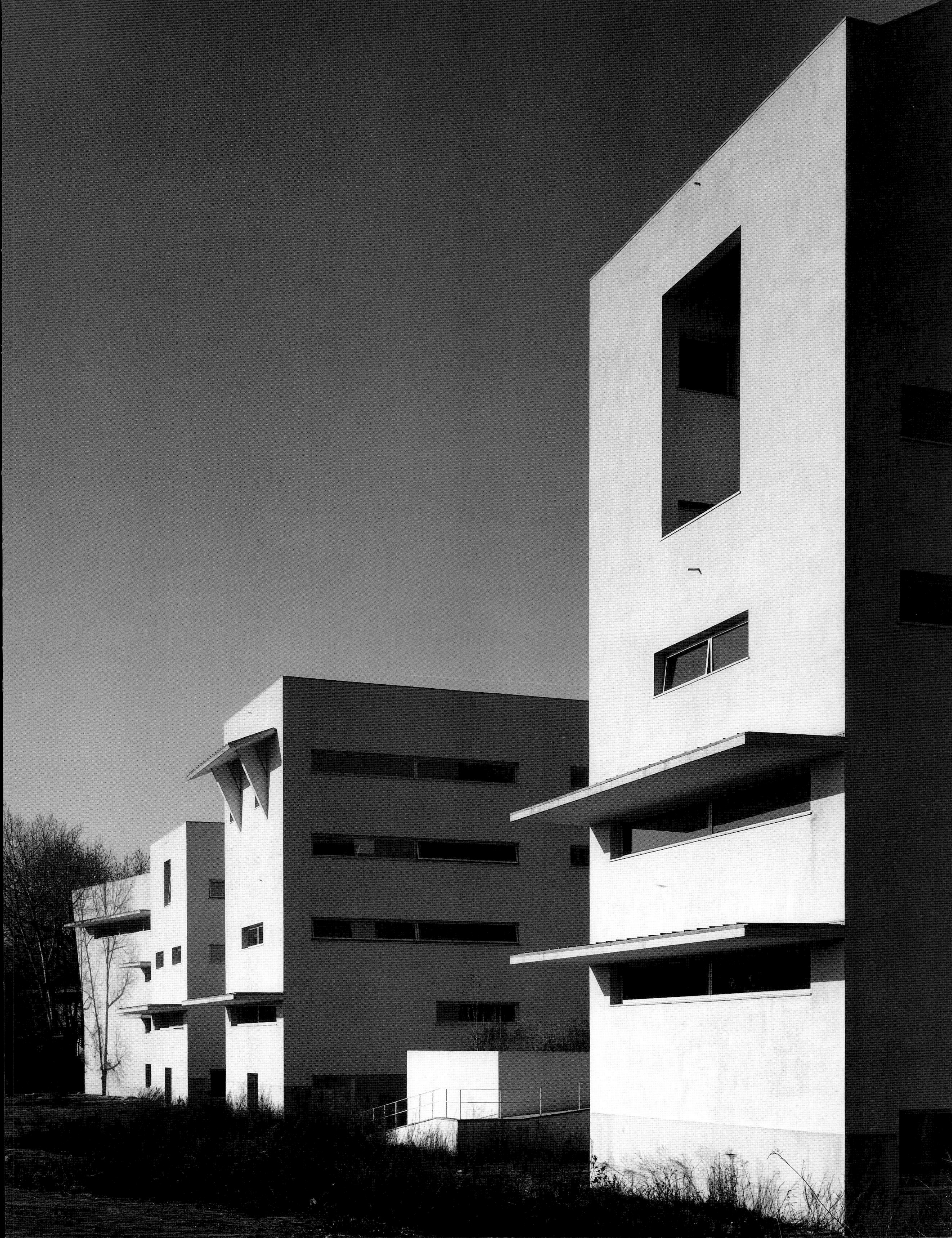

Studio on south wing　南棟のスタジオ

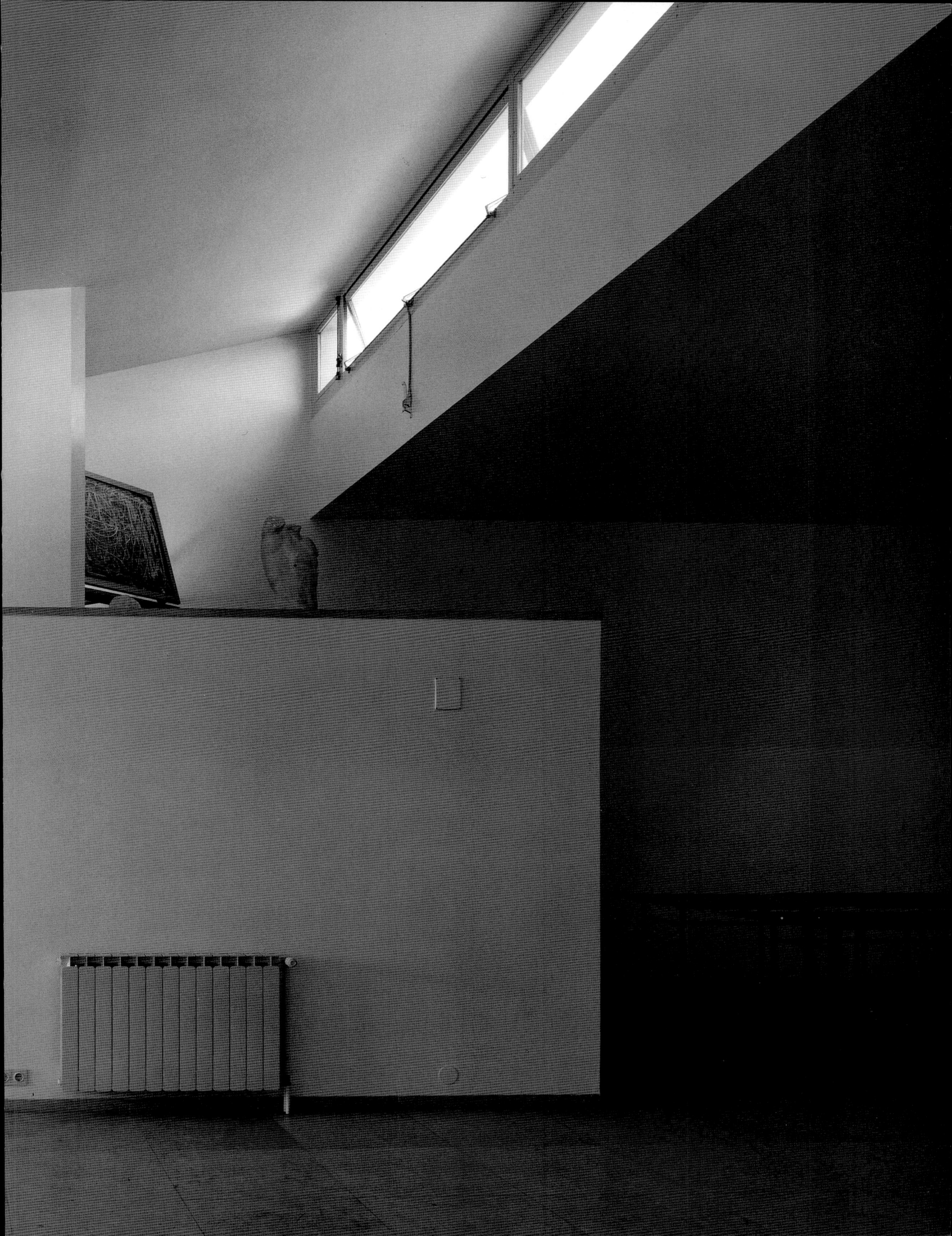

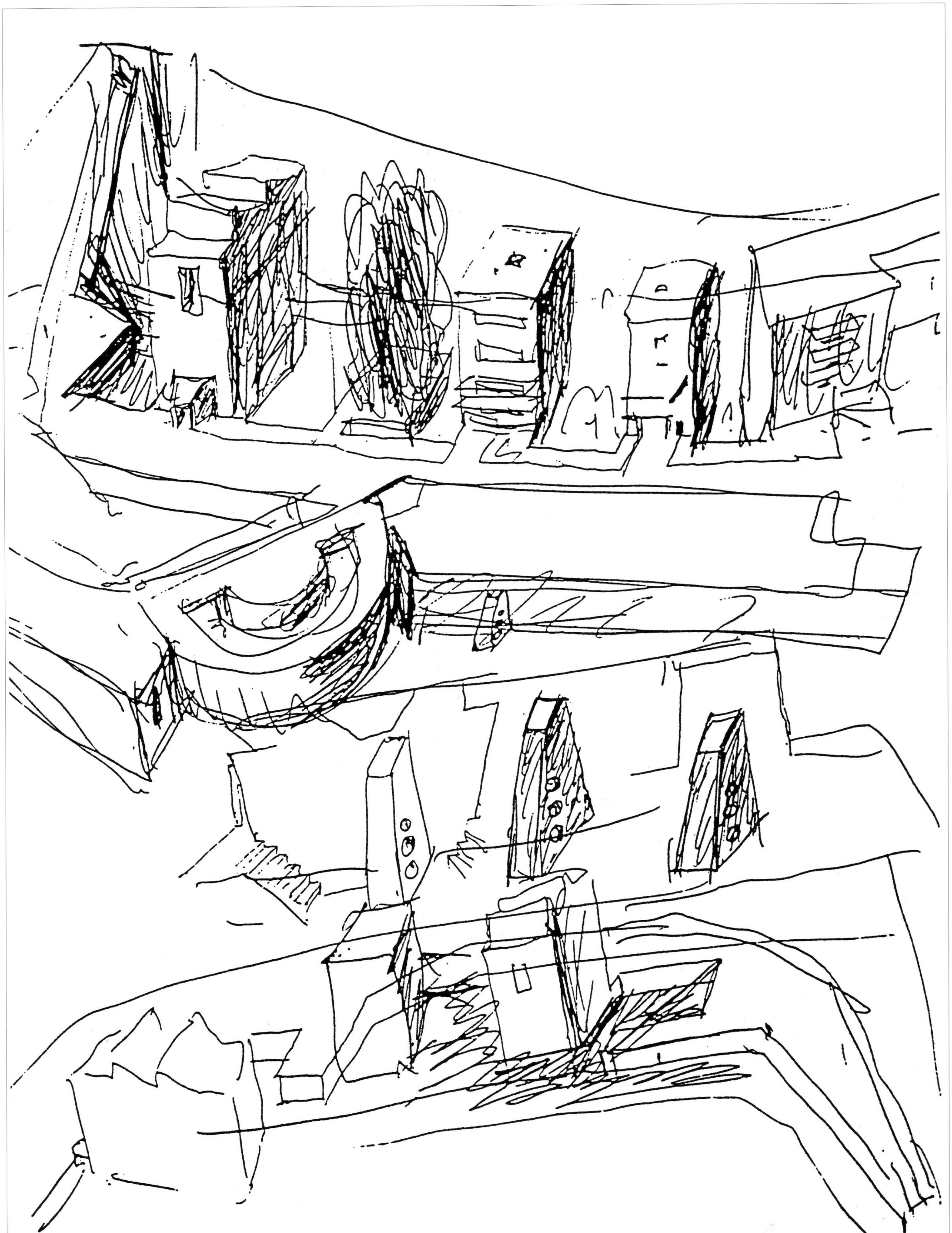

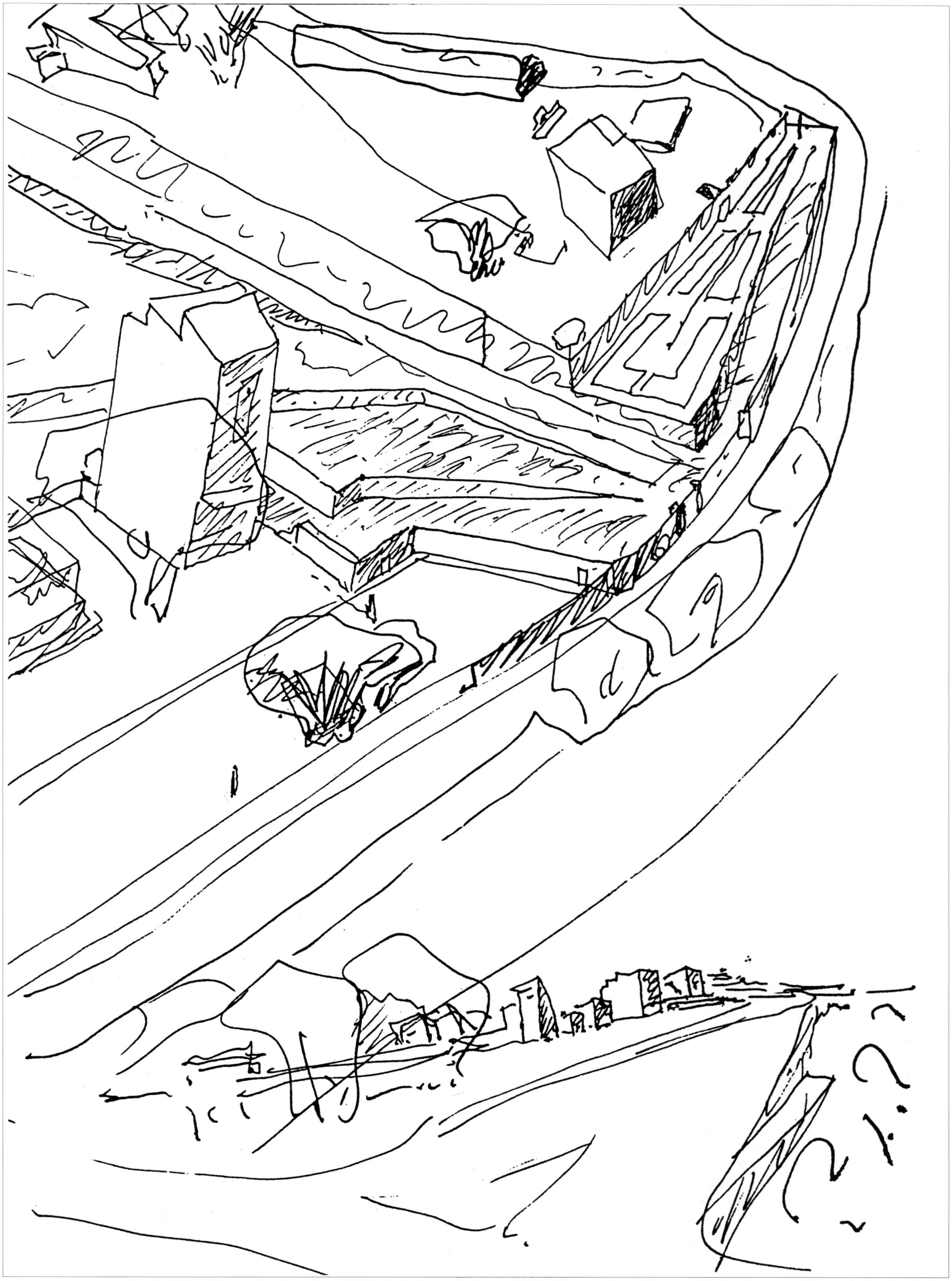

Semicircular corridor　半円形の通路

Corridor of north wing　北棟通路

Library 図書室

Library : upper level　図書室上階△▽

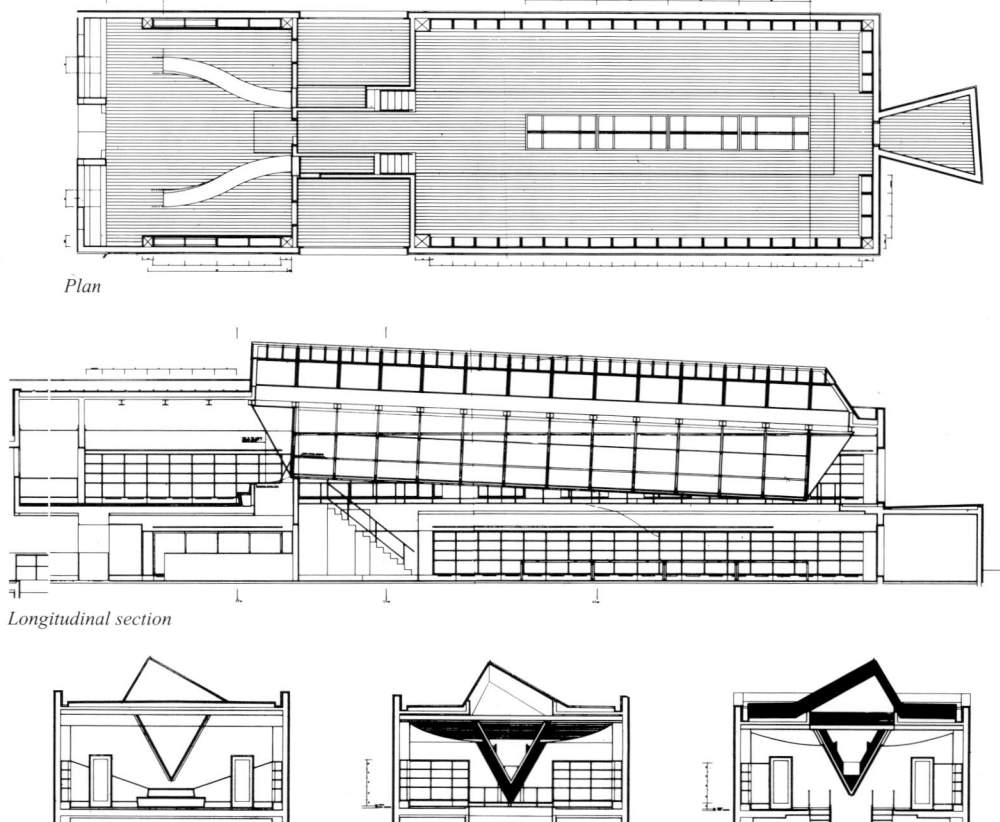

Plan

Longitudinal section

Cross sections

101

Rectory of University of Alicante
アリカンテ大学管理／教室棟

Alicante, Spain

Client: University of Alicante, Spain   Design period: 1995–97   Construction period: 1996–98   Architects: Álvaro Siza Arquitecto, Lda—Elisiário Miranda, Luis Martinez Planelles, principals-in-charge   Project team: António Morata Ortiz, Avelino Silva, Carlos Seoane, Cristina Ferreirinha, Hana Kassem, Luís-Diaz Mauriño   Structural engineer: José Luis Perez Molina   Mechanical engineer: Joaquin Solbes Llorca   General contractors: Gines Navarro, S.A., foundation; Constructora S. José, structure and finishes   Structural system: reinforced concrete structure

View from north 北より見る

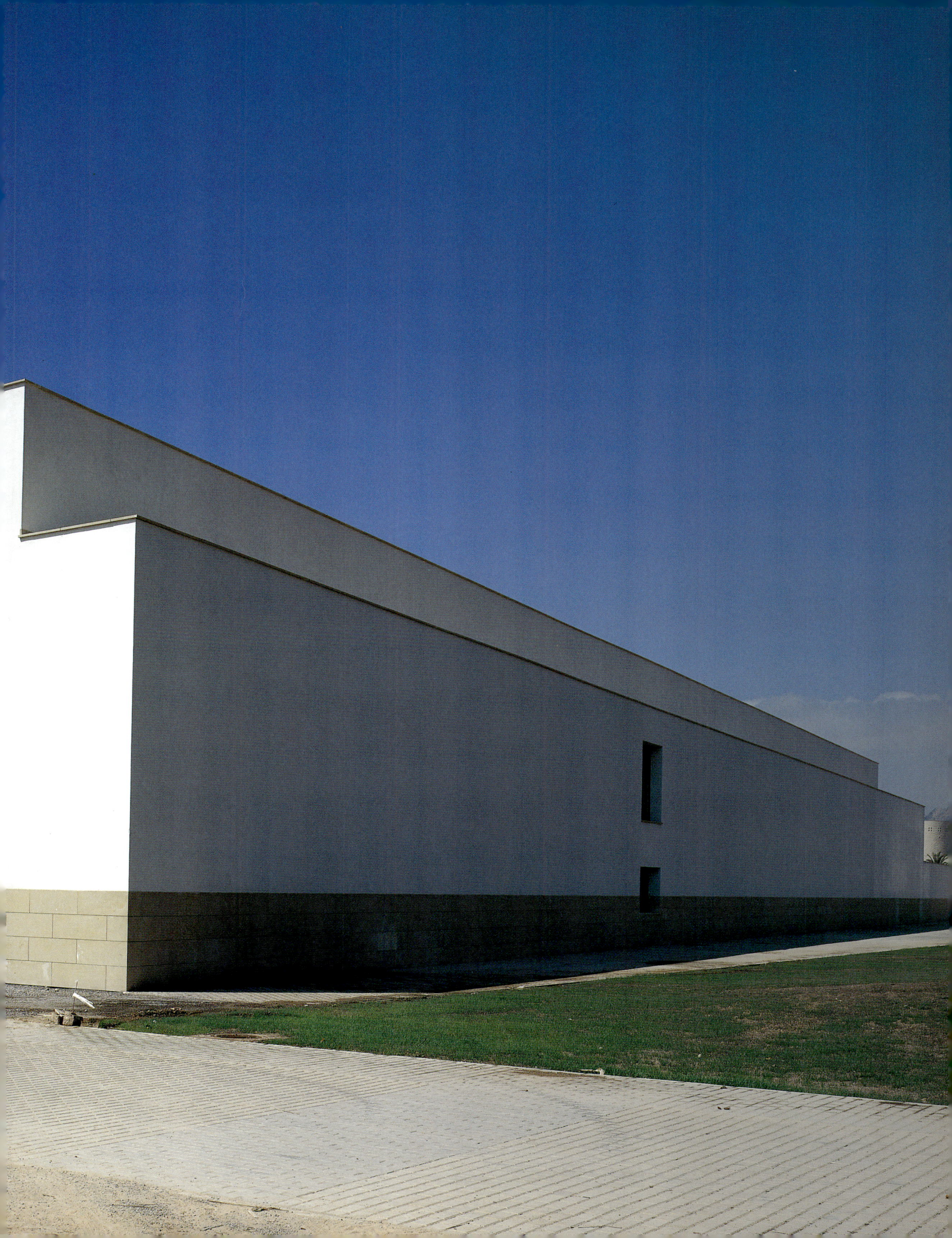

Section A-A

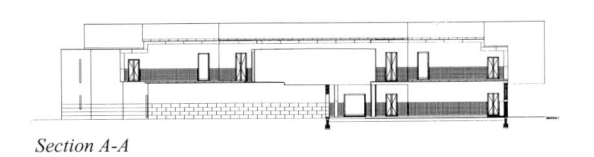

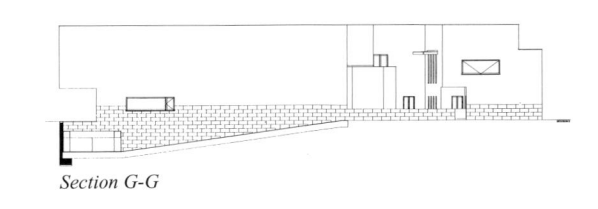

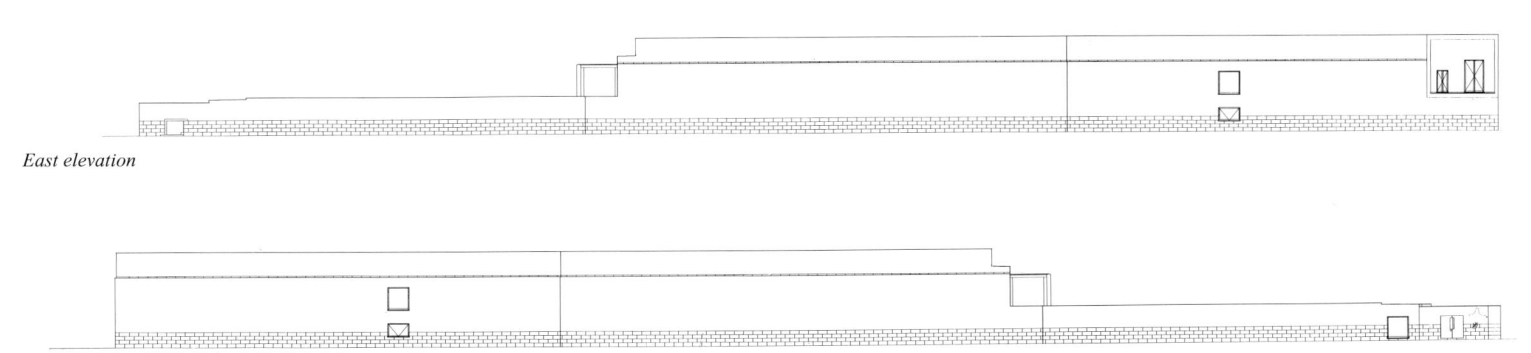

Section G-G

East elevation

West elevation

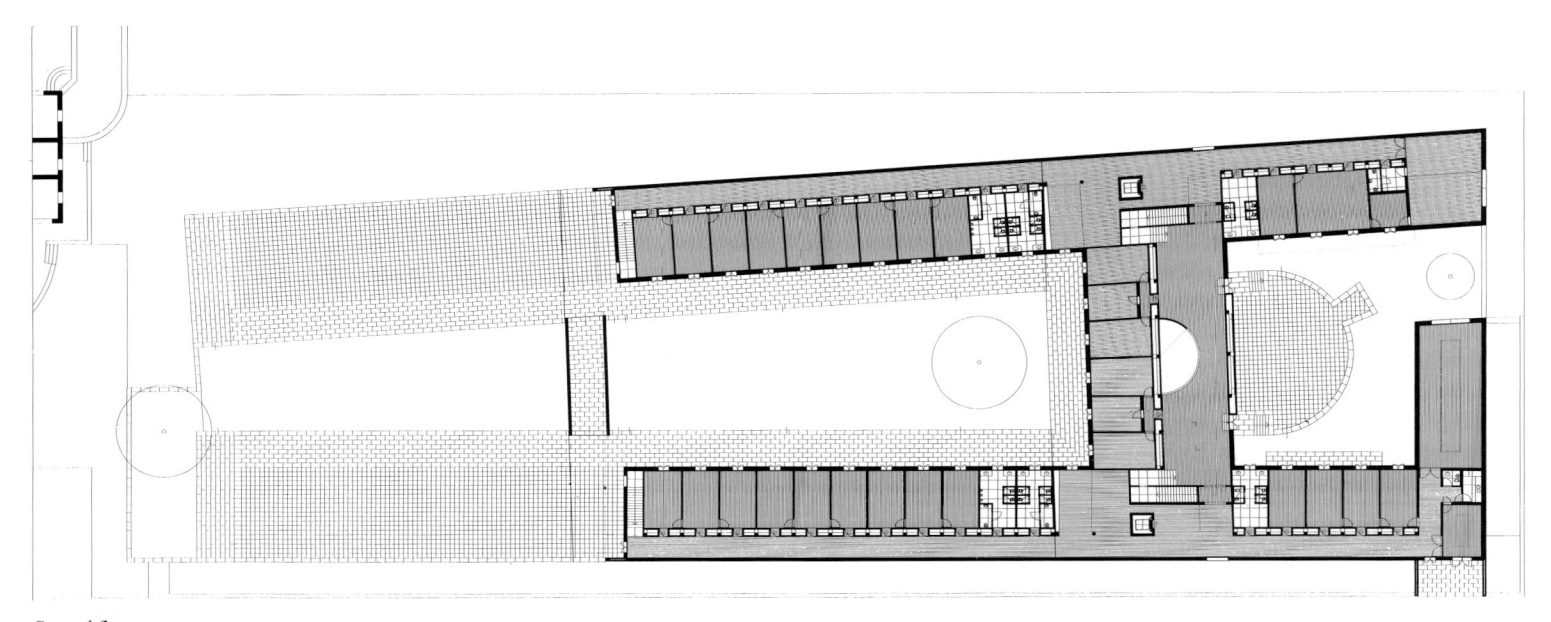

Second floor

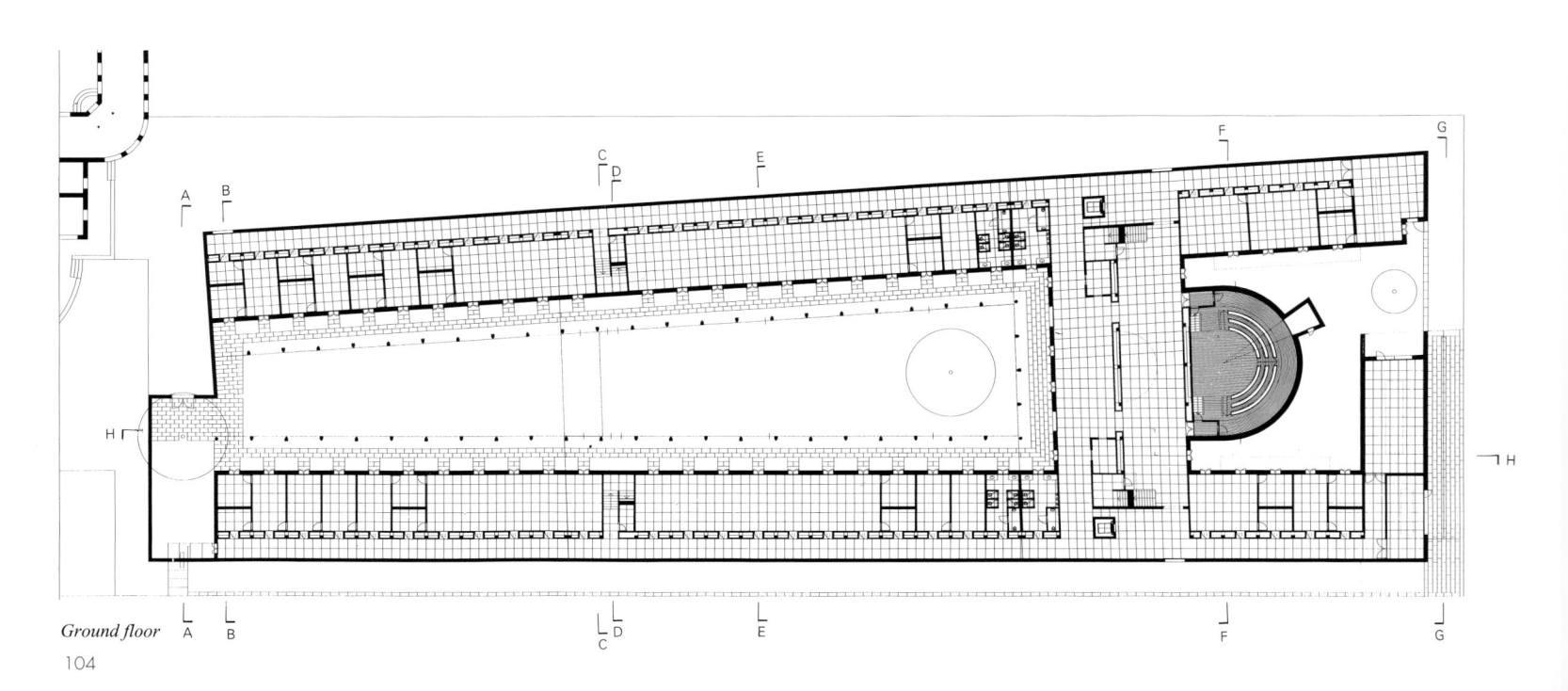

Ground floor

104

GA: In addition to designing several museums, you also do a lot of work for university campuses. In either case there is a lot of attention paid to outdoor spaces.

Álvaro Siza: This is true. In the case of the Alicante University project the design revolves around a double patio. You have offices, in part two floors, and a big hall, and a patio. Inside this patio, there is a covered auditorium. These are the facilities for the director of the university. So in this patio you have offices and meeting rooms for the most important people at the university.

It's part of the new campus at Alicante, which is under construction. The plan is efficient, and they already had built the infrastructure and gardens. These were well planned but the architecture was not so good. When I began the project, they told me to build on two floors. So I chose the scale of the volumes according to that. The project was developed along this two-floor restriction, but after the project was under construction for six months, they made a central space with a higher building. I proposed to renovate an existing building, which had been a military airport, and also a big hangar. I proposed to maintain this structure to create a roofed garden. It is in the Arab tradition of patios and roofs. It is extremely appropriate for the kind of climate in this area. I tried to make the interior spaces related to the outdoors. You have all the offices opening onto the portico, protected from the sun.

GA: So the building itself is organized in a traditional college campus fashion.

Siza: Yes. It is modulated. On the second floor you have more offices, and rooms for professors. Then you have access to the roof of the auditorium. In general the details for the project are very simple, since the project is far from our office. I wanted to make sure that the structure would be simple and clear so that it would be easy to manage. Of course we have a young associate architect over there and someone from our office goes to watch over its progress. I try to visit every few months or so, or if something difficult needs to be resolved.

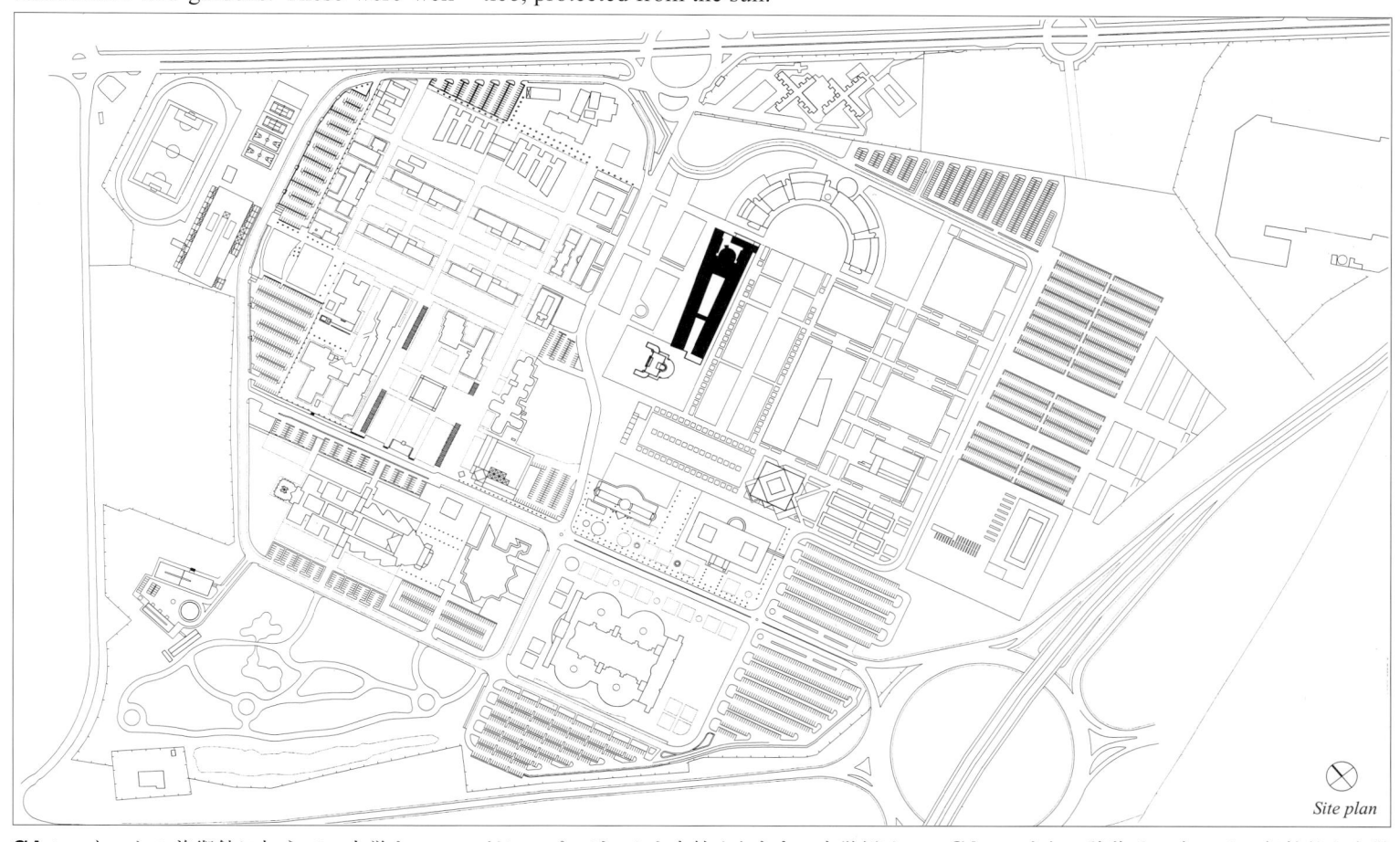

Site plan

South entrance to patio　パティオへの南側エントランス

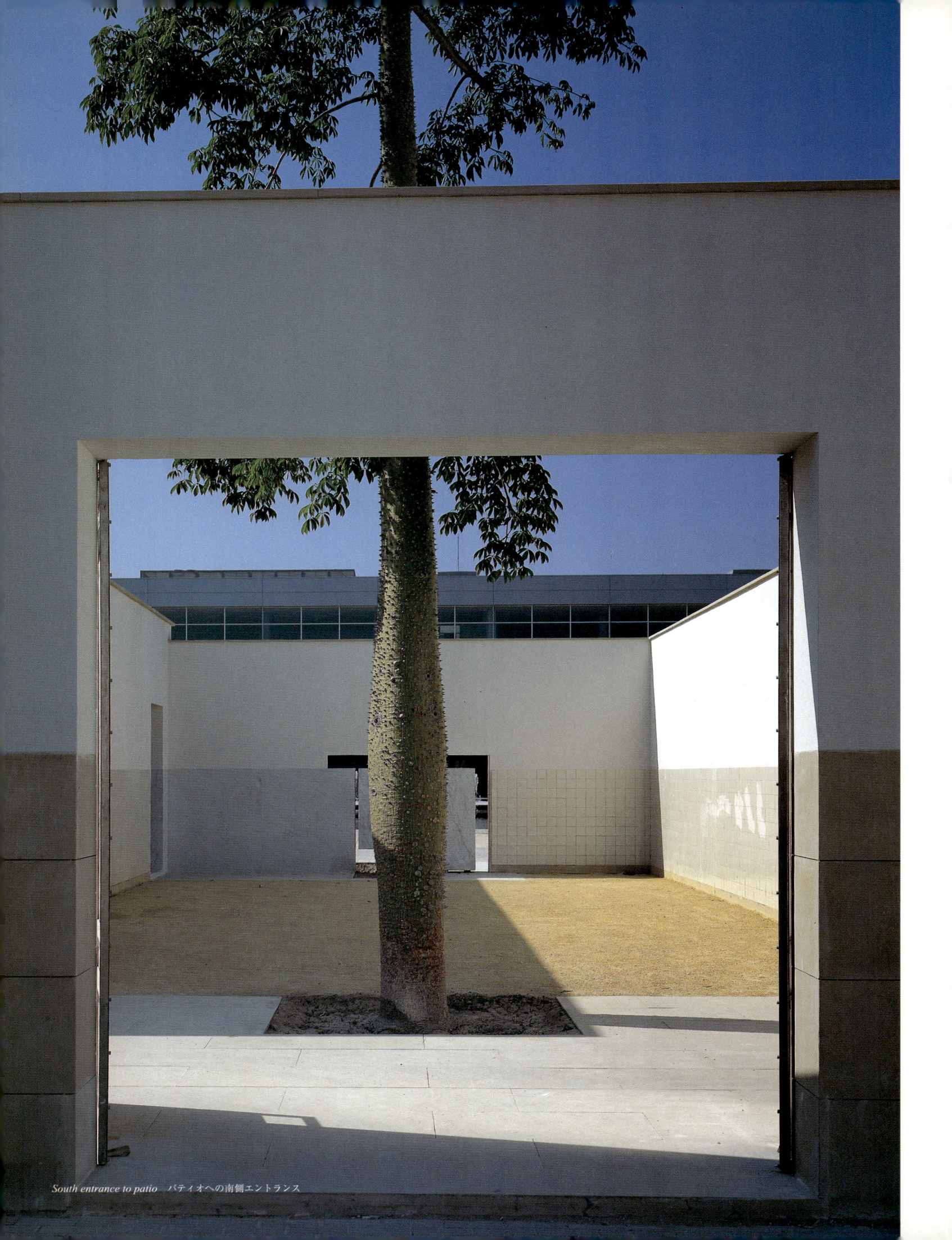

Northeast corner 北東角部

Overall view from south 南側全景

＜解説＞
敷地
サン・ヴィチェンテ・デル・ラスペイグにあるアリカンテ大学の敷地は，もとは軍で使っていたラバーサ空港の跡地である。この校舎のために用意された敷地は，北東―南東に方位を向けた長方形の区画である。北東端の境界には教室棟が，反対側には幸い保存された，明らかに近代建築の影響を受けている航空管制塔が立ち上がっている。

ジオメトリーとヴォリューム
明快な水平性を持つこの建物は，スペインのイスラム建築に見られる方法を用い，激しい暑さから身を守る，閉ざされた要塞として構成され，非常に平坦なキャンパスのなかで強い存在感を示している。この方式により，外側には明快な形態を見せることなく，その内側に幾何学的な輪郭，さまざまなオープン・スペースを包み込むことができる。

教室エリアを包摂しながら，学長室や管理事務局なども置かれる建物であることがそのスケールを決める要因になっている。建物は，管制塔に近づくに従って広さも高さも減らしていき，注目に値する建物である航空管制塔を強調する。

簡素なヴォリュームに対する好みは，航空管制塔にもこの建物にも共通する。この建物は，2つの中庭を持つH字型の構成で，それぞれの機能は明快に分けられている。内向する空間構成をもち，屋根付きのギャラリーや日除けで日差しを防ぐ一方，内蔵された開口が全体を貫き，このキャンパスで最も制度化された性格を持つ建物の厳しく，堂々とした外観は，隣接する建物とは異質なものである。

空間構成とアクセス
建物は基本的に2階建てであるが，航空管制塔に一番近い三分の一の部分は1層である。小さな地下階が建物を完結する。

平面構成はその用途に対応したヒエラルキーを明快に持ち，中庭がそれらの区別をつけ，性格を与えている。つまり，長手に沿って広がる，大きい方の中庭は，管理部門組織に，小さい方の中庭は，この建物の機能を代表するソシアルな領域に対応している。両方の中庭をつなぐ部分は，前室，アトリア，さまざまなアクセスといった，水平性のある共有領域として使われる。

建物のほぼ全体に反復される内部空間の構成システムは，中庭に面する部屋の連なりに基づいている。中庭の反対側には，部屋とは機械設備を収めた二重壁で分けられた，各部分をつなぐ廊下が通っている。

建物への主要アクセスは，航空管制塔に近い所にある。この部分で建物は一番低く，主軸線と正接する位置にある。古代の建物の迂回する進入路の一つを思わせるそのエントランスは，水に沿って進み，唐突に，人を大きな方の中庭に導く。建物に入る前に，2つの中庭を分ける部分を通ることによって，中庭の全長を横切ることになる。

建物の反対側，教室に近い所に，もう少し用途の限られたアクセスが別に2つある。一つはこの学部の中庭に続く歩行者用のアクセス，もう一つは地階に直接続く自動車用のアクセスである。

プログラム
―地階レベル（－3.00m）：一般的な収納と機械設備室を含む，職員用駐車場，積み荷／荷降ろし用の駐車スペースが置かれる。
―地上階レベル（＋0.30m）：広いパティオを囲む教室群が，ワーク・エリアを異なった性格を持つ管理事務，サービス・エリアから分離する。レストルーム・エリアがこの領域を完結する。コントロール・ポイントやアトリウム同様，エントランスが，前述したように，水平と垂直方向の連結部を形づくるパティオを分ける部分を構成する。同じ部分から，オーディトリアム／半円形の大ホールへも導かれる。

この連結部の象徴的重要性は，その囲みとし

Northeast corner 北東角部

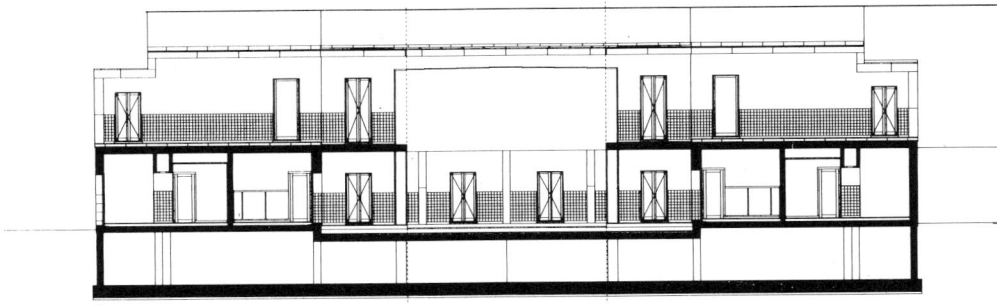

Section B-B

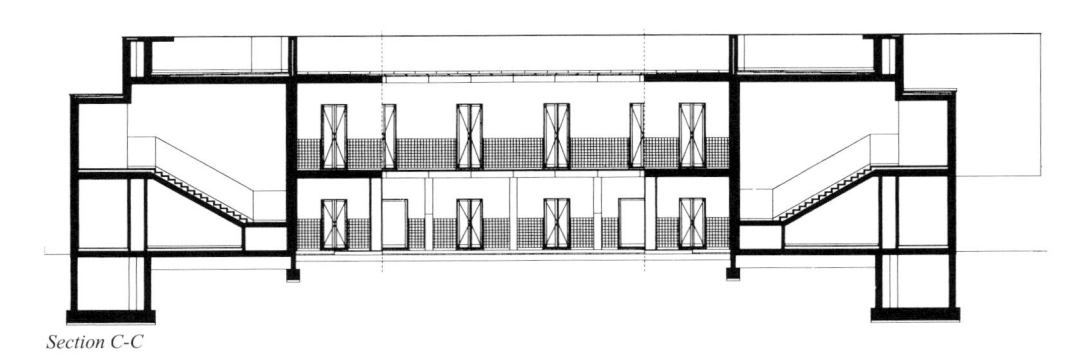

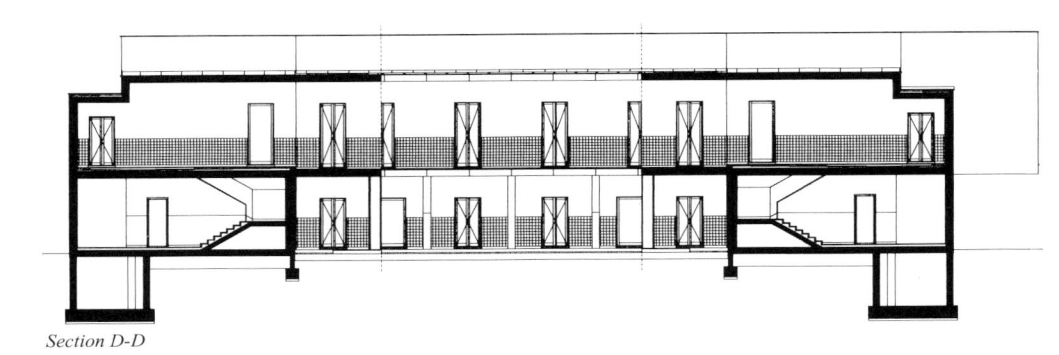

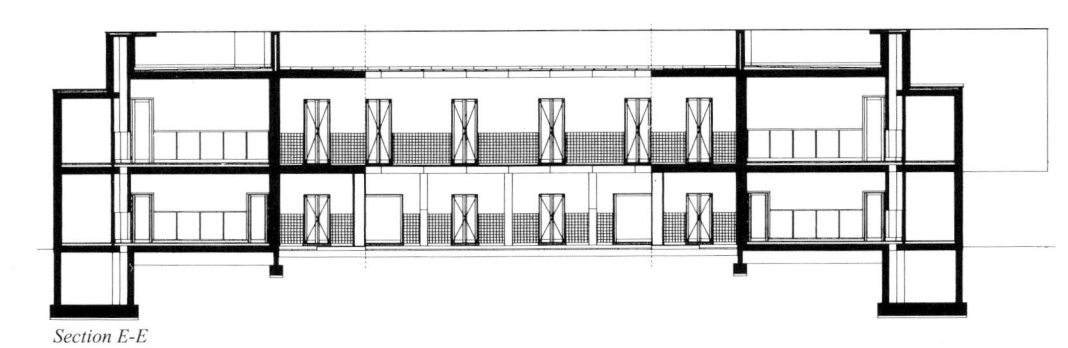

Section C-C

Section D-D

Section E-E

Section H-H

DESCRIPTION

Siting

The University of Alicante in San Vicente del Raspeig occupies the site of the former military airport of Rabasa. The site destined for use as a rectory is a rectangular parcel of a northeastern-southeastern orientation.

At the extreme northeast, the site is defined by the classrooms, while at the opposite side emerges, fortunately conserved, the control tower, with its obvious modern references.

Geometry and Volumetrics

The rectory building, with its clear horizontality, is thought of as a closed fortress defending itself, in the Hispanic-Muslim manner, from the torrentially hot climate, accentuating the distinctly planar character of the campus. This gives the building the needed closure permitting a geometric definition and a detachment from the various open spaces without clear form that appear throughout the university campus.

Comprising the width of the classroom volume, the rectory is a factor in its scaling. It gradually diminishes in area as well as in height as it approaches the airport tower, emphasizing the value of that noteworthy structure.

A preference for simple volumes is common to both the tower and the rectory. The rectory is established as a double-courtyard building, a letter "H," with clearly differentiated uses. As an interiorized spatial organization the building permits solar protection through the careful use of covered galleries and sunshades; while overlooking through contained openings, the austere, imposing and unifying exterior character of the most institutional building of the campus, given the disparity of the adjacent structures.

Spatial Organization and Accesses

The rectory is basically laid-out in two floors above grade except for the third of the building closest to the tower when it unfolds into a single floor. The structure is completed by a small underground level.

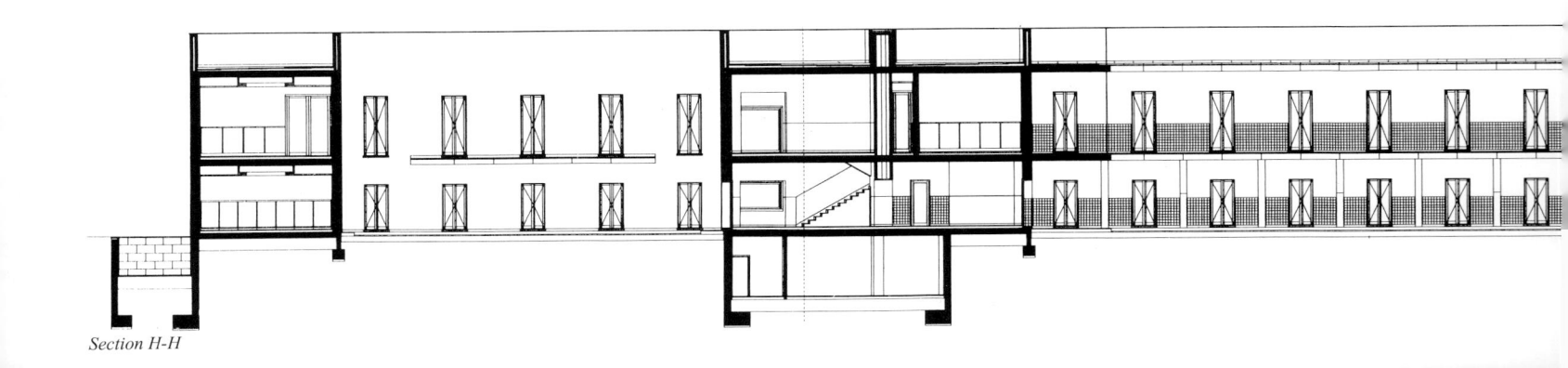

The plans clearly mark the hierarchies of use as the courtyards distinguish and qualify them. Thus, the larger courtyard, of a longitudinal form, is dedicated to the organization of the administration; while the smaller courtyard distributes the social and representative functions. The piece linking both courtyards is devoted to the horizontal and common-use spaces such as vestibules, atria and various accesses.

The organizing scheme of the interior spaces, repeated throughout most of the building, is based upon a sequence of rooms facing the courtyard with a distribution hallway on the opposite side separated from the room by a double wall containing technical and mechanical functions.

The principal access to the rectory area occurs close to the control tower, where the building is at its lowest, and at a tangent to its main axis. That entrance, reminding one of the indirect accesses of ancient structures, along with appearance of water, transports the visitor, almost suddenly, to the large courtyard. The entire length of the courtyard would have to be crossed before the visitor enters the building, through the piece which separates the two courtyards.

There exists as well two other accesses, of more restricted use at the extreme opposite of the building, close to the classrooms. The first, a pedestrian access to the Representative Department courtyard; the second, a direct car access to the underground level.

Program
—Underground level (at -3.00m)
Parking requirements for staff vehicles and loading/unloading vehicles are resolved at the underground level which includes general storage spaces as well as technical equipment rooms.
—Ground floor (at +0.30m)
The classrooms surrounding the large patio separate the work areas from the distinct administrative functions and services of the rectory; they are completed by rest room areas. The entrances as well as the control points and atrium constitute the piece separating the patios where are comprised, as already mentioned, the horizontal and vertical connections. The same piece leads also to the auditorium/semicircular grand hall.

The symbolic importance of the linking piece manifests itself in the exterior as a volume in the smaller patio which appears as a closure to it. Surrounding the smaller patio and to its southeast area the Law and Linguistics Departments as well as the office of International Relations. At the opposite side one finds the press and public relations halls.
—First floor (at +4.10m)
The first floor completes the programmatic requirements of the rectory with its more institutional functions. Thus, the vice-presidents' offices are laid-out along the arms of the longitudinal patio, dividing-up the various administrative zones among them such that each administration is situated directly above its respective department (which have been described with the ground floor area).

This sectional unity is realized with the use of internal staircases in which act as end pieces on the first floor, where the classrooms are shorter. The circulation is completed by an exterior passageway that underlines the introverted nature of the project. At their other extremities, the arms are terminated, as occurs at the ground floor, by two access blocks.

The location of a skylight in the main body signals its identity as a vertical connector which unites physically the two floors. In that spot one finds, complementing the vice-presidents' offices, the conference and management halls.

Finally, the Social Council is located independently in the smaller patio, at the northeastern arm. At the opposite extremity, opening towards the campus, the director's quarters are situated and terminate in a large balcony oriented towards the exterior. This moment being the only element signalling the more noble aspect of the program.

Technical Equipment
Technical and mechanical functions are always resolved through a continuous double-wall which separates the classroom from their accesses. The hot/cold air distribution units are independent for each room, while the generators are centralized and located at the roof level. They are sheltered from view through the use of a parapet wall. The organizational system of the technical equipment offers low-cost maintenance and flexible usage.

Construction and Finishes
The concrete structure is comprised of columns and lightweight two-way slabs with openings of moderate dimensions which do not elevate the costs.

The structural simplicity allows for the creation of an exterior brick cavity wall containing an air-space and thermal insulation, thus protecting the project from intemperate weather.

The exterior finish will be a stucco mixed with pulverized brick complemented by a 1.80 meter high stone base which helps protect the wall. In the large patio however, the stone base is replaced by a ceramic tile one, a traditional finish of the region which brings the desired coolness to the space.

The flat roof will be finished with a bed of gravel which protects the waterproof membrane. The exterior fenestration (window and door frames) is a painted wood-steel combination, permitting adequate protection and durability along with the appreciable quality of the wood towards the interior.

The interior finishes further accentuate the hierarchical character of the distinct floors: the ground level will have a stone floor while the upper level, of a more noble identity will have tongue-in-grove wood flooring.

The interior walls and ceilings will be plastered and eventually lined with a high density DM plywood; wainscoting painted at the ground floor and covered in ceramic tile at the upper floor. All of the interior carpentry is of wood to be painted.

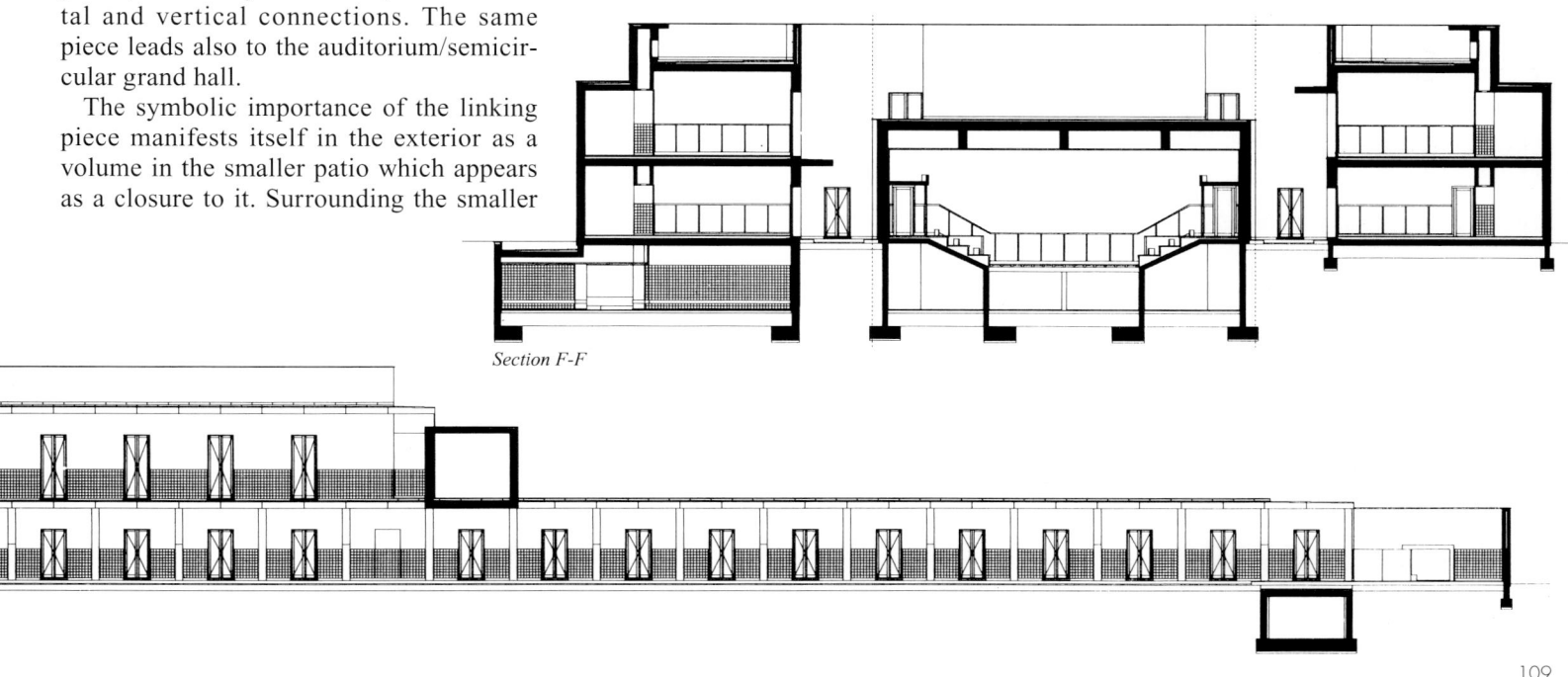

Section F-F

Overall view from south　南側全景

<解説>
敷地
サン・ヴィチェンテ・デル・ラスペイグにあるアリカンテ大学の敷地は，もとは軍で使っていたラバーサ空港の跡地である。この校舎のために用意された敷地は，北東―南東に方位を向けた長方形の区画である。北東端の境界には教室棟が，反対側には幸い保存された，明らかに近代建築の影響を受けている航空管制塔が立ち上がっている。

ジオメトリーとヴォリューム
明快な水平性を持つこの建物は，スペインのイスラム建築に見られる方法を用い，激しい暑さから身を守る，閉ざされた要塞として構成され，非常に平坦なキャンパスのなかで強い存在感を示している。この方式により，外側には明快な形態を見せることなく，その内側に幾何学的な輪郭，さまざまなオープン・スペースを包み込むことができる。

教室エリアを包摂しながら，学長室や管理事務局なども置かれる建物であることがそのスケールを決める要因になっている。建物は，管制塔に近くなるに従って広さも高さも減らしていき，注目に値する建物である航空管制塔を強調する。

簡素なヴォリュームに対する好みは，航空管制塔にもこの建物にも共通する。この建物は，2つの中庭を持つH字型の構成で，それぞれの機能は明快に分けられている。内向する空間構成をもち，屋根付きのギャラリーや日除けで日差しを防ぐ一方，内蔵された開口が全体を貫き，このキャンパスで最も制度化された性格を持つ建物の厳しく，堂々とした外観は，隣接する建物とは異質なものである。

空間構成とアクセス
建物は基本的に2階建てであるが，航空管制塔に一番近い三分の一の部分は1層である。小さな地下階が建物を完結する。

平面構成はその用途に対応したヒエラルキーを明快に持ち，中庭がそれらの区別をつけ，性格を与えている。つまり，長手に沿って広がる，大きい方の中庭は，管理部門組織に，小さい方の中庭は，この建物の機能を代表するソシアルな領域に対応している。両方の中庭をつなぐ部分は，前室，アトリア，さまざまなアクセスといった，水平性のある共有領域として使われる。

建物のほぼ全体に反復される内部空間の構成システムは，中庭に面する部屋の連なりに基づいている。中庭の反対側には，部屋とは機械設備を収めた二重壁で分けられた，各部分をつなぐ廊下が通っている。

建物への主要アクセスは，航空管制塔に近い所にある。この部分で建物は一番低く，主軸線と正接する位置にある。古代の建物の迂回する進入路の一つを思わせるそのエントランスは，水に沿って進み，唐突に，人を大きな方の中庭に導く。建物に入る前に，2つの中庭を分ける部分を通ることによって，中庭の全長を横切ることになる。

建物の反対側，教室に近い所に，もう少し用途の限られたアクセスが別に2つある。一つはこの学部の中庭に続く歩行者用のアクセス，もう一つは地階に直接続く自動車用のアクセスである。

プログラム
―地階レベル（－3.00m）：一般的な収納と機械設備室を含む，職員用駐車場，積み荷/荷降ろし用の駐車スペースが置かれる。

―地上階レベル（＋0.30m）：広いパティオを囲む教室群が，ワーク・エリアを異なった性格を持つ管理事務，サービス・エリアから分離する。レストルーム・エリアがこの領域を完結する。コントロール・ポイントやアトリウム同様，エントランスが，前述したように，水平と垂直方向の連結部を形づくるパティオを分ける部分を構成する。同じ部分から，オーディトリアム/半円形の大ホールへも導かれる。

この連結部の象徴的重要性は，その囲みとし

て現れる小さなパティオのなかのヴォリュームとして外にも表現されている。小さなパティオを囲んで，その南東部に，国際関係のオフィスと法律および言語学部がある。反対側には，報道および広報のホールがある。

―1階（+4.10m）：この建物のなかのインスティテューショナルな機能要求に対応する。長手に延びるパティオの腕に沿って副学長室が並び，さまざまな管理事務ゾーンに分割され，それらは地上階の各学部エリアに合わせてその上に配置されている。

この部門別の構成をまとめるのは，1階の端に設置した内部階段で，この部分で教室は短くなっている。動線は，このプロジェクトの内向する性格を強調する，外部通路で完結する。

もう一方の端部では，パティオの構成する長く延びる腕は，地上階の2つのアクセス・ブロックによって終結する。

主要躯体のスカイライトの位置が，物理的に2つの階を結ぶ垂直のコネクターとしての存在を知らせている。その地点に，副学長のオフィスを補足する，会議室，マネジメント・ホールがある。

最後に，北東のアームのところにある小さなパティオのなかに，ソシアル・カウンシル棟が独立して建っている。この反対側の端には，キャンパスに開いた，学長のための諸室が位置し，その端に向いて大きなバルコニーがついている。これは学長室の存在を知らせる唯一の要素である。

機械設備

機械設備は，教室とアクセスを分けている連続する二重壁のなかに常に配置される。

暖／冷の給気ユニットは各部屋に独立して設置され，発電機は集中管理され屋上に設置されている。それらはパラペット・ウォールで隠されている。この機械設備による組織システムはメンテナンスも安価で，フレキシブルに使える。

建設および仕上げ

コストを押し上げないように適度な寸法の開口，柱，軽量の二方向スラブで構成したコンクリート造。

この構造の単純性によって，空気層をとり絶縁材を入れられるレンガの中空壁を外側につくることが出来，これによって厳しい気候から建物を守る。

外壁の仕上げは，レンガの粉末を混ぜたスタッコを塗り，壁を保護するために1.80mの高さの石の基壇を巡らす。しかし，大きな方のパティオでは，この空間に望まれる涼しさを運び込むために，石の基壇はこの地方の伝統であるセラミックに取り替える。

陸屋根には，防水の薄膜を保護するために砂利が敷かれている。外壁の窓割りは（窓と扉の枠），ペンキ塗りの木とスティールの組み合わせで，内部に向けては木のやわらかさを，外部に向けてはスティールによる保護と耐久性を提供する。

内部の仕上げは，階ごとに異なっている階層性をさらに強調する。地上階の床は石になるが，上の階は，より荘重な雰囲気が感じられるように，さねはぎ継ぎの木の床とする。

内壁と天井は，プラスター塗りで，最後に，非常に目の詰んだDM合板で補強する。腰壁は，地上階はペンキ塗りで，上階はセラミックで覆う。内部の木の造作部分はすべて塗装する。

Patio パティオ

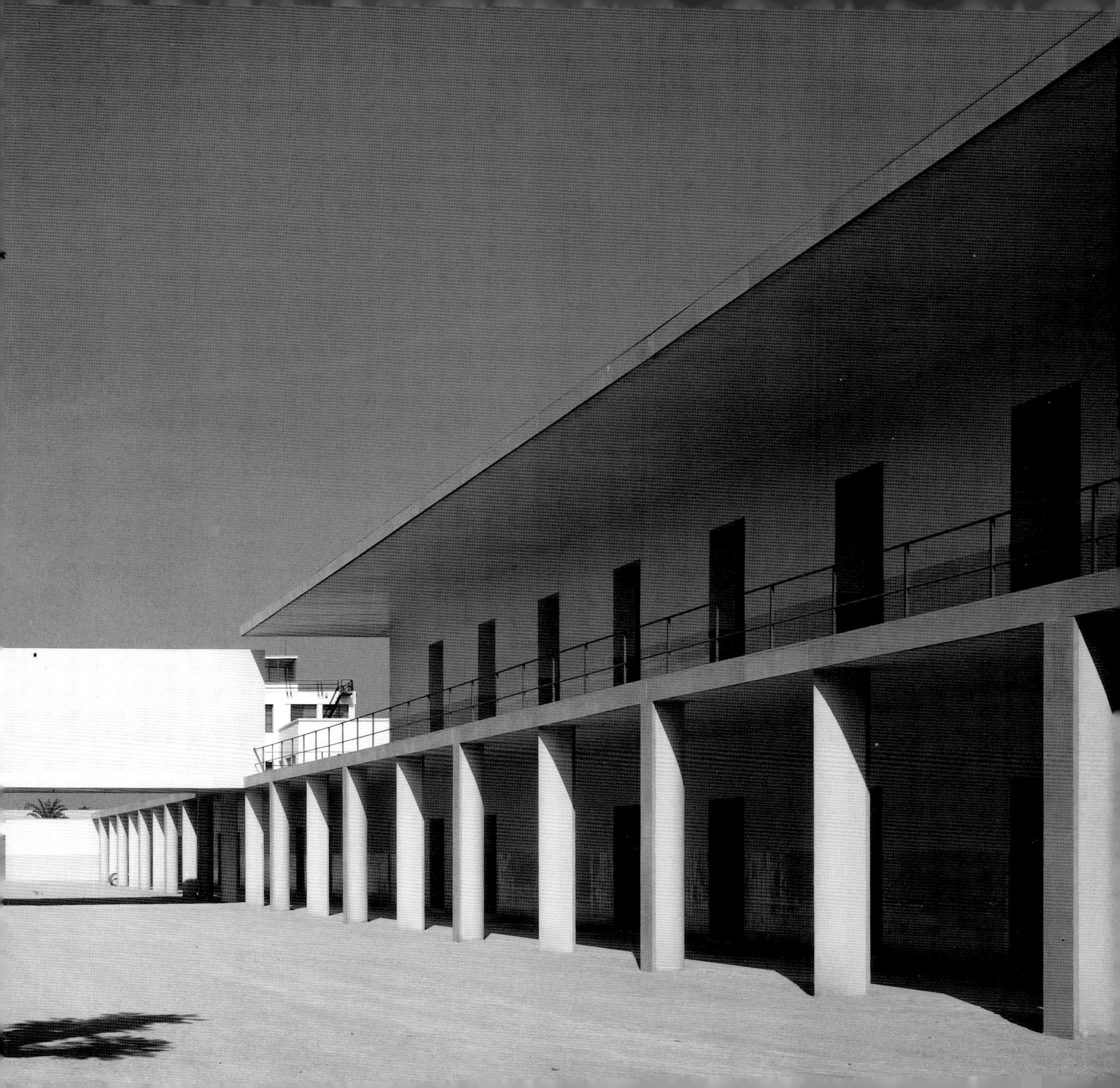

Atrium アトリウム

Second floor 2階

Staircase 階段室

115

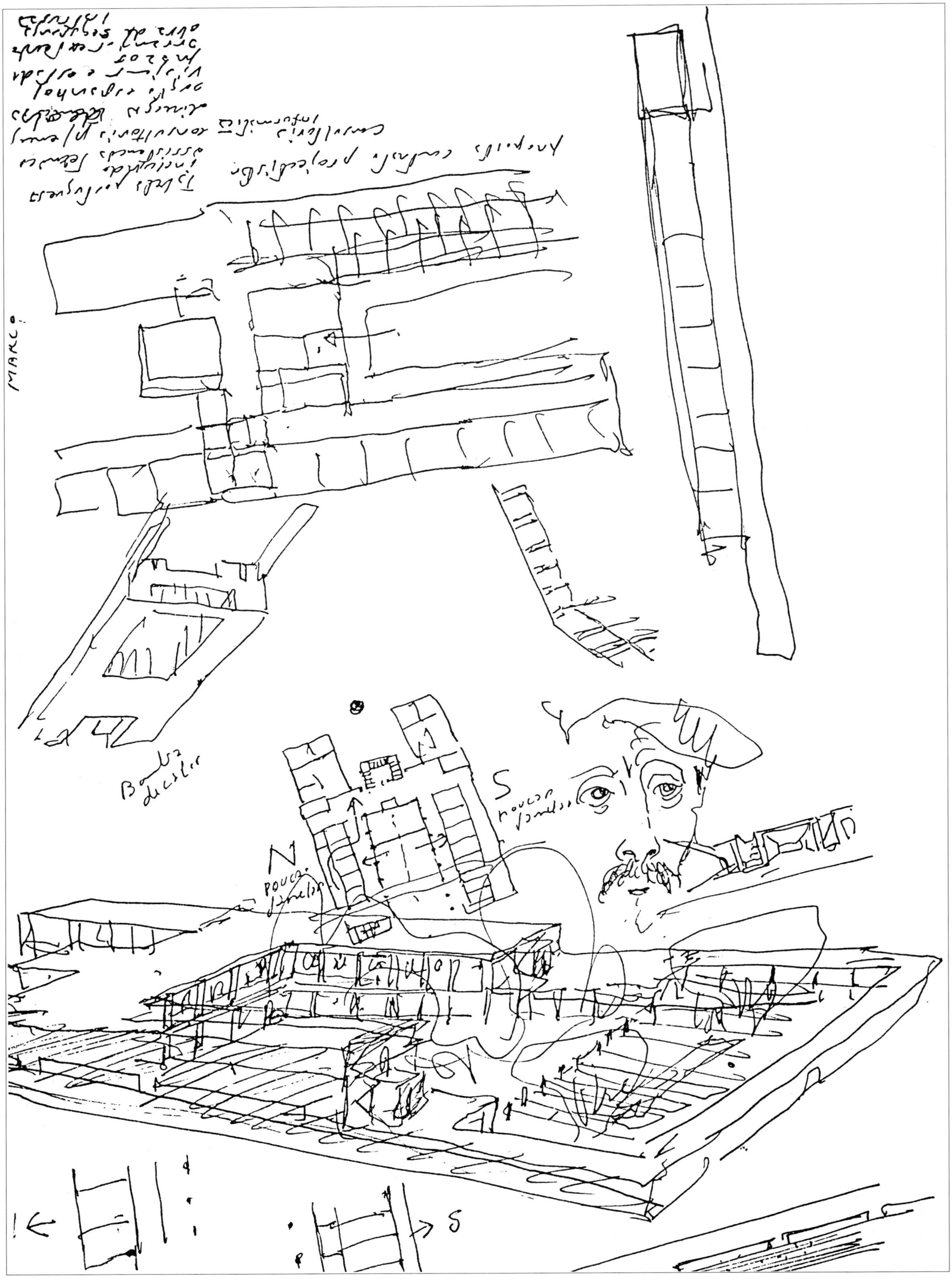
MARCO
S
N
poucas janelas

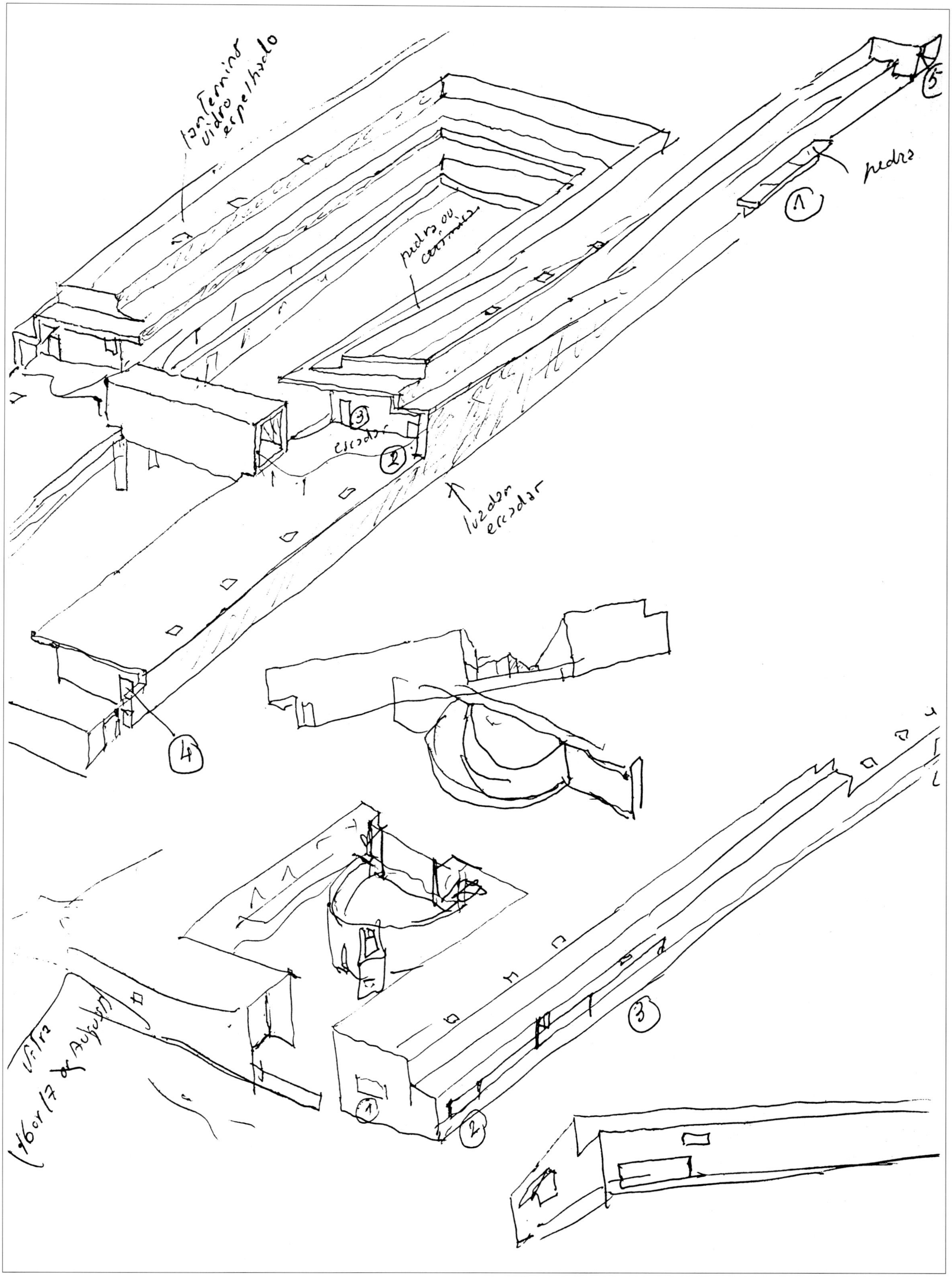
lanternim vidro espelhado
5
pedra
1
pedra ou cerâmica
3
escadas
2
luz das escadas
4
Vitra
3
1
2

Expo '98 Portuguese Pavilion
Expo '98 ポルトガル・パヴィリオン

Lisbon, Portugal

Client: Expo '98   Design period: 1995–97   Construction period: 1996–98   Architects: Álvaro Siza Arquitecto, Lda—Rui Castro, principal-in-charge   Project team: Daniela Antonucci, Hana Kassem, Luís Antas de Barros, Luis-Diaz Mauriño, Taichi Tomuro   Engineers: [Design phase] Ove Arup & Partners—Alfredo Ilidio, structure; Mike Gilroy, electricity; Martin Walton, Erin McConahey, air conditioning; Rod Green, water systems; Andrew Minson, security; Malcolm Wright, acoustic; [Execution phase] STA Lda—Segadães Tavares, Ana Bártolo, structure; Vieira Pereira, electricity and security; Carlos Palma, air conditioning and water systems   Landscape architect: João Gomes da Silva   Installation: Eduardo Souto Moura   Structural system: reinforced concrete structure

Overall view—全景

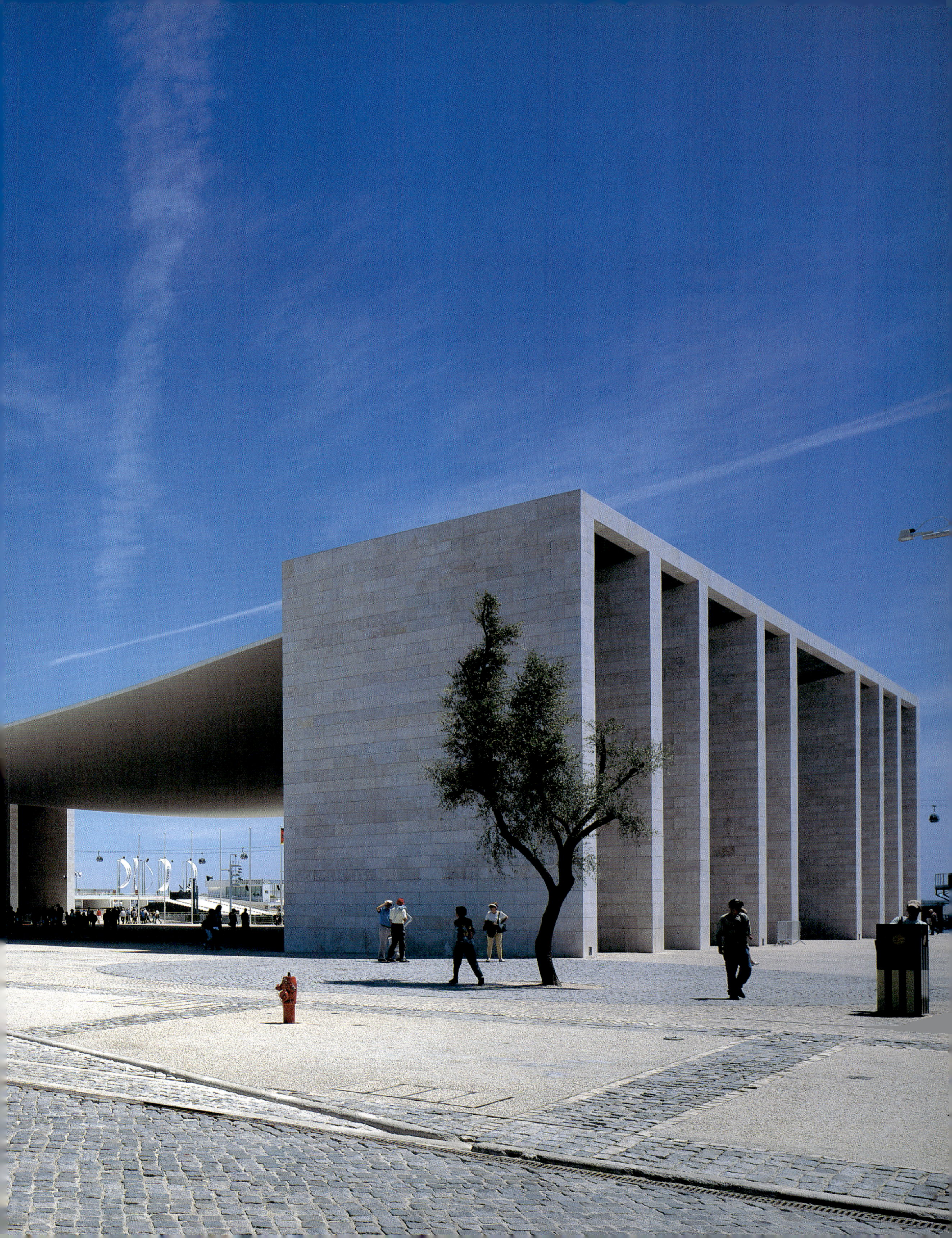

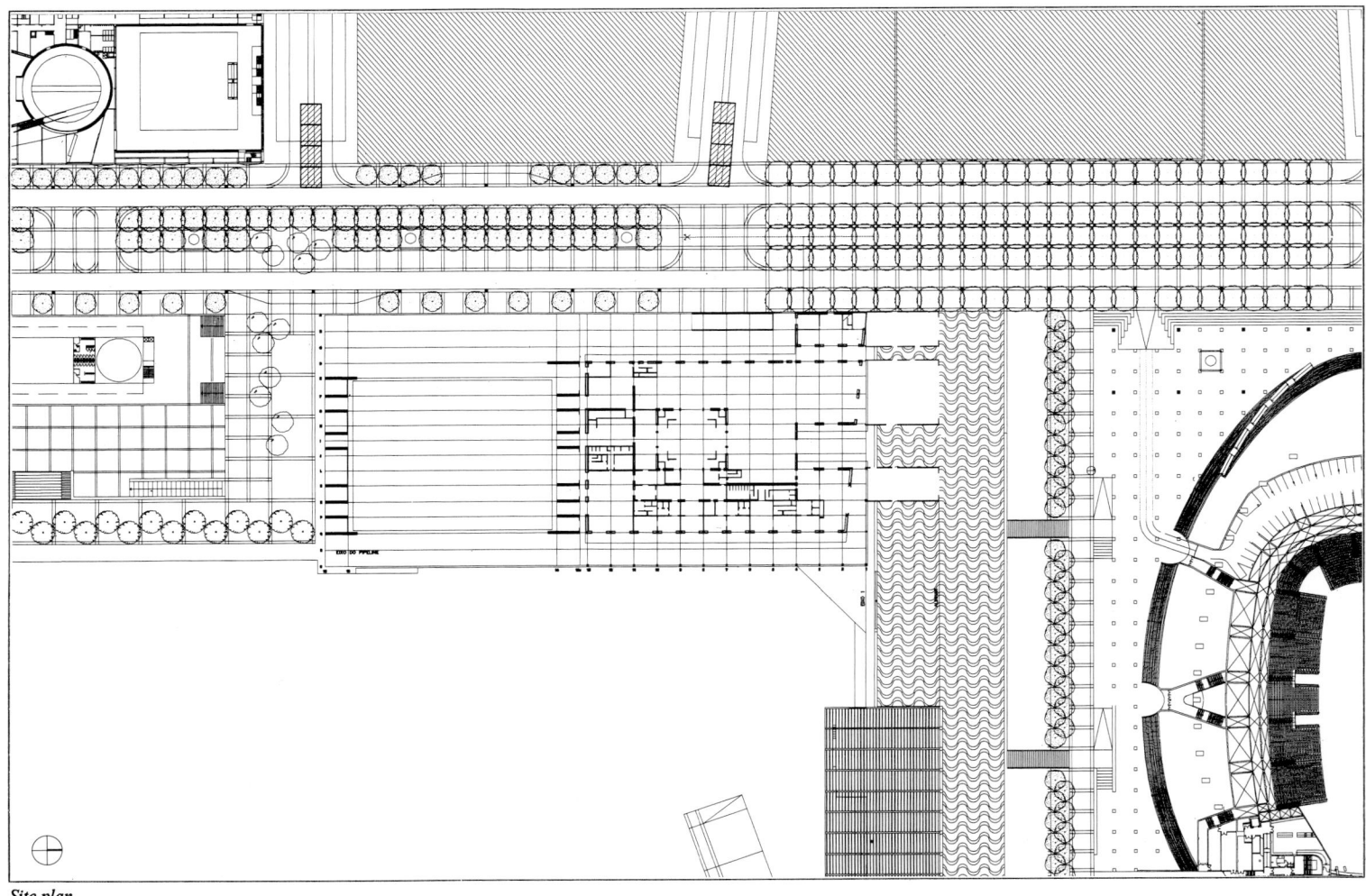

Site plan

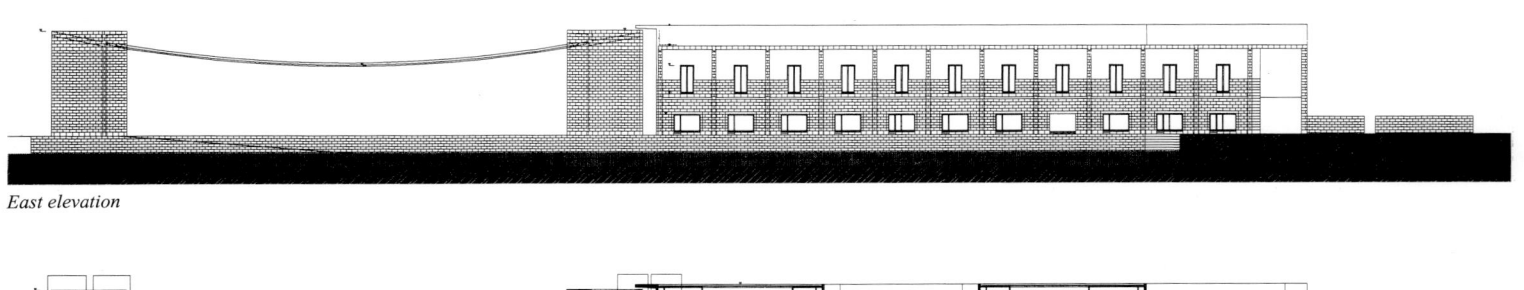

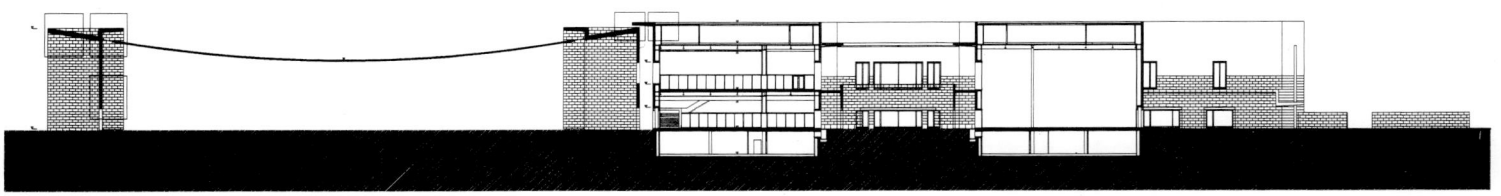

East elevation

Section

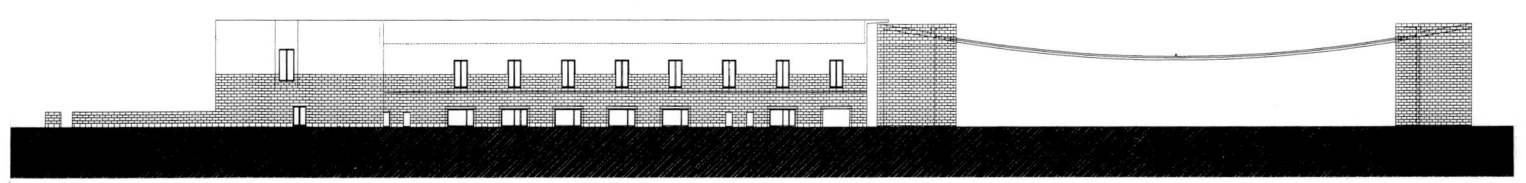

West elevation

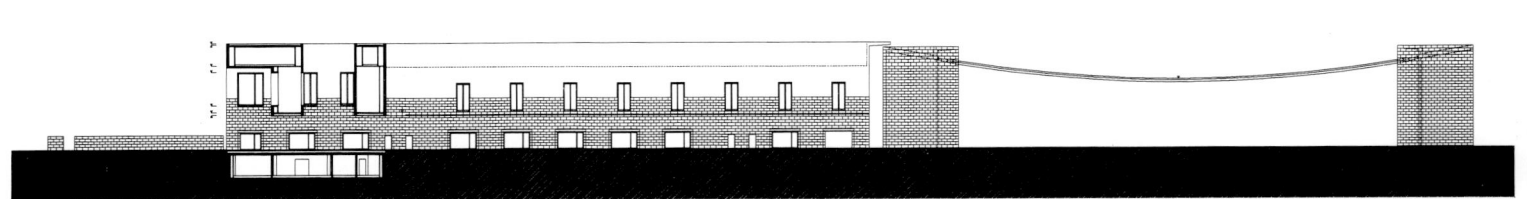

Section

Roof

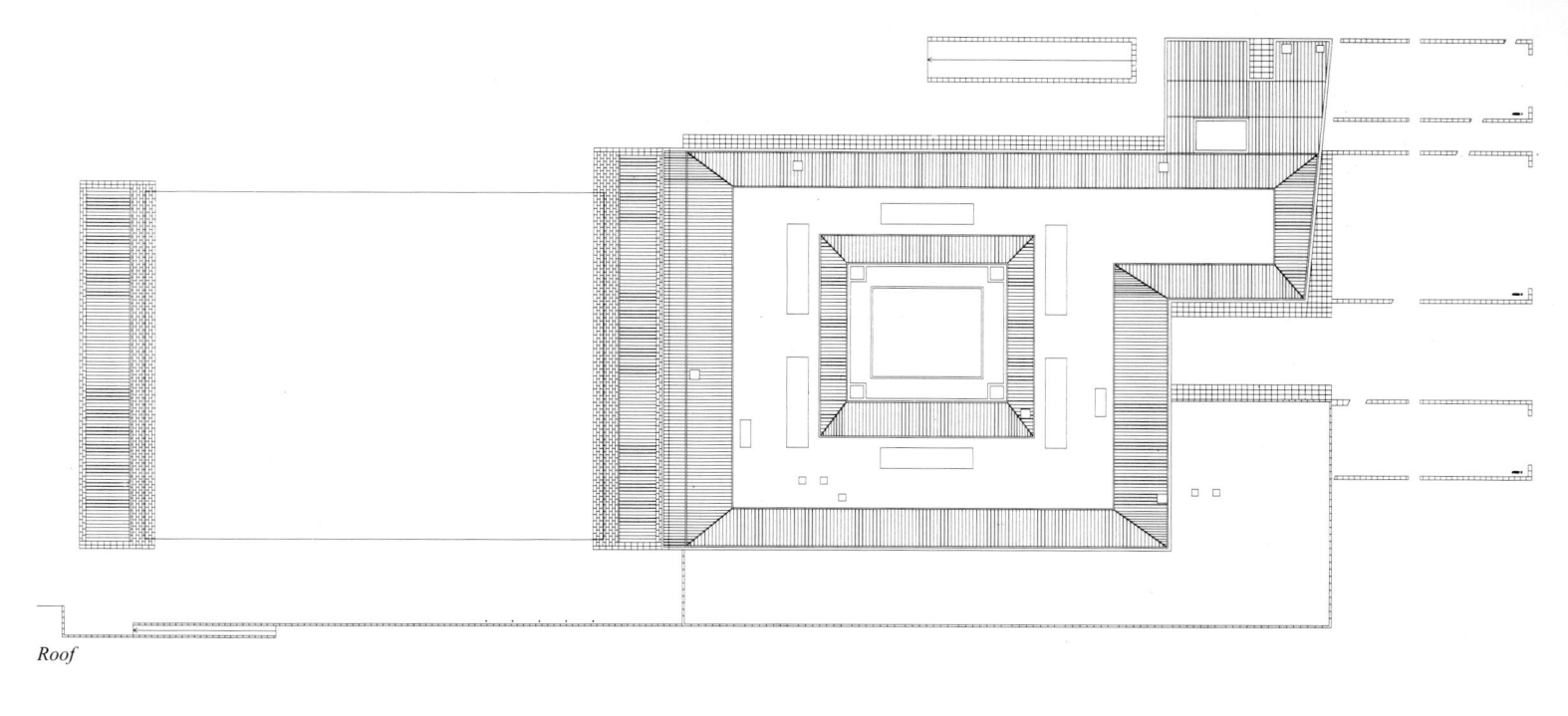

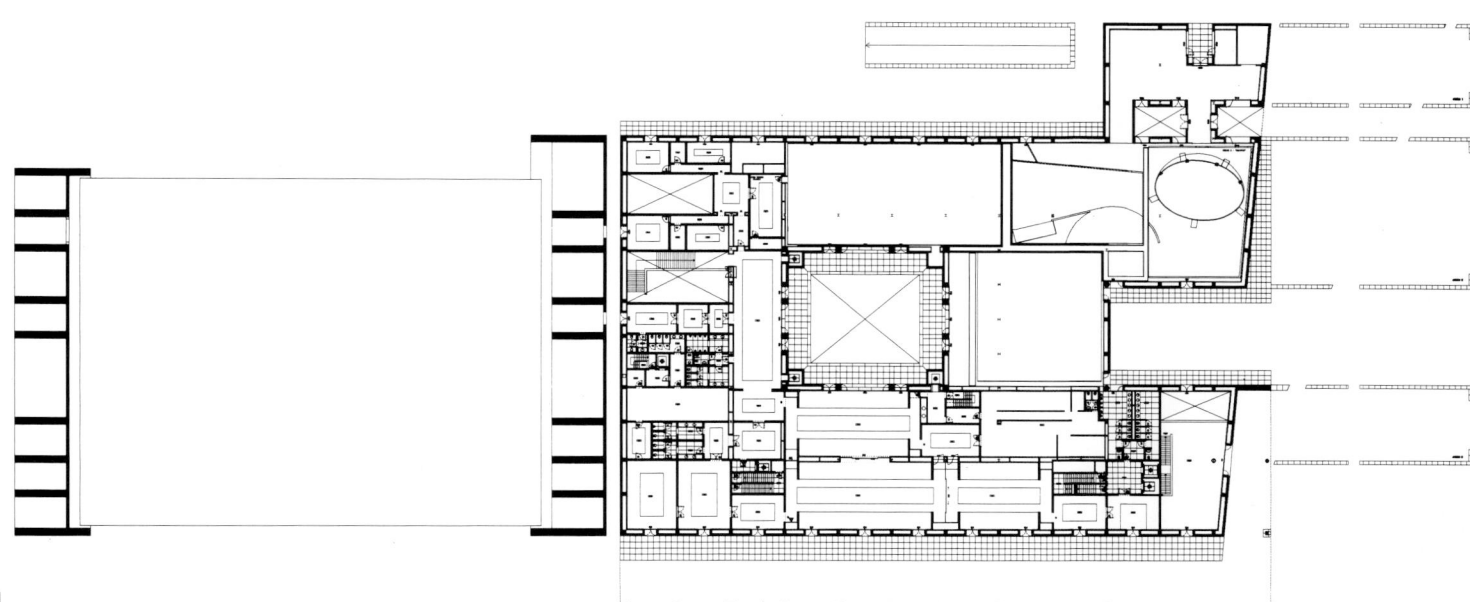

Second floor

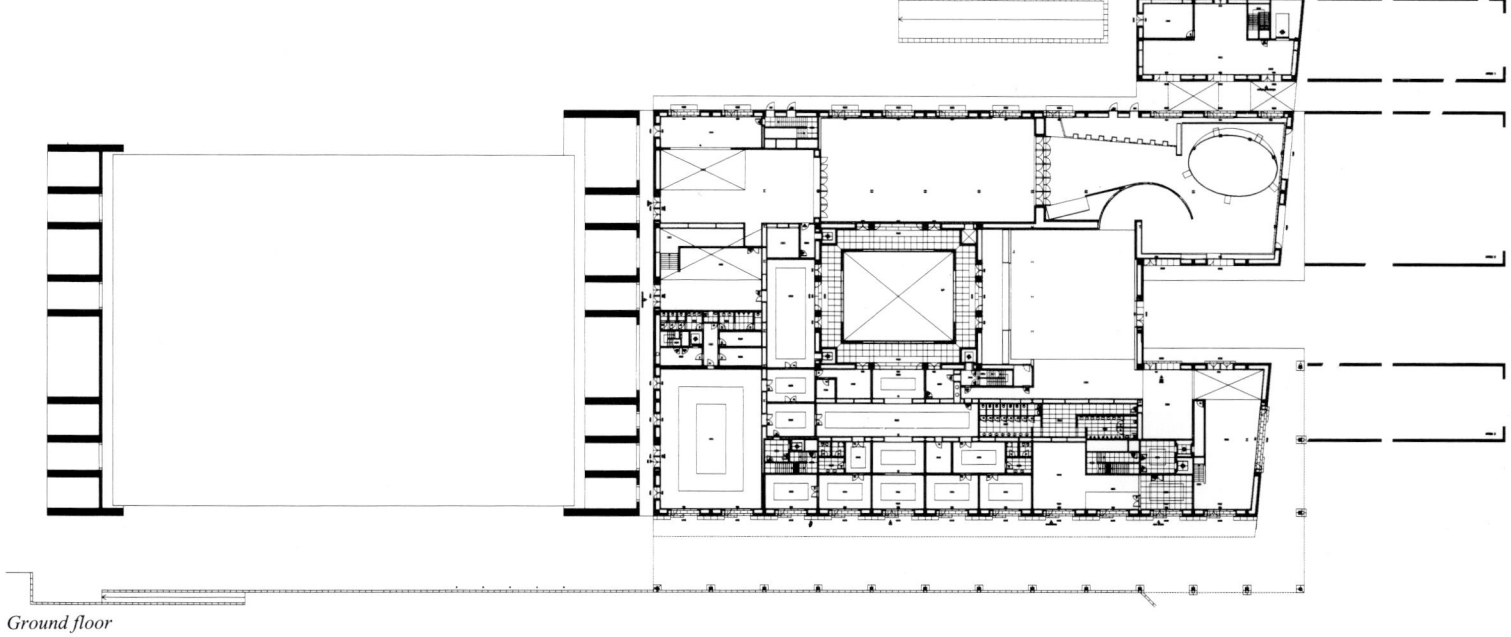

Ground floor

121

View from northeast 北東より見る

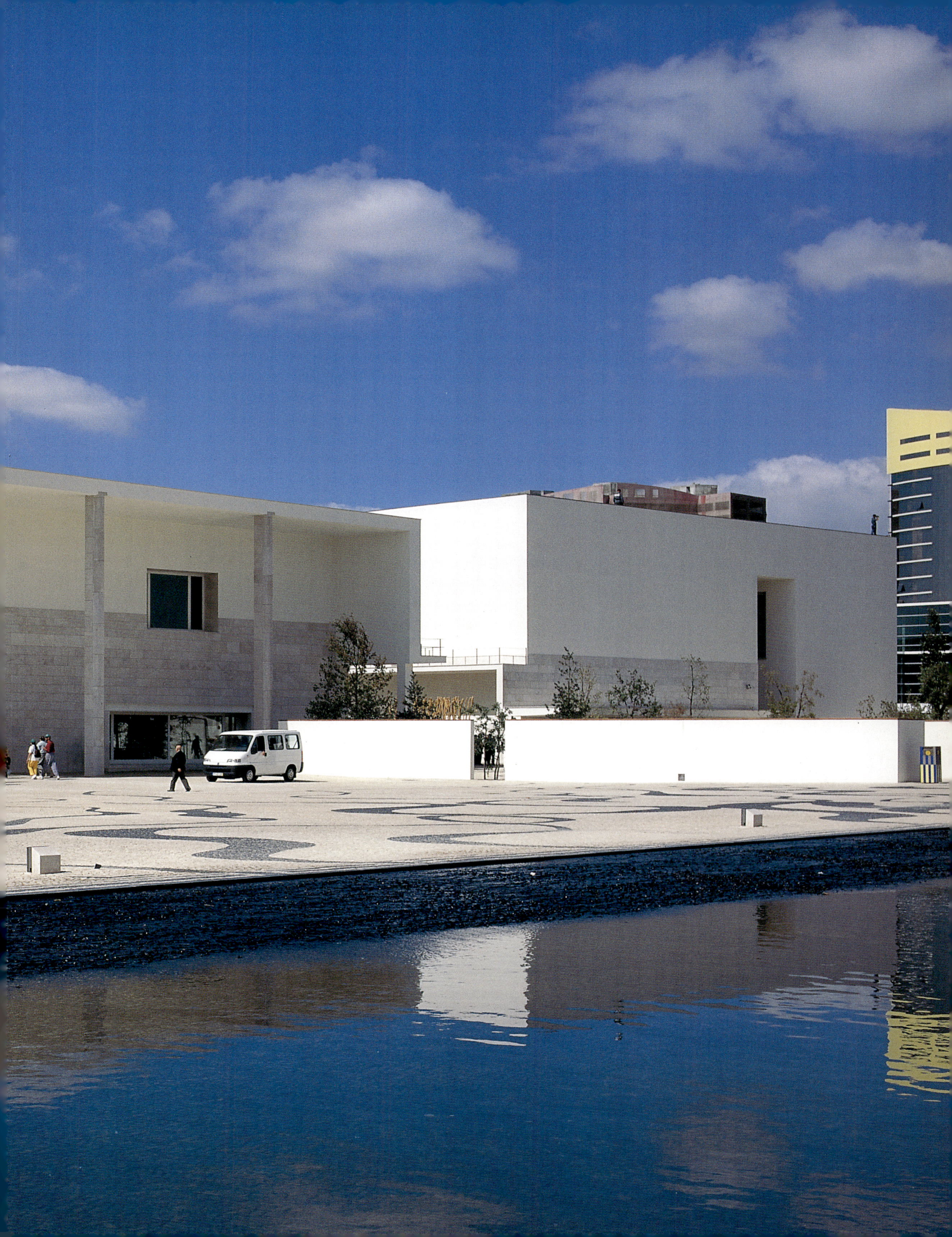

GA: Do you think it is difficult to design a temporary building?

Álvaro Siza: The history of contemporary architecture is full of temporary buildings and many are extremely important in the evolution of modern architecture. They are moments of research and examples of particular manifestoes. In that way they are not always directly related to the particular things that are going to be put inside of it. There is a similar kind of distance. They are interested in investigating a particular moment in architecture. For instance, the Stockholm Exhibition of the 30s. They built to last just a very short time, and they were not designed for particular programs. They were much more than that. They were fantastic buildings. Temporary buildings are like a concentration of the expression of an architectural idea and they created the possibility to read and react to those ideas for a brief moment. But again, that is totally different than designing just to be seen or just for it's impact or presence.

GA: One of the unique things about the Expo this time is that they weren't thinking of these buildings as temporary buildings but intend to reprogram them after the Expo is finished.

Siza: That's right. The strategy for the Expo was to reduce the number of temporary pavilions. The stands for the foreign countries will be in two big structures. One will be the fair of Lisbon, for industrial expositions. The other big building is a prefabricated structure that will be divided and put into different towns after the Expo concludes. So there will not be this problem like they had in Seville where many of the buildings are there without any use for them. In the case of Portuguese Pavilion, I thought a lot about this problem of future use.

GA: How does the Expo plan to use this building later on?

Siza: That's the problem. They are not sure. There was a definition of the objectives of the exhibition but beyond that I had no idea. This was a very difficult project because there were no fixed conditions. There was a schematic masterplan, but I didn't know what the other architects around me would create and of course they didn't know what I would make. So this was a very interesting exercise. I was forced to project a building that was very flexible, but that should have a firm image and that eventually would have a strong role in the town. In the end, what happens is the same thing that happens with all buildings, and that is that even if you have a very precise program, the problem is not only to solve for the program. Do you know what I mean?

GA: So the Expo committee was very vague in what they wanted?

Siza: The only thing the Expo told me is that the building might be used as a government building but it might also become a museum. That obligated me to make a structure that could be anything. It could be offices, administration, exhibition space, anything. What I did was to create a modulated structure with modulated windows so that the distribution of light is uniform. I determined dimensions that would allow each wing to have a central corridor double loaded with rooms. That's the reason for the interior patios. I placed the vertical accesses next to the patios at the four corners so that you can have convenient distribution of people along the spaces. Of course this yielded a very simple building. I also didn't have fixed interior conditions. The program included a big ceremonial space which gives that roof in concrete with cables. I had to create a structure that fit the image of the Expo but that could also be used later on.

GA: The siting is different from what was dictated in the mater plan. What's the reason for this?

Siza: I needed something to react against. I didn't know how the buildings around this one would be. The architects all began

---

GA：仮設的な建物を設計するのは難しいと思っていらっしゃいますか。

アルヴァロ・シザ：近代建築の歴史は仮設の建物であふれていますし，その多くが近代建築の展開のなかで非常に重要な位置を占めています。それは研究の機会となり，固有なマニフェストの例証となっているわけです。ですから，それらが，中に展示されるであろう特定のものとの直接的な関係を常に持つというわけではないのです。同種の距離がおかれています。建築における特定の時期を探求することに興味が向けられている。たとえば，30年代のストックホルム博。非常に短い期間開催されるために建てられ，特定のプログラムのために設計されたものではなかった。それ以上のものでした。ファンタスティックな建物でした。仮設の建物は建築的アイディア表現の凝縮のようなもので，つかのまの時間に対するこうしたアイディアを読解し反応する可能性をつくりだしてくれます。しかしまた，これは，ただ見られるための，その衝撃や存在感だけのためのものをデザインすることとはまったく違うことです。

GA：今回のExpoの特徴の一つは，これらの建物が仮設的なものとして考えられているのではなく，Expo終了後，リプログラミングされる予定だということですね。

シザ：その通りです。今回のExpoの戦略は，仮設的なパヴィリオンの数を減らすことでした。外国からの出展スタンドはすべて2つの大きな建物に入ることになります。その一つはリスボンで行われる産業展の会場として使われる予定です。もう一つの大きな建物はプレファブ構造で，Expo終了後，分割していくつかの町に設置されます。ですから，セビリャでのように，多くの建物が使われぬままに残ってしまうという問題は生まれないでしょう。ポルトガル・パヴィリオンでは，将来の利用法というこの問題について私はずいぶん考えました。

GA：Expo側は，この建物を後でどう使おうと計画しているのですか。

シザ：それが問題なのです。彼らは確かではないのです。この博覧会の目的は定義されていますが，それ以上は，私にもアイディアがありません。固定した状況というものがなかったのですから，これは非常に難しい計画でした。スキマティックな全体計画はありましたが，私の担当する建物の周りに他の建築家が何を建てるのか分かりませんでしたし，もちろん，彼らも私がどんなものをつくるかを知りません。つまり，これは非常に面白い実習でした。建物を，高度にフレキシブルではあるが，強固なイメージを持ち，最終的に街のなかで強い役割を持つであろうものを計画するように強制されました。結局，あらゆる建物に起こるのと同じことがここでも起こりました。つまり，非常に詳細なプログラムを持っていても，問題はそのプログラムを解くことだけではないのです。言っている意味が分かりますか。

GA：つまり，Expo事務局は，自分たちが何を望んでいるのか非常に曖昧だったわけですね。

シザ：Expo側が話してくれた唯一のことは，建物は政府が使うことになるかも知れないが，美術館になることも有り得るということでした。それは，私にどのようにでも成り得る建物をつくることを義務づけることになりました。オフィス，管理事務局，展示スペース，何でも有り得る。私がしたことは，光の配分を均質にするように，調整された窓の付いた調整された建物をつくることでした。部屋を二重に詰め込んだ中央廊下を各ウィングに備えることが出来るようにディメンションを決めました。それがインテリア・パティオがある理由です。各スペースに沿って人がなめらかに流れるように，四隅にあるパティオの隣に垂直方向へのアクセスを置きました。もちろん，これは非常に単純な建物を生むことになる。また，内部空間も固定されたものにしていません。プログラムには，ケーブル吊りのコンクリート屋根の付いた，式典などの開けるスペースも含まれていました。Expoのイメージに相応しく，かつ後でも使える建物を創造しなければなりませんでした。

around the same time and the master plan was rather schematic. So in fact what I did was to propose a different site for the building to create a point of departure. Before the building was on the other side of the street. But since I didn't know what the other buildings would be like around this axial situation which calls for symmetry, what I did was to create an asymmetric situation.

I related it more directly with the water. I discussed a strategy with the architect in charge of the open space, and we agreed basically in leaving a big space of the porch of the building, limited by the street and by a smaller long building along the street. Then it would be possible to create a relationship between the two structures with this open space. You have a more unified composition, with balance. Unfortunately later, this square was not as completely free as I wanted it to be. An area had to be elevated for parking and there were problems with the water line. You can still see through it but it is not ideal.

GA: What was your strategy when the building was in the older site?
Siza: I never really studied it. I didn't know how to begin this project without knowing any of the parameters. So I had to look for a fixed point to start thinking. That's why I proposed this and was happy when this idea was accepted.

GA: Tell me more about the building itself.
Siza: The structure is very flexible. There is a system along the walls and the ceiling is suspended. It all relates to the fixed module developed for this building.

GA: How did you develop this cable roof?
Siza: I had many different solutions I was trying in the beginning. Then I began working with the engineers to see all of the possibilities. The way to make the roof came through many experiments. I had many different concepts. When I came to this idea of a hanging roof, I didn't want a temporary one of canvas. I wanted a fixed thing. I spoke with the engineers about this possibility and they were very enthusiastic about this and started developing this concept. It's 20-centimeter slab with cables and two important porticos. Of course there were a lot of technical problems, for instance before one of the porches was part of the building, we realized that there should be allowances for movement, so I divorced the structures and created a very narrow space between them. The roof cantilevers and doesn't actually touch the building, so it can move a little without

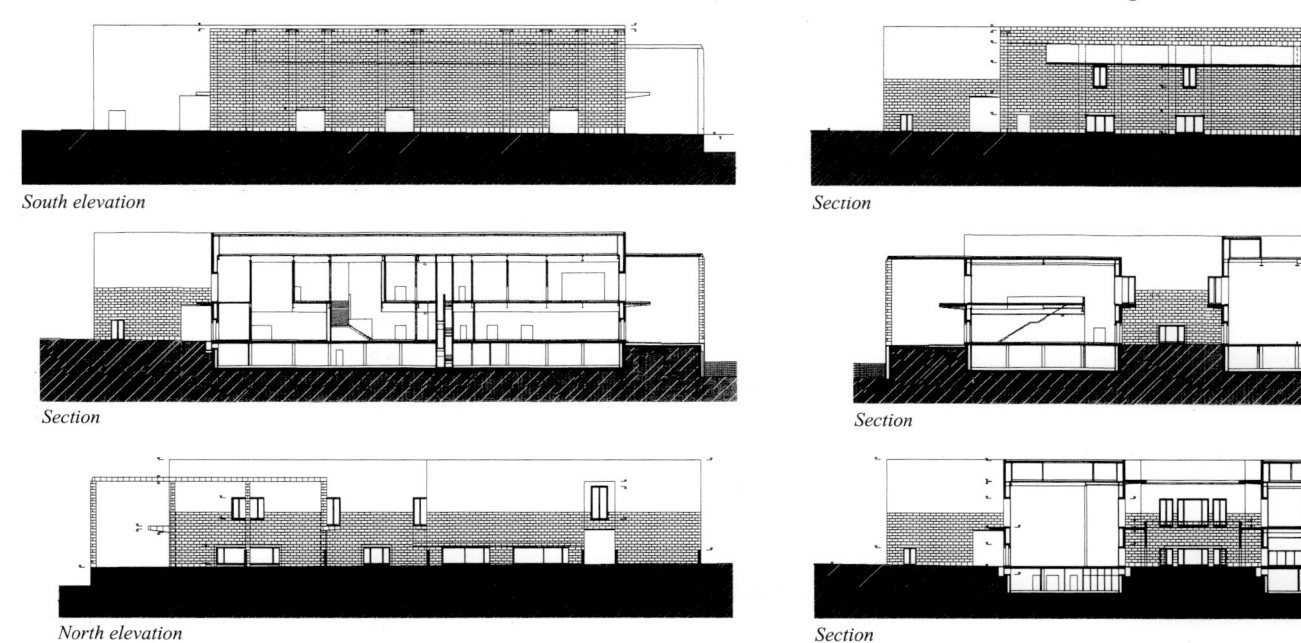

South elevation

Section

Section

Section

North elevation

Section

GA：敷地は全体計画が指示していた場所とは違っています。なぜでしょうか。
シザ：私は全体計画に対抗する何かを必要としていました。この建物の周りにどのような建物がくるのか分からなかったのです。建築家は皆，ほぼ同時に設計を始め，全体計画はかなりスキマティックなものでした。それで，実際に何をしたかといえば，出発点をつくりだすために，この建物に対し違う敷地を提案しました。それまでは，建物は通りの反対側に面していたのです。しかし，対称性を要求されるこの軸線の周囲に他の建物がどのようなものとして並ぶのかが分からなかったので，非対称的な状況をつくったのです。

私はそれをもっと水と直接の関係をもたせるようにしました。オープン・スペースを担当した建築家とストラテジーを討議して，道路と道路沿いのこちらより小さな細長い建物に限られた建物のポーチというかたちで，広い空間を残すことに決めました。それによって，2つの建物とこのオープン・スペースの間に関係をつくりだせる可能性が生まれるはずです。均衡のとれた，より一体感のある構成になります。残念ながら，後になって，この広場は，私が期待していたような完全に自由なスペースとはならなかった。そのエリアは駐車場のために高くする必要があり，水位との問題がありました。それでもまだ，広場を通して水が見えます。しかし理想通りではありません。

GA：元の敷地のときは，どのようなストラテジーをたてていたのですか。
シザ：実際にはスタディしませんでした。パラメーターを少しも知ることなしに，このプロジェクトをどう進めたらよいのか分かりませんでした。ですから，考え始めるために固定点を探す必要がありました。これを提案した理由はそのためで，このアイディアが受け入れられて嬉しかったですね。

GA：建物そのものについて，もう少し説明して下さいませんか。
シザ：構造はとてもフレキシブルです。壁にそって一つのシステムがあり，天井は吊られています。すべてが，この建物のために開発された固定されたモデュールに対応しています。

GA：このケーブル・ルーフはどのように開発されたのですか。
シザ：はじめに，さまざまな解法を試しました。つぎに，技術者と一緒に，そのすべての可能性を検証する作業を始めました。屋根をつくる方法は，多くの実験を通して生まれたものです。数多くの違ったコンセプトを持っていました。吊り屋根というこの考えに至ったとき，カンヴァス製の一時的なものを望んではいませんでした。固定されたものが欲しかったのです。私はこれについて技術者に話したところ非常な興味を持ち，このコンセプトを展開しはじめたのです。ケーブルと2つの重要なポルティコの付いた，20センチ厚のスラブです。もちろん，技術的問題が無数にありました。たとえば，最初は，ポーチの一つは建物の一部でしたが，人の流れのために許容度をとるべきであることに気づきました。そこで，私は建物を分離し，間に非常に狭いスペースをとったのです。屋根は片持ち

damaging the structure and yet still creates this interesting narrow space between the two. Other problems included how the roof would shed water. In the first concept we had a slight angle and a cut so that shed water would fall directly into the water below but in the end they ran pipes across the area and we couldn't do this so now the water has to fall on the ground. My new idea is to put a special tree here that would break the fall before the water hits the ground.

GA: Couldn't those pipes be moved?

Siza: Of course this could be solved but it would just be another conflict. The Expo administration decided not to pursue that. I was very angry, but I forgot about it and found another solution. I thought it would have been nice to see the rain water falling directly into the docks but you can't get everything. I know that when I designed it, the pipes weren't there, but they appeared, so what could I do. There are many stories like this, especially with large projects when you have to plan and coordinate many companies and individuals. The coordination of large projects is not a strong point in Portugal.

GA: Are you working with Souto de Moura with the interior installations?

Siza: He's doing it by himself. They originally asked me to do everything, exterior and interior. But I realized that it would be difficult for me, because to put up the presentation of the exhibition which is based on video images and so on, would need a lot of coordination. It would be difficult to oversee all of these things. So I proposed that someone else would do the interiors. I recommended Souto de Moura whom I know very well. We have both a lot of engagement in architecture. So he did it on his own, but we are always in contact.

GA: I think this is a good arrangement, because if you did the installation as well it might have been more integral to the architecture and may have affected it's flexibility after the Expo. This way the installations are separate from the building.

Siza: Yes. But what was important to me was that I was able to choose someone with which I have a good relationship so that it would be simple to coordinate. But for him it is a lot of work because it is a very technical installation.

GA: The other day you mentioned that the exterior would be tile?

Siza: Yes. It's stone from Lisbon. It's a marble. It goes around the whole first floor and a part of the second floor. The rest is stucco. The slab is concrete which will be painted white, which will work well with the artificial lighting.

で，建物には実際は触れていません。ですから，構造体を傷めることなしに少し動かせるのです。それでいて，依然として，2つの間にこの面白い狭いスペースがつくりだせるのです。他の問題には，屋根からどのように水を流し落とすかということも含まれていました。最初のコンセプトでは，少し勾配をつけて開口をとり，水は下の水面に直接落ちるようになっていましたが，結局，彼らは，そのエリアを横切るパイプを通し，われわれはこれをすることができず，今，水は地面に落ちざるを得なくなっている。私の新しいアイディアは，そこに特別な木を植え，水が地面に達する前にはじき散らすというものです。

GA：これらのパイプを，移動することは出来ないのですか。

シザ：もちろん，出来るはずです。しかし，別な対立が生じるだけでしょう。Expo事務局はそれを進めないことに決定したのです。とても腹が立ちましたが，それを忘れることにして，他の解決案を見つけました。雨水がドックのなかに直接落ちて行くのを見るのは素敵だろうと思いますが，すべてを手に入れることは出来ないのです。私がデザインしたときはパイプはそこにないことを知っていました。ところがそれは出現したのです。私に何が出来るでしょう。これに類した話はたくさんあります。特に，多くの会社や人たちと調整し，計画しなければならないビッグ・プロジェクトの場合はそうです。大規模計画の調整は，ポルトガルの得意技ではないのです。

GA：展示のインスタレーションは，ソウト・デ・モウラさんと一緒に仕事をされたのですか。

シザ：彼はその仕事を一人でしています。事務局側は外部も内部もすべてを私に依頼してきたのですが，私はそれは難しいことに気づいていました。ヴィデオ・イメージなどに基づいた展示構成には，多くの協働作業が必要となるでしょう。それをすべて監督するのは無理がありま

す。ですから，インテリアに誰か他の人を提案することにしました。自分がよく知っているソウト・デ・モウラを推薦したのです。私たちは建築設計で何度も協力してきました。そんなわけで彼はその仕事を一人で担当しましたが，常に連絡を取り合っています。

GA：それは良い方法なのではないかと思います。もしシザさんがインスタレーションもされたとしたら，展示構成が建築そのものにもっと統合されてしまい，Expo後の柔軟な対応性に影響したのではないかと思うからです。この方法ですと，インスタレーションが建物から明快に切り離されます。

シザ：そうですね。しかし，私にとって重要だったのは，良い関係を持てる人を選ぶことが出来たことでした。それによって，調整も簡単に行くでしょうから。しかし，彼にとっては手のかかる仕事です。非常にテクニカルなインスタレーションですから。

GA：前に，外観はタイルになるだろうとおっしゃっていましたね。

シザ：ええ。リスボン産の石です。大理石なのですが。1階全部と2階の一部を包み込みます。残る部分はスタッコです。スラブはコンクリートで白く塗る予定です。人工照明によく映えるでしょう。

North end 北端▷

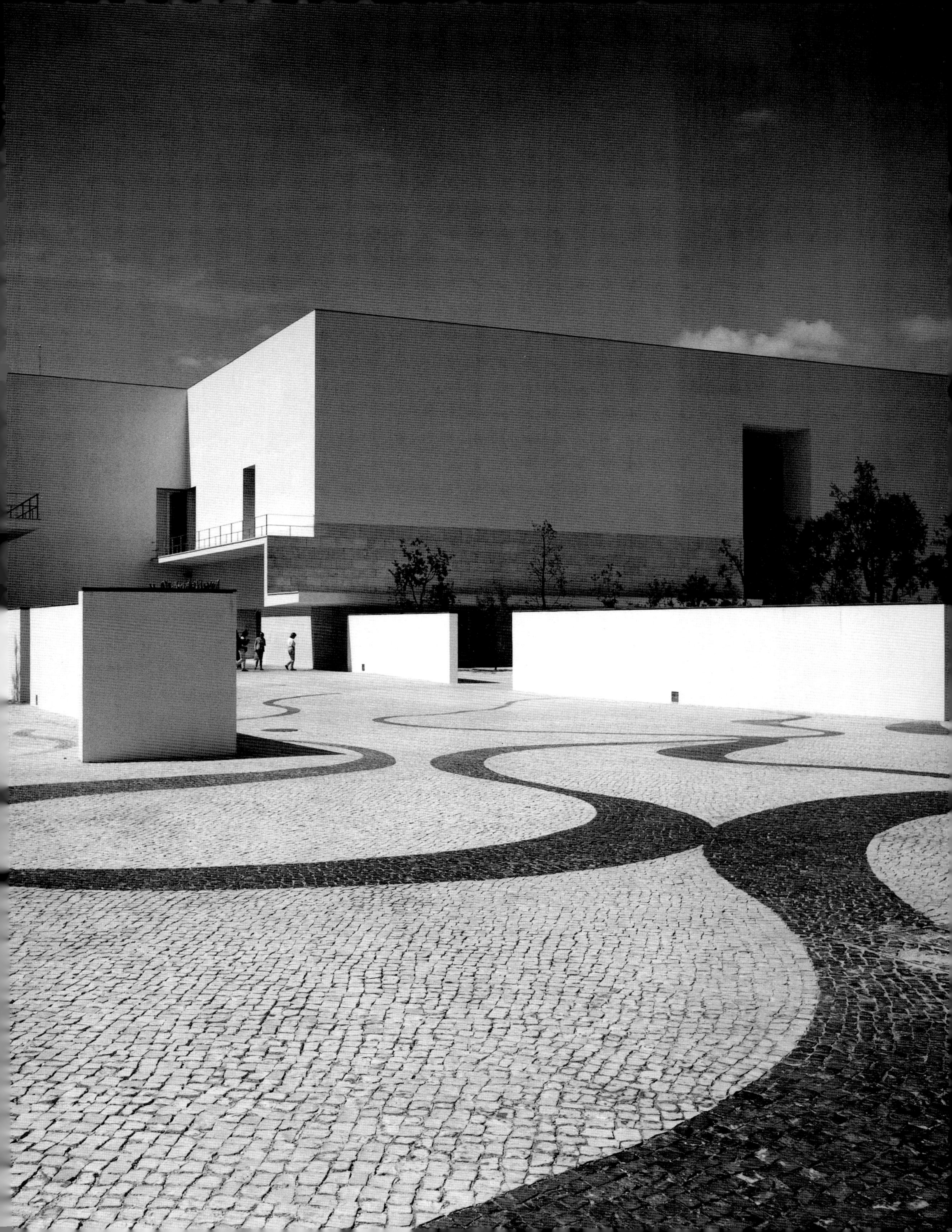

128

Roof　ケーブル・ルーフ

PROJECTS

Manuel Cargaleiro Foundation, Lisbon, Portugal, 1992-　マヌエル・カルガレイロ財団

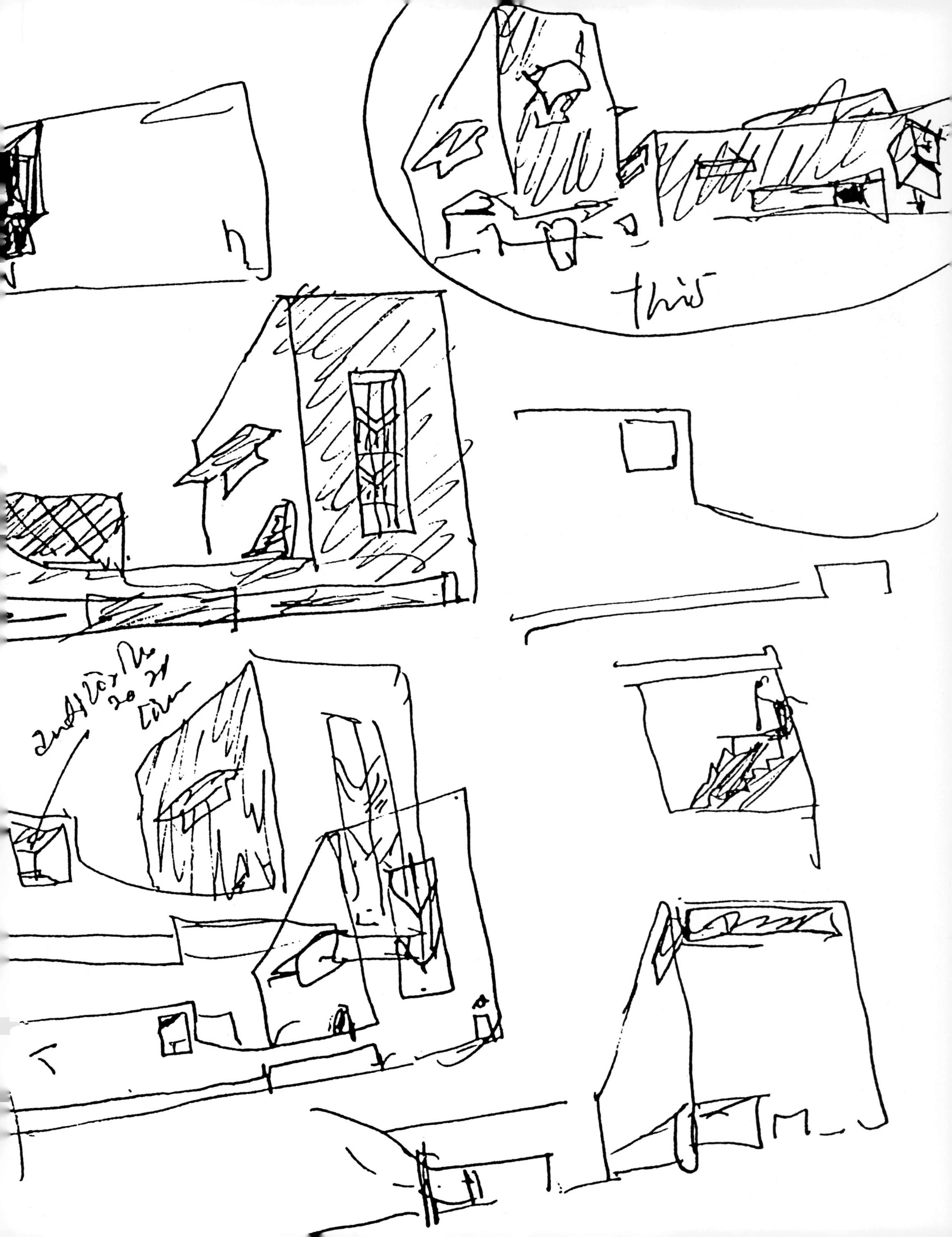
this

Manuel Cargaleiro Foundation
マヌエル・カルガレイロ財団

Client: Manuel Cargaleiro Foundation   Design period: 1992–   Architects: Álvaro Siza Arquitecto, Lda   Collaborators: [Design phase] Peter Testa, project architect; Clemente Menéres Semide, Gonzalo Benavides, Rudolf Finsterwalder, assistants; [Execution phase] Rudolf Finsterwalder, João Sabugueiro, Luís-Diaz Mauriño, Roberto Cremascoli, project architects; Cristina Ferreirinha, assistant   Structural engineer: Triede—Víctor França   Mechanical engineer: Luis Malheiro   Structural system: reinforced concrete structure

Lisbon, Portugal

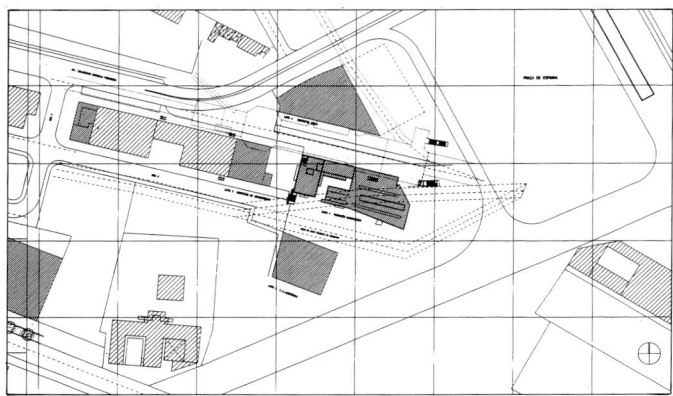

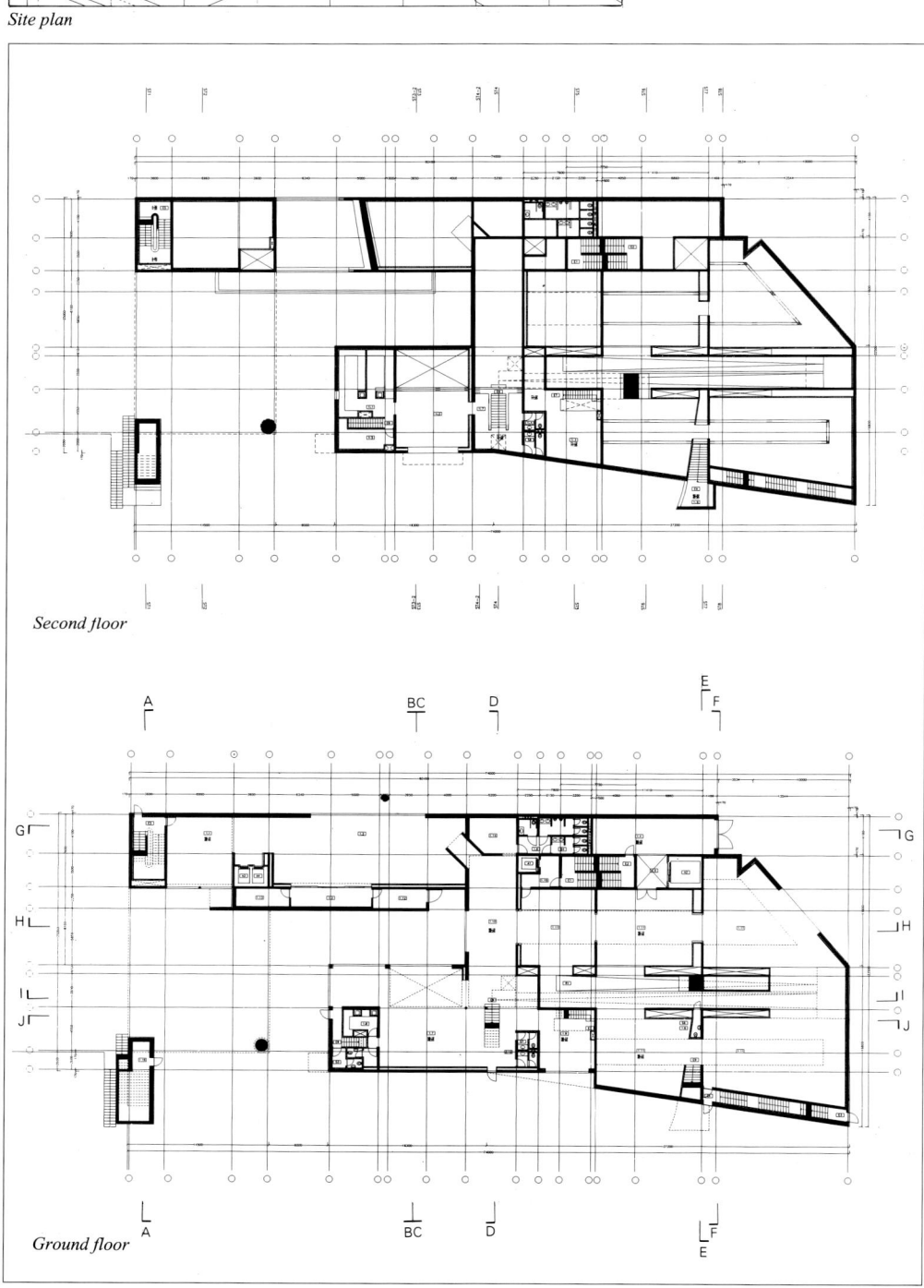

Site plan

Second floor

Ground floor

Álvaro Siza: This project was very much conditioned by the site. There is a new rank of buildings, big buildings. Some built, some in the project stage. The town called me to see what was possible to improve what had begun to be a monstrous and chaotic bunch of buildings. The problem was that the town had made an exception to allow larger buildings here, but they weren't in relation to any urban order.
GA: This is not the urban texture of the town.
Siza: That's right. The buildings were beginning along a street but there was no overall plan or strategy. In the beginning there was an existing viaduct, so it was even more chaotic. So when this was already absolutely out of control they asked me to come and try to make sense of it. They asked me to propose how this area might develop in the future. I began by negotiating with the architects working on

アルヴァロ・シザ：このプロジェクトは，敷地状況に大きく左右されています。新しい種類の建物，大きな建物があります。いくつかは既に建てられ，いくつかは計画段階です。巨大化し，混沌の様相を見せ始めた建物群を改善するために何が可能かを考えて欲しいと，市が頼んできたのです。問題は，市当局はここに大きな建物の建設を許可する特例を設けたのですが，それがいかなる都市的秩序とも結びついていないことでした。
GA：これは，この街の都市構造ではありませんね。
シザ：その通りなのです。建物群は道路に沿って始まっていますが，全体的なプランやストラテジーに欠けています。最初の頃には，高架橋があったのでさらに混沌としていました。この地域がまったく制御不能なものに陥ったとき，市はここに来て，どうにかして欲しいと依頼してきたのです。この地域を将来どのように開発して行くか提案することを求めてきました。ここで新しいプロジェクトを進めている建築家たちと，何らかの秩序を確立するための調整を始めました。強力なヴォリュームを持つ建物群の系統化を試みたのです。彼らは広場を欲しがっていましたが，いくつかの建物には既に大きな庭がありましたから，伝統的な都市型の広場をつくることは難しかったのです。代わりに私が

new projects in this area to establish some sort of order. I tried to organize these strong volumes. They wanted to have a square but several of the buildings already had large gardens so it would be difficult to establish a traditional urban kind of square. What I proposed instead was to organize the new volumes in relation to the existing ones to try to create a kind of magnetic force between them. It was a consideration of Le Corbusier's idea of free volume in space. To help this work, I proposed building a museum amidst these tall buildings. It would be a museum for the work of a particular artist. The artist also had a good collection of Parisian art since he used to live in Paris, and so he could offer his own work and this collection to the town. A bank and insurance company would pay for the building, and the building would be for the town.

The form of the building comes from the constraints I spoke of before. But in addition to the problems I spoke of, there is a metro passing and it wasn't very deep in the ground. As you can see it has a taller part which relates to some existing buildings and other projects that have already been approved when I took on the project. The exhibition area is developed on two floors, and there is an underground area for storage. The tower is lifted free off the

Fifth floor

Fourth floor

Third floor

提案したのは，既存建物との関わりのうえで，新しい建物を構成することで，両者の間に一種の磁力をつくろうとするものです。空間のなかに立つ自由なヴォリュームというル・コルビュジエのアイディアについて考えたものでした。この作業を支援するために，これらの高層の建物の真ん中に美術館を建てることを提案したのです。ある芸術家の作品を収めるものです。この芸術家はパリに住んでいたので，パリで集めたなかなか良いコレクションを持っており，自分の作品とそのコレクションを市に寄贈することが出来ます。銀行と保険会社が美術館建設の費用を出すことになる予定で，建物は市のものになるでしょう。

この建物の形態は前に説明した制約から生まれています。お話しした問題に加えて，地下鉄が通っていることがあり，しかも地下のあまり深くない所を走っています。ごらんのように，いくつかの既存建物と，私がこのプロジェクトを受けたときにはすでに認可されていた他のプロジェクトと関係づけた高層の部分があります。展示エリアは2層分を占め，地下に倉庫があります。高層部は地上階を開放して持ち上げられています。

パブリックやパティオに開放できるレストランがあります。エントランスは高層部の下からで，そこから広いホールに出ます。そこから，

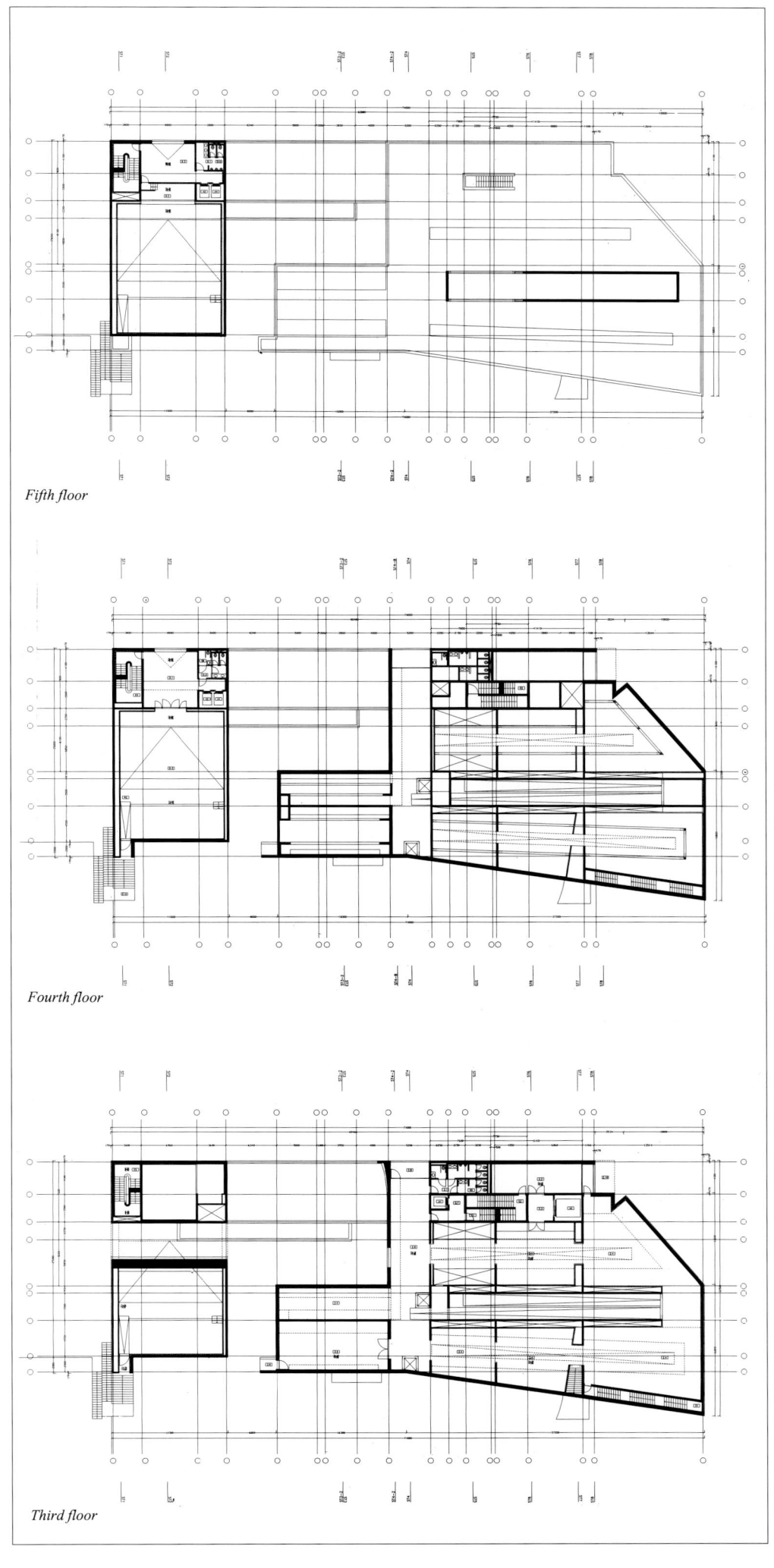

North elevation

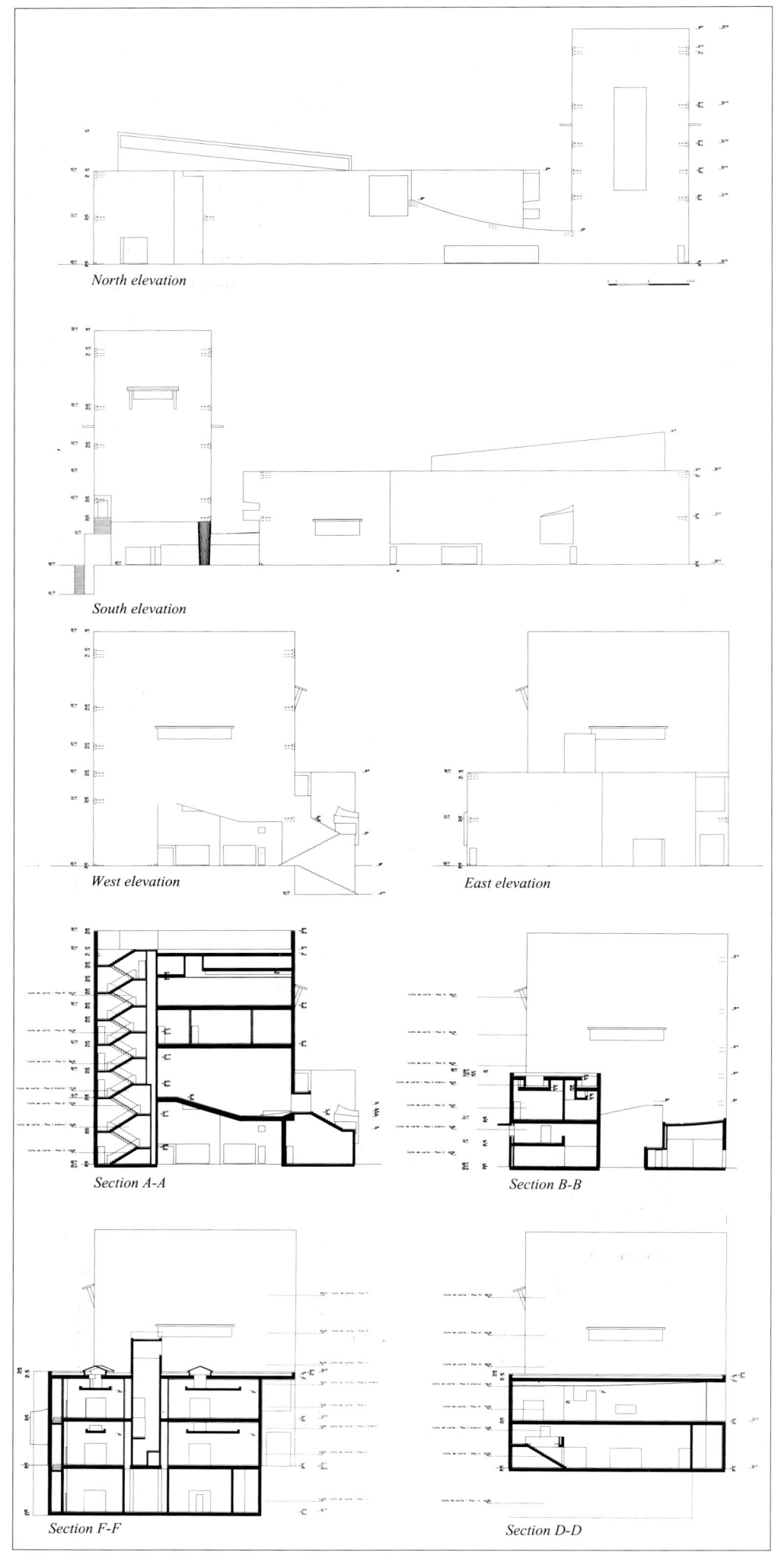

South elevation

West elevation

East elevation

Section A-A

Section B-B

Section F-F

Section D-D

ground floor.

You have a restaurant which can be open to the public and a patio. The entrance is under the tower and leads you to a big hall. There you enter a second hall that leads you to the exhibition area and to the restaurants. There is a stair taking you up where you have the second part of the restaurant and you have another space. Here you also have a small bookshop. Then you enter and you have a central nucleus with a ramp going to the above floors, and with spaces around it. It is much freer. It's a whole space but with well-defined smaller spaces of different dimensions within it. The ramp takes you up to a double-height atrium. So the organization works around a central nucleus with the ramp which then took you to the various other rooms around it.

GA: Where does the project stand now?
Siza: This project has been blocked because Lisbon doesn't want to spend the money and the bank feels the same way. I'm afraid it probably won't be built. Conditions changed very rapidly within a few years. Originally they wanted this for offices, and today they can't sell a single square meter of office space. The town is presently trying renegotiated uses for this area and to make it less dense.

展示エリアやレストランに導く，2番目のホールに入ります。レストランの上層，そして別な空間に連れて行く階段があります。ここにはまた小さなブックショップがある。次に，中央の核のなかに至る。ここには上層とその周囲の空間につながるスロープがある。そこはさらに自由な空間です。一体化した空間ですが，そのなかに異なったディメンションを持つ巧みに区画された小さな空間が内包されている。スロープは2層の高さを持つアトリウムに続いている。つまり空間は，スロープの付いた中央の核のまわりに構成されており，このスロープがその周囲のさまざまな部屋へと運んでくれるようになっています。

GA：プロジェクトは今，どのような状態にあるのですか。
シザ：ずっと停止されたままの状態です。リスボン市は費用を負担することを望まず，銀行も同じように感じているようですから。たぶん建てられないかもしれないと心配しています。数年の間に状況が急速に変わったのです。最初は彼らはオフィスにすることを希望していたのですが，今では，数平方メートルのオフィスも売れないのです。市は目下この地域の用途について再交渉中で，もっと密度の低いものにしようとしています。

Section G-G

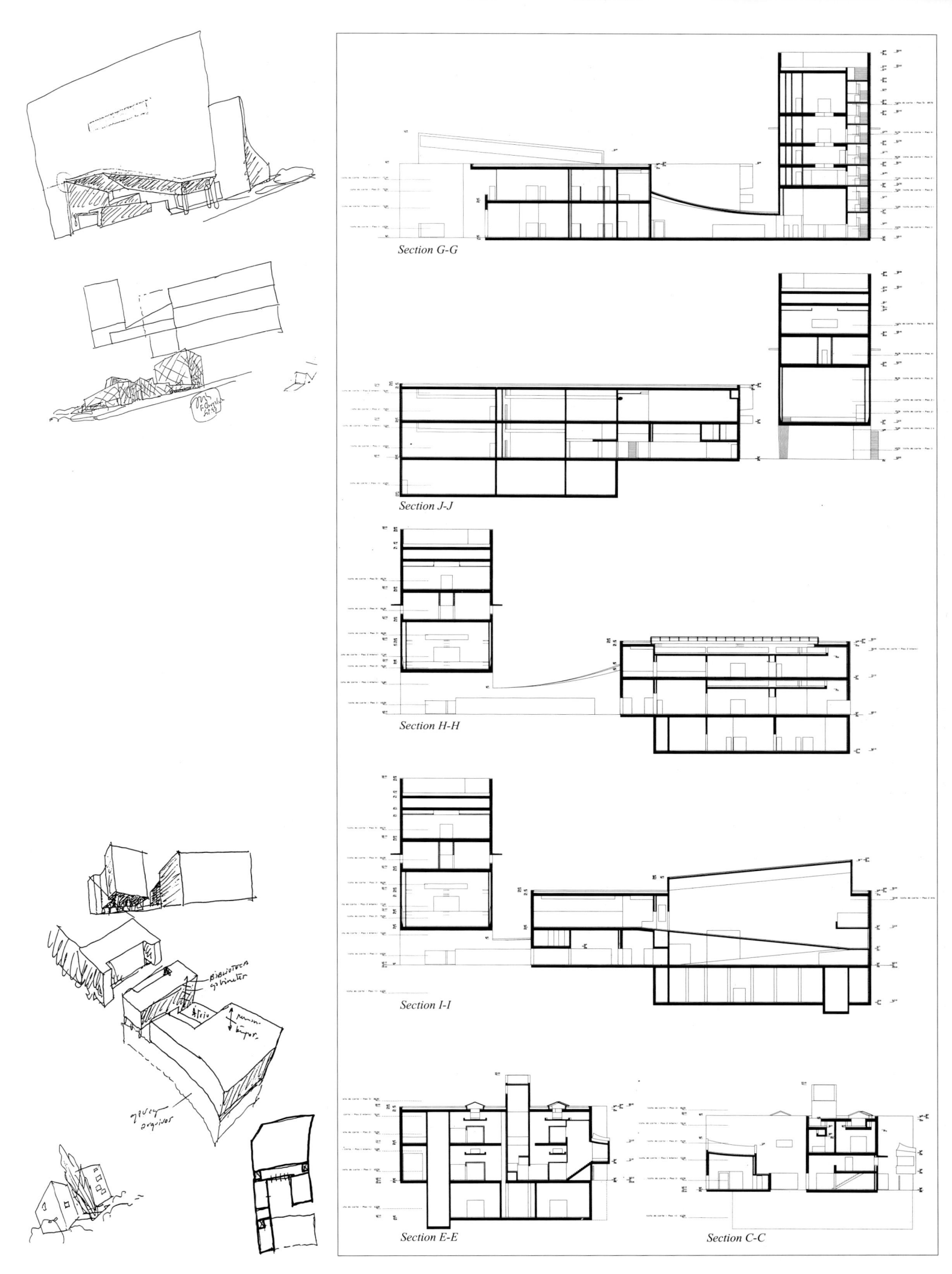

Section J-J

Section H-H

Section I-I

Section E-E

Section C-C

DESCRIPTION

1. The building conforms to the volumetrics of the Plan for the Praça de Espanha and the principles laid down in this plan. However, some modifications on points of detail were introduced, essentially with regard to the lay-out and relationship with the building to be erected against the gable end on the west of the lot in such a way as to define a new small square.

2. The characterization of the building is founded on a patio at datum 66.00 being surrounded by a volume 15 meters high, from which a 30-meter high parallelepiped, partially standing on pillars, rises on the west side.

3. The program for the Foundation is developed on two floors and a basement in the larger area of the building. The tower on the west side contains four floors (and two mezzanine floors, between the first and second and the second and third floors. The ground floor (datum 68.10, which corresponds to the Avenida Columbano Bordalo Pinehiro) is only partly used. The larger part of this space forms a spacious entrance gateway. The overall area is 4800 m² (including 840 m² basement area).

4. The distribution of the program is as follows.
—Floor 0 (basement, datum 62.10): Spare areas, machine room, store and workshop
—Floor 1 (ground floor, datum 68.10): Atrium, reception, cloakroom, exhibition rooms, shop, cafeteria and service atrium.
—Floor 1 (intermediate level, datum 71.10): Mezzanine floor housing cafeteria and shop
—Floor 2 (datum 74.10): Exhibition rooms, restoration workshop, audio-visual room
—Floor 2 (intermediate, datum 76.50): Auditorium
—Floor 3 (datum 80.00): Projection and Interpreter rooms
—Floor 4 (datum 83.50): Administration
—Floor 5 (datum 88.40): Office area

5. The accesses to the various floors of the tower on the west side include a stairway and two lifts. In the exhibition area, the circulations include a ramp, lift, stairway and an emergency staircase. Service access is via a spacious door on the east side; the reception area has a staircase and a goods lift. All the staircases have fire doors.

6. There are no plans for a car park in the grounds of the Foundation. The small loading and unloading bay accommodates only three vehicles. Ample parking space will be provided on the adjoining site in an underground car park to be built by the Companhia de Segruos Lusitânia. The area below the small square on Avenida Columbano Bordalo Pinheiro may also be used for parking, with access from the property on the west side which is at a lower level.

7. The designs for the structures and installations will be presented in due course. The structure includes reinforced concrete walls, columns, beams and roofing. The building has air conditioning throughout. For this reason, the outer windows are generally fixed. Windows which can be opened are fitted only in areas where secondary ventilation is necessary and in parts of the building in which communication with the outside is necessary or advisable (the cafeteria, which may be extended into an esplanade). The planned artificial lighting is basically indirect lighting; it complements the lantern-type lighting in the areas on the top floor.

8. Thermal insulation is provided by hol-

low-brick walls, which duplicate the concrete walls on the inside, and by an external expanded polystyrene covering, with acrylic resin coating. The entire roof area has thermal insulation. It is planned to have a limestone base and partially tiled walls.

Wood and stainless steel frames have been chosen for the outer windows, with double-glazed thermal/acoustic insulation. The outside pane is security glass.

For the finishing of the interiors, it is planned to use marble and wood on the floors, with wood paneling or marble facing in the circulation areas, walls and plastered ceilings and washable floors in the sanitary facilities. The window frames will be wooden.

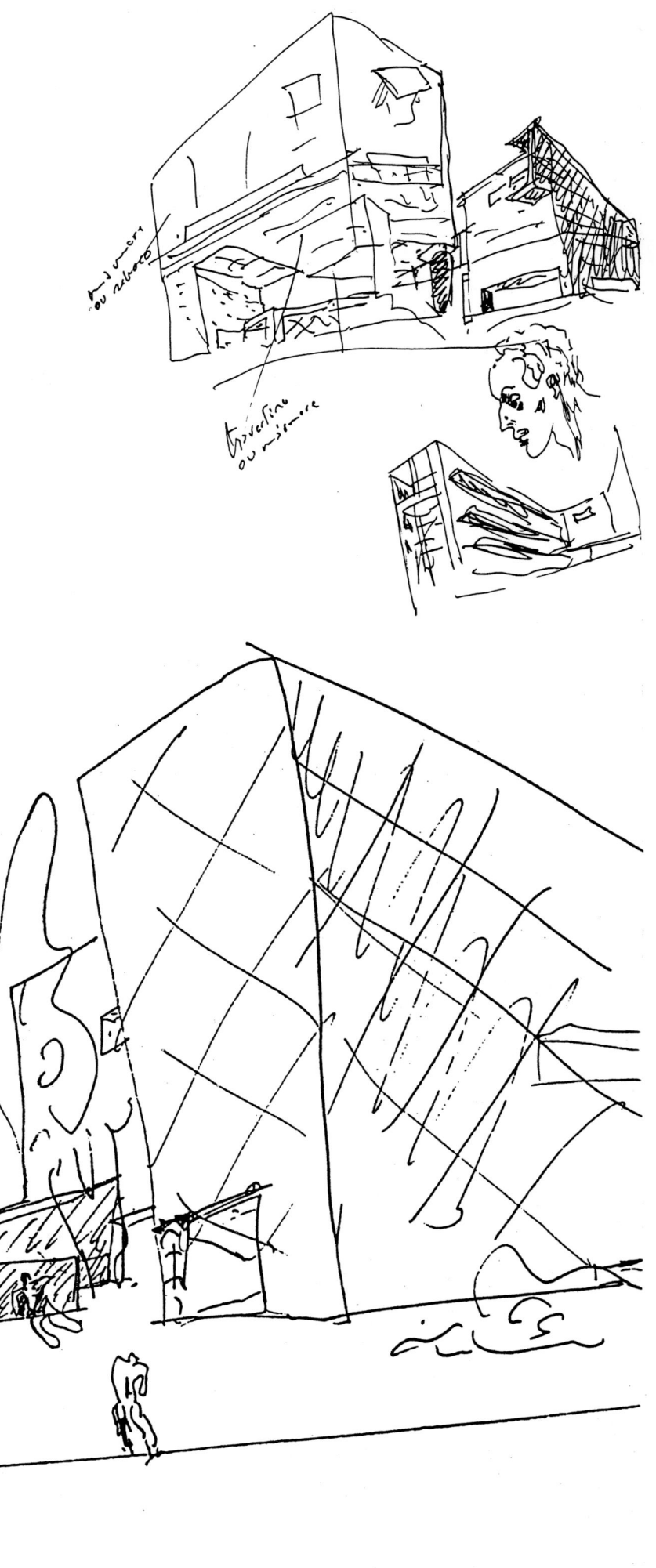

〈解説〉
1）建物は，プラサ・ドゥ・エスパーニャ計画の規模とこの計画のなかで規定されている原則に従っている。しかし，ディテールに関していくつかの修正が加えられている。主には，敷地の西端に面する切妻壁に向かって建てられる建物とのレイアウトと結びつきを，小さな広場を新しくつくるように構成することである。

2）建物の性格づけは，15mの高さのヴォリューム——そこから，部分的に脚柱に乗った，30mの高さの平行六面体の建物が西側に建ち上がる——によって囲まれた，基準面66.00の所に位置するパティオに基づいている。

3）財団のプログラムは，2層にわたって，また，建物の大きな方のエリアにある地下階に配される。西側に面した建物は4層で（1階と2階の間，2階と3階の間に計2つのメザニン階がある）。地上階（基準面68.10。コロンバーノ・ボルダーロ・ピネヒロ通りのレベルに相当する）は一部のみが使われる。このスペースの大部分は広いエントランス・ゲートウェイを形成する。

4）プログラムの配分は以下の通りである。フロア0（地下階。基準面62.10）：予備エリア，機械室，倉庫，ワークショップ／フロア1（地上階。基準面68.10）：アトリウム，レセプション，クロークルーム，展示室，店舗，カフェテリア，サービス・アトリウム／フロア1（中間階。基準面71.10）：カフェテリアや店舗のあるメザニン階／フロア2（基準面74.10）：展示室，修復のための工房，オーディオヴィジュアル室／フロア2（中間階。基準面76.50）：オーディトリアム／フロア3（基準面80.00）：映写・通訳室／フロア4（基準面83.50）：管理事務／フロア5（基準面88.40）：オフィス。

5）西側に面する建物のさまざまな階へのアクセスは，階段と2基のリフトである。展示エリアの動線は，斜路，リフト，階段，非常階段が構成する。サービス・アクセスは東側の大きな扉から入る。レセプション・エリアには階段と荷物用リフトが備えられる。階段にはすべて防火扉が設置される。

6）財団のある1階には駐車場の計画はない。積荷，荷下ろし用のベイには3台分の余裕しかない。充分な広さを持つ駐車場は，隣接する敷地の地下にコンパーニャ・ドゥ・セグルオス・ルシターニャが建設予定の駐車場が提供することになろう。コランバンド・ボルダーロ・ピンへ

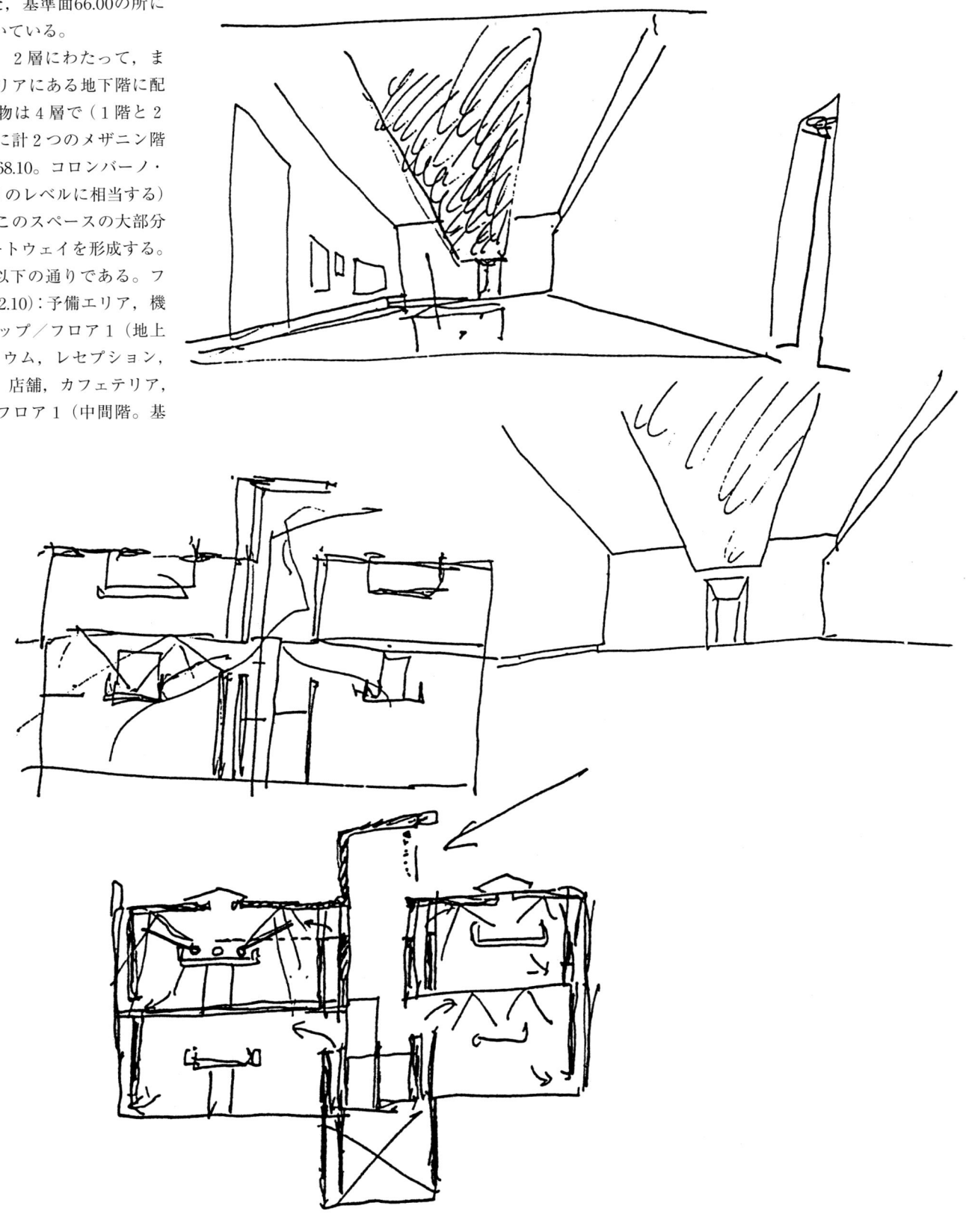

イロ通りに面した小広場下のエリアもまた駐車場に使われるかもしれない。ここには低いレベルにある西側に面した敷地からアクセスする。

7）構造とインスタレーションのためのデザインは以下のようになる予定。壁，柱，梁，屋根は鉄筋コンクリート造。建物は全体が空調されている。このため，外壁の窓は全般にはめ殺しである。開放できる窓は二次的な換気が必要な場所，また，屋外との交流が必要なあるいは望ましい（遊歩道のなかへと広げられる可能性のあるカフェテリア）一部の箇所にのみ設置される。計画されている人工照明は基本的に間接照明である。これは，最上階のランタン型の照明を補足する。

8）断熱は，内側のコンクリート壁を複製した中空煉瓦の壁，および，アクリル樹脂を被せた外側に広げられたスチレン樹脂の覆いが提供する。屋根のあるエリアは全体に断熱されている。そこはライムストーンの基部に部分的にタイル貼りの壁を使う計画である。

外側の窓枠は木とステンレス・スティールで，断熱／防音のために二重ガラスがはめられる。外側には安全ガラスが使われる

内部仕上げは次の通り。床は大理石と木，動線部分は木製パネルまたは大理石貼り。サニタリー設備はプラスター塗りの天井に，洗い流せる床。

Restaurant of Ocean Swimming Pool
レサのスイミングプール・レストラン

Leça da Palmeira, Portugal

Client: Municipality of Matosinhos   Preliminary design: 1966   Design and execution: 1993–95   Architects: Álvaro Siza Arquitecto, Lda   Principals-in-charge: Antonio Madureira, Beatriz Madureira, preliminary; Guilherme Páris Couto, design and execution   Project team: Luís Cardoso, Cristina Ferreirinha, Marco Rampulla, Roberto Cremascoli   Structural engineer: G.O.P.—João Maria Sobreira   Mechanical engineers: Rita/Paul Serafim, electricity; Alfredo Costa Pereira, Paulo Queirós Faria, mechanical; Inês Sobreira, plumbing; Manuela Castra, gas   Structural system: reinforced concrete structure

GA: So this is an addition to a project you did over thirty years ago.
Álvaro Siza: Actually the original design for the pool, included a restaurant.
GA: In the first stage?
Siza: Yes. I made the first drawings in 1962 but they never built it. Then two years ago, more than thirty years after, they asked me to do the working drawings for it. I didn't change the design much.
GA: How did you feel about realizing a project thirty years after it's design?
Siza: I felt good. The only problem is that it is not yet in construction. They're currently looking for a promoter that will take it on. So now I don't feel good because I went ahead and made all of the drawings and it's still not going anywhere. I'm waiting.

It's funny because it's like being hired by somebody to execute the project of another architect. But I must say that I like this project so I don't mind at all. It's like working for Siza long ago.
GA: Tell me a little about the project history.
Siza: The idea for a swimming pool actually came from an engineer. He was the brother of Távora, and was a very good engineer. He was then asked to also create changing facilities and so he said he needed an architect and brought me onto the project. He had a rectangular swimming pool, but I suggested that we let the rocks determine the boundaries and only use walls where they were needed to contain the water. So that created the original concept.

GA: Is this natural water?
Siza: The water here is very strong. It needs to be treated and then brought in by pipe. There are a lot of pools that use natural water in Casablanca and Morocco along the Atlantic. I didn't know about them. In fact, when I designed this pool in relation to the rocks I thought it was an entirely new idea. Later I went to Morocco, I found a lot of them. I designed the architecture along the Marginal Street. I designed the section in a way that used the level changes from the street down to the shore. The idea was not to interrupt the view, so when you pass along the street you see the sea. Then, you go down via a ramp and you pass the changing facilities. Then there is a wall where you lose the view momentarily, and then you arrive to another area and you see the ocean again. Then you cross a bridge underneath which is the swimming pool for kids.

As you can see, the overall composition needed another element. And I felt that we needed a restaurant for the people. And there was a mass of rocks that I liked so I designed it on these rocks. It would also help protect from the wind which is strong here at times. A natural ditch was included in this area so you can go into the ocean when it is warm. The water here is always a little warmer because it is contained. So the restaurant structure was the closing of the composition which has this dense linear quality. The older buildings had to be strong to resist the water since it can comes up pretty high during the winter. It is concrete with some stainless steel and then wood at the roof. The restaurant is on a much more exposed site. It is protected by the rocks. A new problem here was how to make a relationship between this new building and a very old wall which happens to be 1.5 kilometers long. The moment they touch is very very critical. So what I did was to create parallel walls that don't touch. Instead they cross. I put the entrance at this level and then elevated the building to be better protected from the water. The existing wall is never interrupted. It goes on and on. And the building sits above it.
GA: Did you have to work on the older elements of the pool at all?
Siza: It's funny. After thirty years, the wood was absolutely perfect. It was wood taken from demolished buildings, nineteenth century buildings. But some of the concrete was damaged. We had to go in with a special concrete.
GA: And did you stay with the same material palette?
Siza: Basically. Everything is concrete. The interior is also all concrete. The roof, the ground, and walls had no finish materials. We had to use special glass to resist the water's force. We also create a terrace to come to on a nice day.

Again it is principally a linear organization. It's not a full service restaurant. It's simple.

This is the first building I have ever done like this. But the exterior is so rich. The presence of the ocean and view are so strong, that the finish materials hardly matter. It should be very simple.

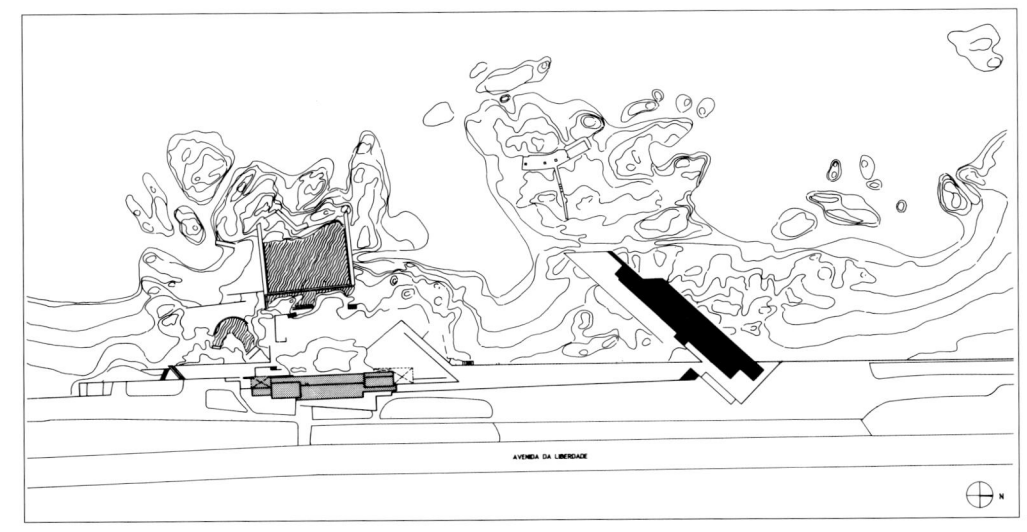

Site plan

Upper level

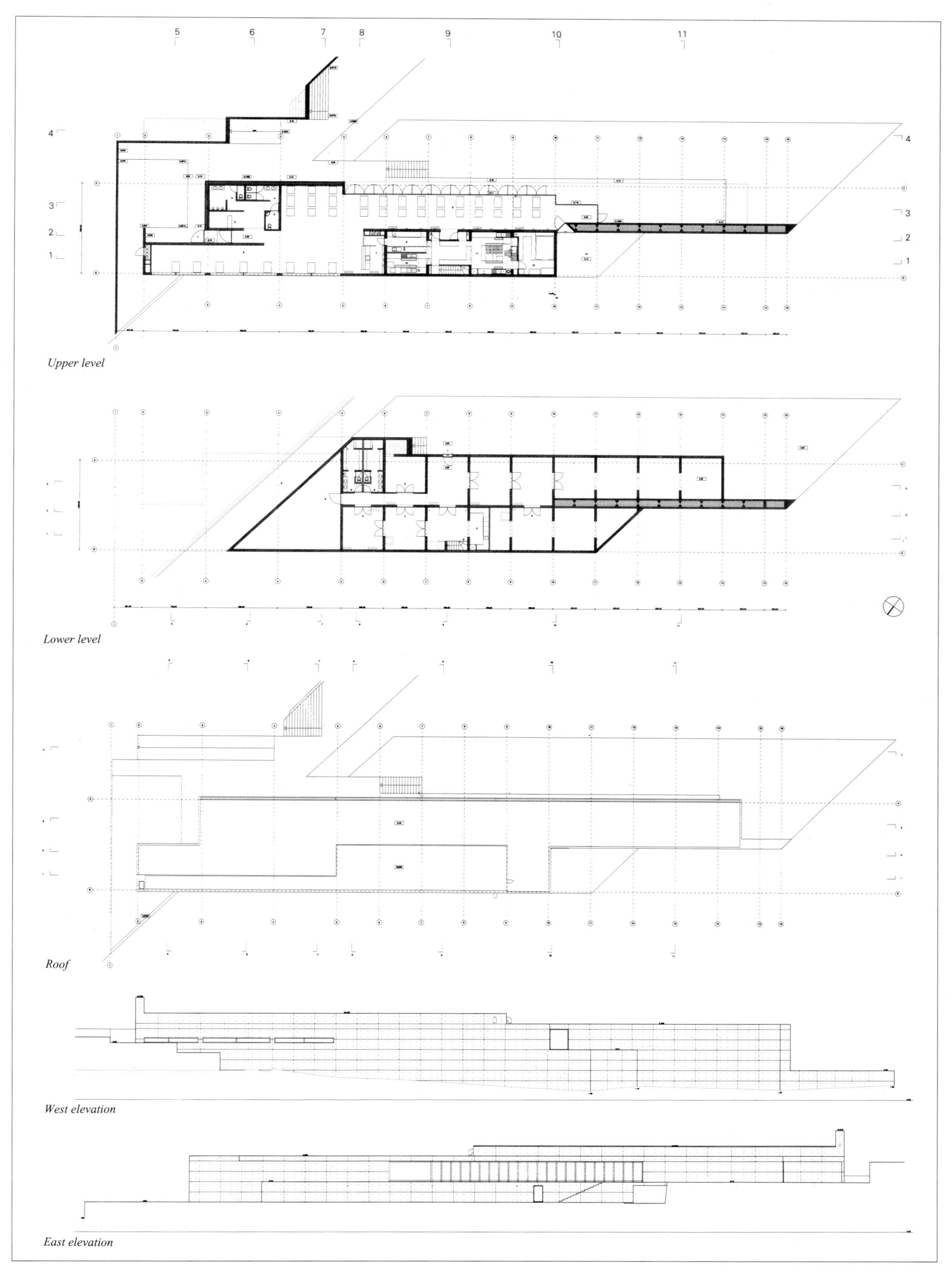

Lower level

Roof

West elevation

East elevation

141

North elevation

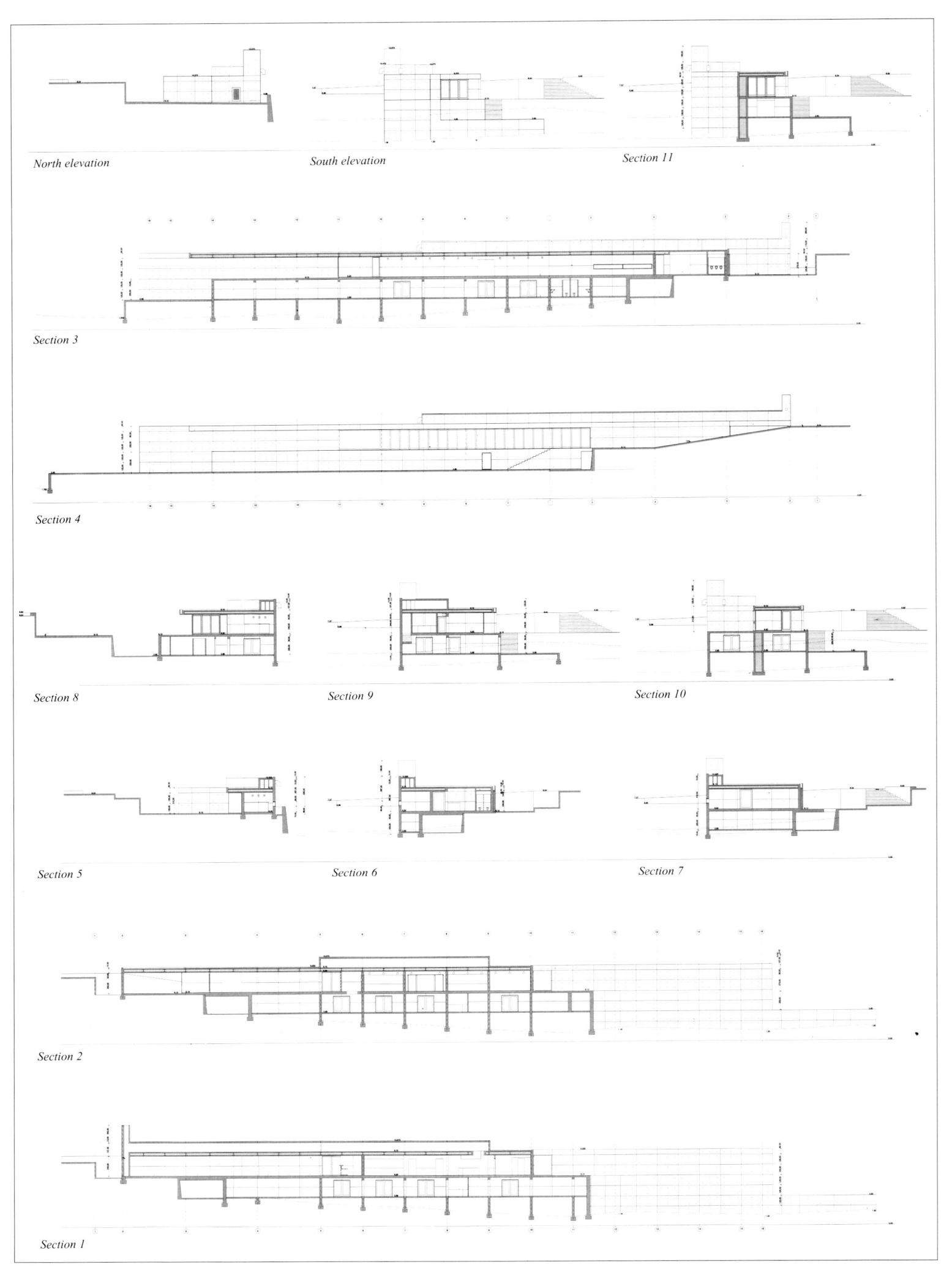

South elevation

Section 11

Section 3

Section 4

Section 8

Section 9

Section 10

Section 5

Section 6

Section 7

Section 2

Section 1

DESCRIPTION

The project of the Restaurant is part of an integrated study of all the land of the Municipal Swimming Pool that was started in 1961. The whole area includes two pools that are partially limited by the rocks that are a feature of this part of the Atlantic coast.

The buildings of the dressing and shower rooms, which are reached by a ramp, stand parallel to the sea wall of the Avenida Marginal (Coast Road) in such a way that they do not impede the view.

The solarium is split up among the rocks, the several parts being of different sizes and suitable for different uses. These natural platforms, supported by small constructions such as stairways, ramps and stretches of wall are adjusted to the lie of the land and establish a natural relationship with the sands to the north and south of the cliffs.

A wall built at 45 degrees to the Marginal is the northern limit of the area and a terrace with a small bar.

This first phase was completed in 1966. The restaurant, the project for which has just been elaborated, stands on another group of rocks at a 45-degrees angle to the Marginal. Like the dressing rooms, it is only a little higher than the marginal, its height being sufficient to give it two floors.

The lower floor leads on to a terrace that can be reached from the beach. It is occupied by storerooms and pantry and is linked to the kitchen by a lift. The upper floor contains the restaurant and public and catering services. As in the first phase, the materials used are almost exclusively reinforced concrete (floors, walls and ceilings) and wood.

The roof, also in reinforced concrete, is protected by a permanent sheet from water. The volume of the restaurant affords protection from the winds to the beach to the north of the swimming pools.

<解説>
このレストラン計画は、1961年に始められた、市営スイミングプールの敷地全体に対する統合的なスタディの一部である。ここには、大西洋岸のこの地域特有の岩によって部分的に囲まれた2つのスイミングプールがある。

スロープを経由して行く、更衣室とシャワー室のある建物はマージナル通り（海岸道路）の海側の壁に平行に、眺めを遮らない位置に建っている。

日を浴びるテラスが岩の間を分けて広がり、大きさの違うそれぞれが、異なった用途に対応する。階段、スロープ、壁の広がりなどの小規模な構造物で支持された、これらの自然のプラットフォームは地勢に適合され、北側の砂浜、南側の崖との関係をつくりだす。

マージナル通りに対し45度の角度で立つ壁は、このエリアと小さなバーのあるテラスの、北側の境界である。

第1期の工事は1966年に終了した。まさに練り上げられ続けてきたレストランは、マージナル通りに対して45度の角度で広がる別の岩の群の上に建つ。更衣室のように、レストランは通りより少し高いだけで、建物の高さは2層分をとるに充分である。

低い方の階は浜辺から上がって行けるテラスへ通じている。そこには貯蔵室と食器室があり、リフトで厨房とつながっている。上階には、レストラン、パブリック、ケータリング・サービスがある。第1期同様、使用材料は、ほぼ全面的に鉄筋コンクリート（床、壁、天井）で、それに木材が使われている。

屋根もまた鉄筋コンクリートで、耐久性のある防水シートにより水から保護されている。レストランのヴォリュームはスイミングプール北側の浜辺へ吹き付ける風避けとなる。

GA：これは，30年以上前のプロジェクトへの増築ですね。

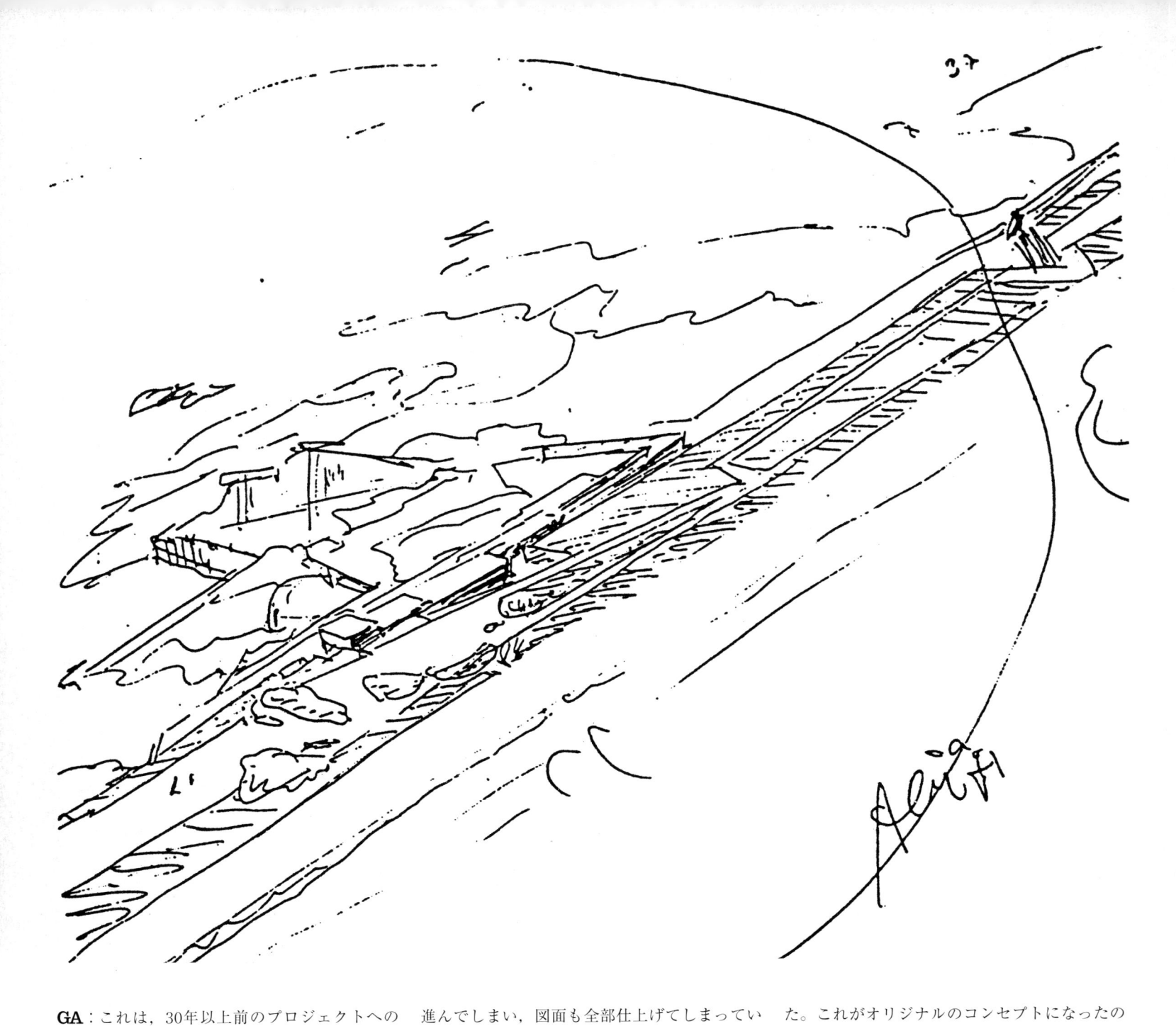

アルヴァロ・シザ：実際には，あのプールのもともとのデザインにはレストランも含まれていたのです。

GA：最初の段階でですか。

シザ：ええ，1962年に最初のドローイングをつくりましたが，それは建てられませんでした。次に，2年前に，30年以上たって，その実施図面を進めるように依頼してきたのです。デザインはそれほど変えていません。

GA：そのデザインから30年を経て，プロジェクトが実現することになって，どのような気持ちですか。

シザ：良い気持ちですね。唯一の問題は，いまだに工事がはじまっていないことです。彼らは目下，レストランを引き受けるプロモーターを探しているのです。というわけで，今，私は気分爽快というわけにはいかない。私の方は先に進んでしまい，図面も全部仕上げてしまっているのに，まだどこへも進めない。待っているのです。

他の建築家のプロジェクトを実施するために誰かに雇われているようで，妙な感じですね。しかし，このプロジェクトが好きですから，何も気にしていないと言うべきでしょう。はるか昔のシザのために働いているような感じです。

GA：このプロジェクトの歴史について少し教えて下さい。

シザ：スイミングプールのアイディアは，実際にはあるエンジニアから生まれたものです。彼はターヴォラの兄弟で，優秀なエンジニアでした。そのうちに，彼は更衣施設をつくることも頼まれたので，建築家が必要だと述べ，そして私がこのプロジェクトへ参加することになりました。彼の案は長方形のプールでしたが，私は，境界をつくるのに岩を使い，水をためるのに必要な部分にだけ壁をつくることを提案しました。これがオリジナルのコンセプトになったのです。

GA：水は海水そのままですか。

シザ：ここの海水は非常に濃いのです。処理が必要で，その後，パイプで運び入れています。大西洋沿いのカサブランカやモロッコでは自然の海水をそのまま使ったプールがたくさんあります。それについては知りませんでした。岩と結びつけたこのプールをデザインした当座は，これはまったく新しいアイディアだと思っていたのです。後に，モロッコへ行き，そうしたプールをたくさん見つけました。マージナル通りに沿って建築を設計しました。その断面を，通りから海岸に降りて行くレベルの変化を利用してデザインしました。このアイディアは，眺めを遮らないということで，通りを過ぎて行くとき海が見えるのです。次にスロープを降りて行き，更衣室を過ぎる。それから，一瞬，眺めを遮る壁にぶつかり，また別のエリアに出ると海

Swimming pool　スイミングプール

が再び見える。次に，子供用プールにかかるブリッジを横切ることになります。

ごらんのように，全体構成は別な要素を必要としていました。そして，私は皆のためのレストランが必要だと感じたのです。そして，ここには私が気に入っている岩の塊がありましたから，私はその上にレストランを設計したのです。岩は，ここでは時々，強く吹く風から守ってくれる助けとなるでしょう。この地域には自然の水路も含まれていますから，暖かいときには，海にも入れます。プールの水温は，海水より常に少し暖かいのです。貯められているわけですから。レストランの建物は，この密度の高いリニアーな性格をもつ構成を締めくくるものでした。古い建物は水に抵抗するために強くなければなりませんでした。冬の間は水位がかなり高くあがるからです。それはコンクリートで，若干ステンレス・スティールも使い，屋根は木造です。レストランの敷地はそこよりずっと晒された場所です。岩によって守られている。ここでの新しい問題は，たまたま1.5キロの長さにわたるこの非常に古い壁と新しい建物の間の関係をどうやってつくりだすかでした。それが接することは非常に危険なことでした。そこで何をしたかといえば，接することのない壁を平行につくりました。接する代わりに両者は交差するのです。エントランスをこのレベルに置き，次に，水から守られるように，建物を持ち上げました。既存の壁は遮られることはありません。それは進み続けます。そして建物はその上方に座るのです。

GA：プールの古い部分について，さわる必要はまったくなかったのですか。

シザ：不思議なことに，30年たっても，木はまったく完璧でした。取り壊された19世紀の建物からとってきた木材でした。しかし，コンクリートの一部は傷んでいました。特別なコンクリートを使うべきでした。

GA：そして，同じ材料パレットを使うことにされたのですか。

シザ：基本的には。全部コンクリートです。内部もまたすべてコンクリートです。屋根，床，壁には仕上げ材は使っていません。水圧に耐えさせるため特殊ガラスを使う必要がありました。気持ちの良い日には外に出られるテラスもつくりました。

再び，これは原則的にはリニアーな構成をとっています。フル・サービスのレストランではないのです。とても簡素なものです。

このようなことをした，最初の建物です。しかし外観はとてもリッチです。海と眺望の存在感がとても強いですから，仕上げの材料はほとんど問題ではない。それは単純であるべきなのです。

Contemporary Art Museum of Oporto
ポルト現代美術館

Oporto, Portugal

Client: Serralves Foundation   Design period: 1991–99   Construction period: 1996–99   Architects: Álvaro Siza Arquitecto, Lda—Clemente Menéres Semide, principal-in-charge   Project team: [1st project] Tiago Faria; [2nd project] Christian Gaenshirt, Sofia Coelho; [3rd project] Edison Okumura, Abílio Mouráo, Avelino Silva, Joáo Sabugueiro, Cristina Ferreirinha, Taichi Tomuro   Structural engineer: João Maria Sobreira   Mechanical engineers: Alfredo Costa Pereira, air conditioning; Raul Serafim, Barros da Silva, Alexandre Martins, electricity and security   Landscape architect: João Gomes da Silva   Acoustics: Daniel Commins   General contractors: Edifer (foundation, structure and finishes)   Structural system: reinforced concrete structure

GA: Oporto is your city. How were you chosen for this project?

Álvaro Siza: In effect the choice came from the government, the minister of culture. It's a national museum, but it belongs to a foundation which includes state, city and private members. The government decided to buy this wonderful site which was the house of an industrial Mogul built in the 1940s. The house is a project of a French architect. It is a Déco house and was executed by the then most important architect in Oporto, Marques da Silva. He had a diploma from Paris and was director of the school of architecture. He was a Rome Prize recipient and was the most important architect in Oporto. He built things such as the main theater, the central station, several houses, public buildings, and churches. He was an eclectic architect, so this Déco project was one of his few modern projects. The garden was designed by a famous French landscape architect, someone who also worked a lot in California, Spain and so on. The client was a rich cultivated man. All of the furniture was by the best French artists of the time. Today several different collectors own this collection. We tried to get them together and put them back into the house which was an interesting process.

We began the project based on a study done by a Danish museum director. The original program was about 5,000 square meters. But then there was a long period where the minister of culture kept changing their minds about whether they supported the project or not and also the specifics of the program. In the end I think I did four projects. Only recently was the program fixed and the decision to build finalized.

GA: When did the project originally begin?

Siza: A long time ago. I forget exactly.

GA: How do you keep your focus over such a long period? You mentioned that the program has changed over time. Do you keep basic strategies and elements? Or do you start over every time?

Siza: It isn't easy. If you look at the plan, you see the house and the big formal garden on the axis of the house. Then there is another garden. The main entrance is on the main street. A street connects the rotunda which is parallel to the axis of the house. So in the first program which was smaller. I planned to place the garden on the side of the big axis in the free space, articulated by the house. But people were afraid of putting an old and new building side by side. Meanwhile, there was an evolution in the program and they proposed something much bigger, so the first concept wouldn't work anyway because of the increased size requirements of the new

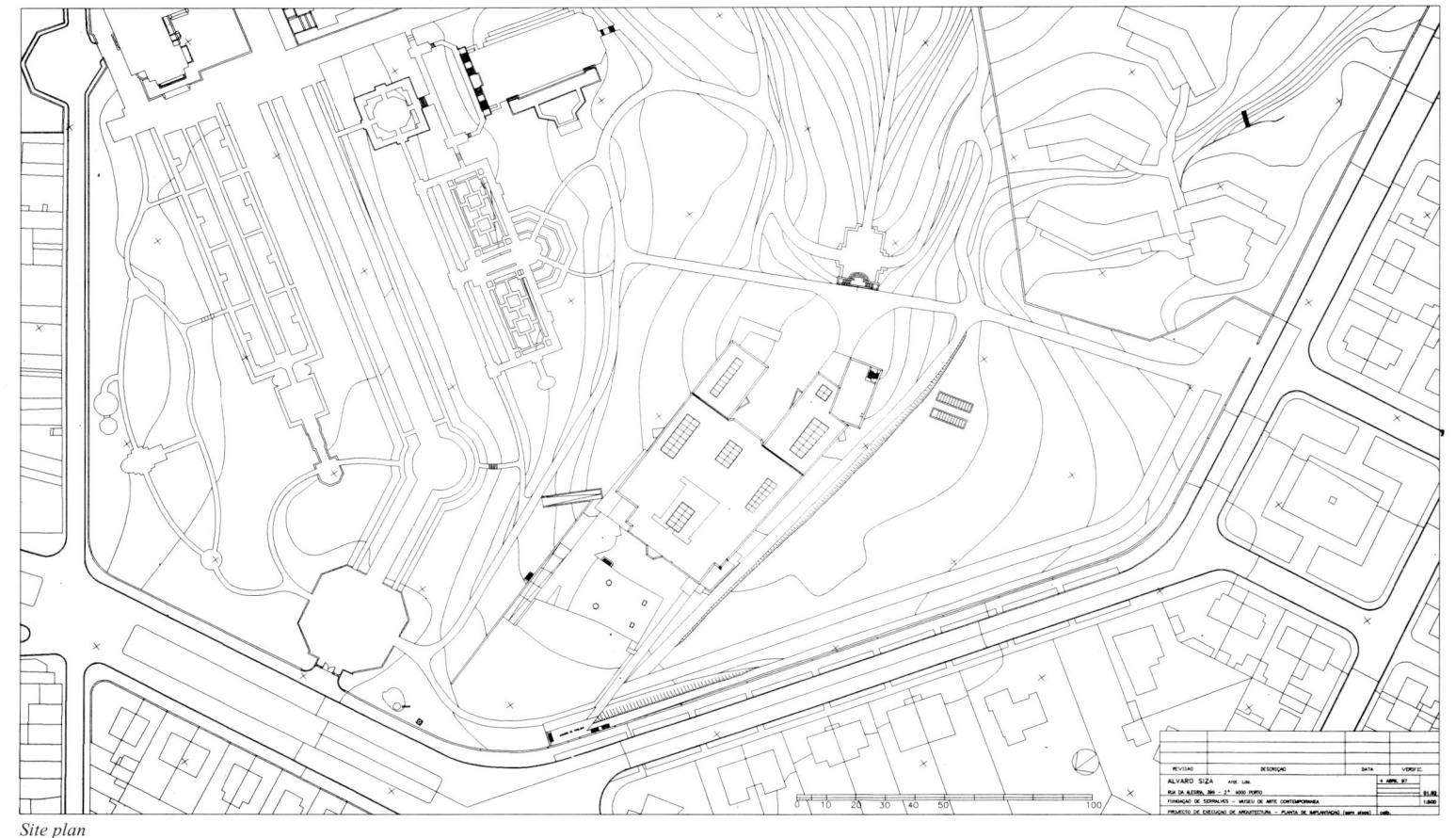

Site plan

structure.

Then I proposed to put the building in the only area that could in effect support this larger program. This also facilitated access for services since there is a square here that would allow larger vehicles to access the structure. I proposed to enter by the main entrance. But people were afraid of security problems and they didn't want to rely on electronic control. In the end I had to accept entry from the side, but I developed the project so that the entry would work from either in the hopes that in the future they would understand that the better access was from the main entry. So the entry sequence is flexible.

The reason I prefer this is that at the rotunda you can feel the two buildings. You cannot see the other building from either building because there are trees planted in between. So you have to rely on memory. If you enter from the main entry, the relationship is very clear even though you never see the two together.

The park consists of the house, the formal garden, natural greenery, a romantic lake, and then a farm. We wanted to maintain the whole and include a new area for the museum.

The museum has only two floors with very high spaces for exhibitions. We have areas for a small bookshop and a restaurant, next to a central two-level atrium near the entry. In a way, this is a reference to the existing house which also has an atrium. I wanted to incorporate a similar kind of element. Then you have another floor underground. The final room connects with the patio which is also a sculpture garden. We have parking underneath for the people who work here, but not for the public. You have a line of trees that we maintained. But we had to reinforce the vegetation in some parts. Largely the volume of the museum can't be seen in it's entirety, which is important because we didn't want the structure to be a dominant element.

GA: So there wasn't an attempt to create a grand facade.

Siza: Exactly. Just the opposite. I wanted to make a building in the park. That is how I saw the project. In a way that is the same thing that happens with the old house. In either case, the buildings are large enough to have extremely rich interior experiences, and so it did not have to project so strongly to the exterior. There are small houses in this area also, so a grand facade would have had too much of an impact. On this point the foundation and I agreed. We wanted to maintain the experience of the park.

GA: So this is the third museum we've talked about. How would you relate this one to the others?

Siza: In this museum, there was more emphasis put on the life of the building and not just on the exhibitions. For instance the auditorium is going to play a very important role in the town. At one point, there was talk of a bigger auditorium, one large enough for conferences of 700 people. It might be a reflection of a tendency to look for ways to finance a project. But eventually they gave up the idea, which I think is good, because it would have been too much for the park to handle in terms of scale. The site is a very attractive and quiet park. So the project has to be more directly related to it's interaction with the day by day life of the town. Of course the exhibits will be important as well. The museum is already part of a circuit of international exhibitions together with other museums. The permanent collection is not very good however, although they've begun a modest acquisitions program. But it is important that the life of the museum extend beyond the exhibits. For instance, the restaurant is more open to the public.

GA: Is there anything in particular you were trying to achieve with the auditorium or exhibition spaces?

Siza: Not really. There are certain elements very much like Compostela, and

GA：ポルトはシザさんの地元ですね。このプロジェクトの設計者にはどのようなことから選ばれたのですか。

アルヴァロ・シザ：実際には，私を選んだのは政府，文化省でした。国立の美術館なのですが，国，州，個人メンバーで構成された財団が所有しています。1940年代に建てられ，ムガル人の産業家が所有していた，この素晴らしい住宅と敷地を政府が購入することに決めました。家はフランス人建築家の設計です。アールデコの邸宅で，当時，ポルトで最も有名だった建築家，マルケス・ダ・シルヴァが実施しました。彼はパリで学位をとり，ポルト大学建築学部の学部長でした。ローマ賞受賞者で，ポルトの最も重要な建築家でした。彼は，中心的な劇場や，中央駅，いくつかの住宅，公共建築，教会などを設計しています。また，折衷主義の建築家でしたから，このアールデコのプロジェクトは，彼の数少ない近代的な作品の一つです。庭園はフランス人のランドスケープ・アーキテクトが設計したもので，彼はカリフォルニア，スペインなどでも多くの仕事をしています。クライアントは金持ちで，教養のある人物でした。家具はすべて，当時の最も優れたフランス人芸術家がデザインしています。このコレクションは現在何人かのコレクターの手にあります。それらを一つに集め，元の場所に戻すことにしましたが，これは楽しいプロセスでした。

私たちはデンマーク人の美術館長によって行われたスタディに基づいてこのプロジェクトを始めました。オリジナルのプログラムは約5,000平方メートルのものでした。しかし，その後，文化省はこのプロジェクトを支援すべきか否か，また，個別的なプログラムについて，考えを変え続けるという長い過程が来ました。最終的に私は4つの案をつくったと思います。プログラムが固まり，建てることに決まったのはごく最近のことです。

GA：そもそもプロジェクトが最初に始まったのはいつのことですか。

シザ：ずいぶん前のことです。正確には忘れました。

GA：このように長い期間，どのようにしてご自分を集中させてこられたのでしょうか。プログラムは変更を重ねたと言われましたが，基本的なストラテジーやエレメントを維持し続けたのですか。あるいは，毎回，はじめからスタートされたのですか。

シザ：簡単ではありませんでした。プランを見ると，住宅と住宅の軸線上に広いフォーマルな庭園があるのが解ります。それから別な庭があります。正面のエントランスは主要道路に面しています。1本の道路が住宅の軸線に平行するロトンダを結んでいる。つまり，もっと小さかった最初のプログラムでは，住宅に縁取られたフリー・スペースのなか，主要軸線の片側に面して庭園を配置する計画でした。しかし，皆は，古い建物と新しい建物を並べて配置することが心配でした。まもなく，プログラムが進展して，彼らはさらに拡大された内容を提案してきました。つまり，新たなプログラムの要求によって規模が増大した結果，いずれにせよ，最初のコンセプトは機能しなくなりました。

次に，私はこの拡大されたプログラムを効果的に支持することの出来る唯一のエリアのなかに建物を配置することを提案しました。これによって，大型車が建物へアクセスできる広場がありますから，サービス関係の出入りも容易になります。正面から入れるようにすることを提案したのですが，皆は安全性の問題を憂慮し，電子制御に頼ることも望まなかったのです。結局，私は側面にエントランスを置くことを受け入れました。しかし，将来，彼らが，より良いアクセスは正面からだということを理解してくれるだろうという望みのもとに，エントランスはどちらにとることも出来るようにこのプロジェクトを展開させたのです。ですから，エントランス構成はフレキシブルなのです。

私がこれを好む理由は，ロトンダのところで，2つの建物を感じることが出来るからなのです。どちらの建物からも他方の建物を見ること

Level 3

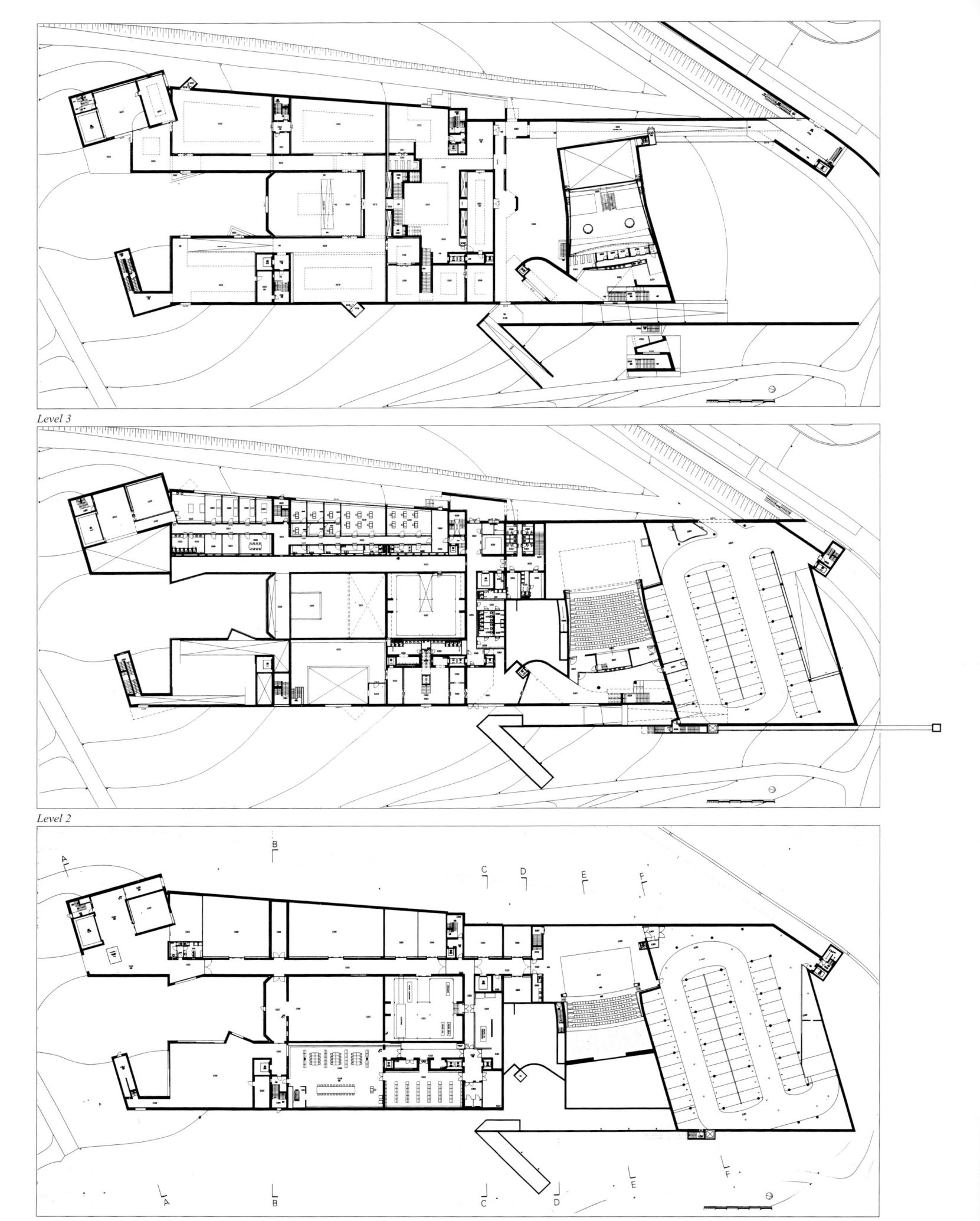

Level 2

Level 1

148

Roof

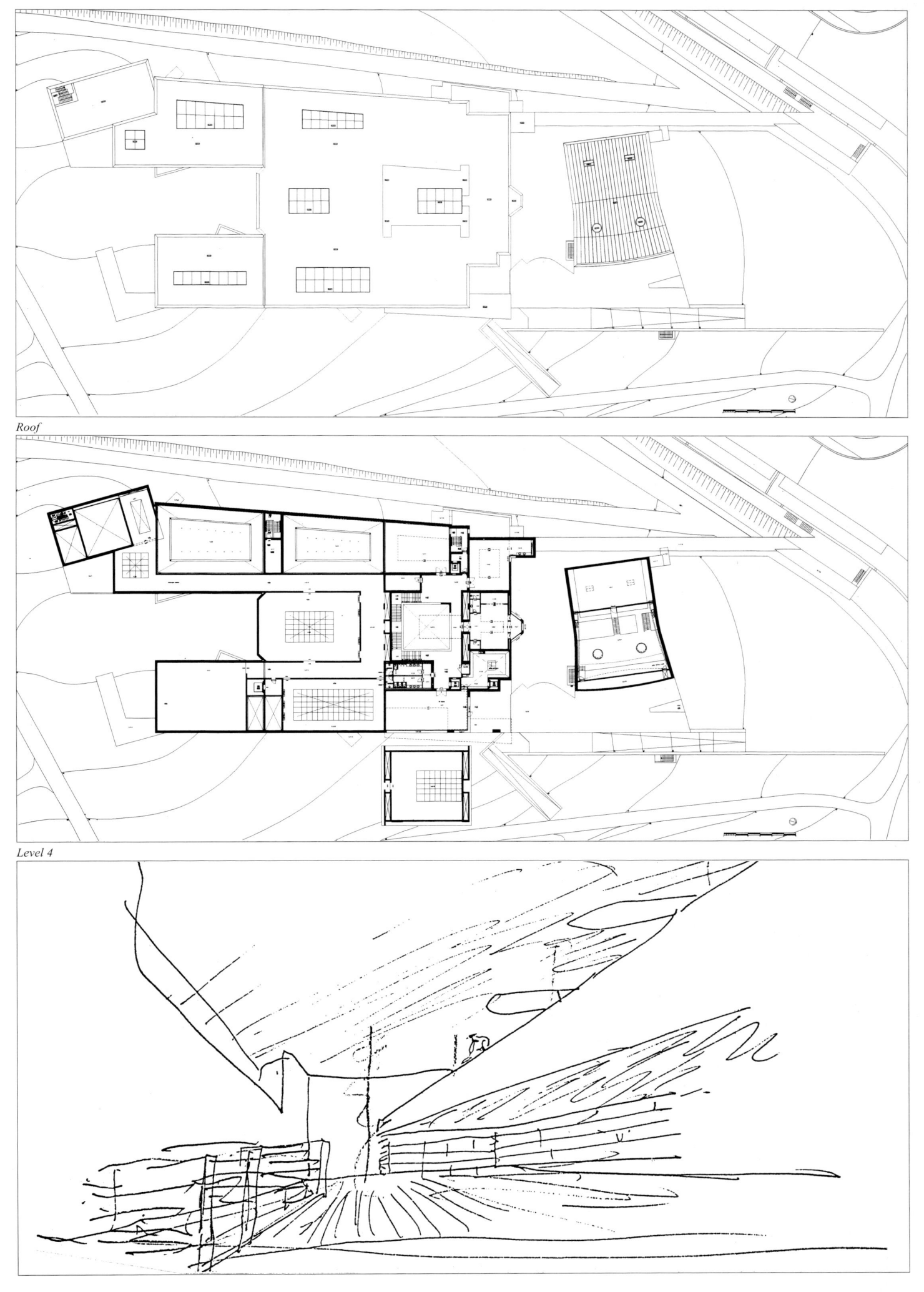

Level 4

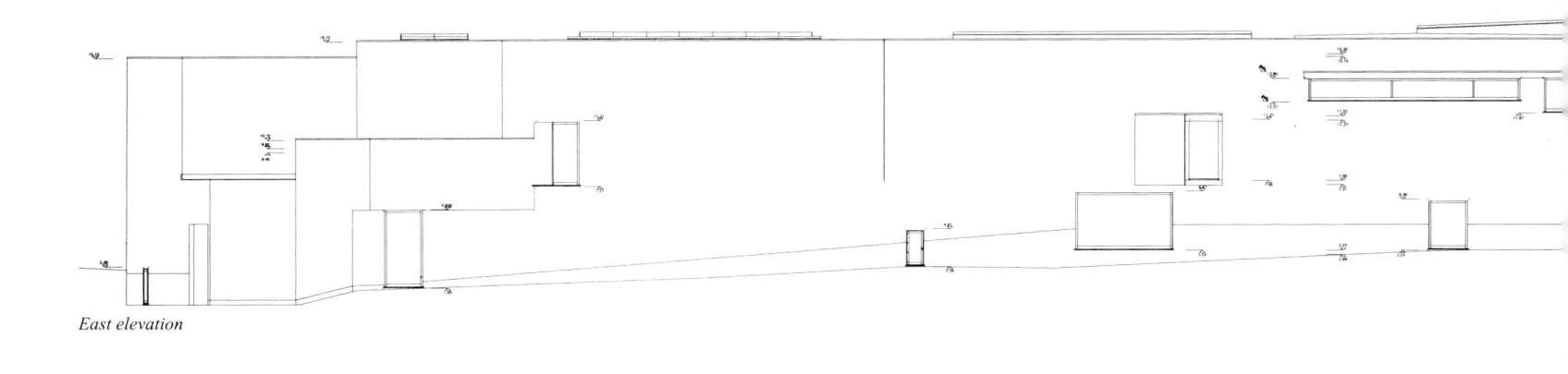

East elevation

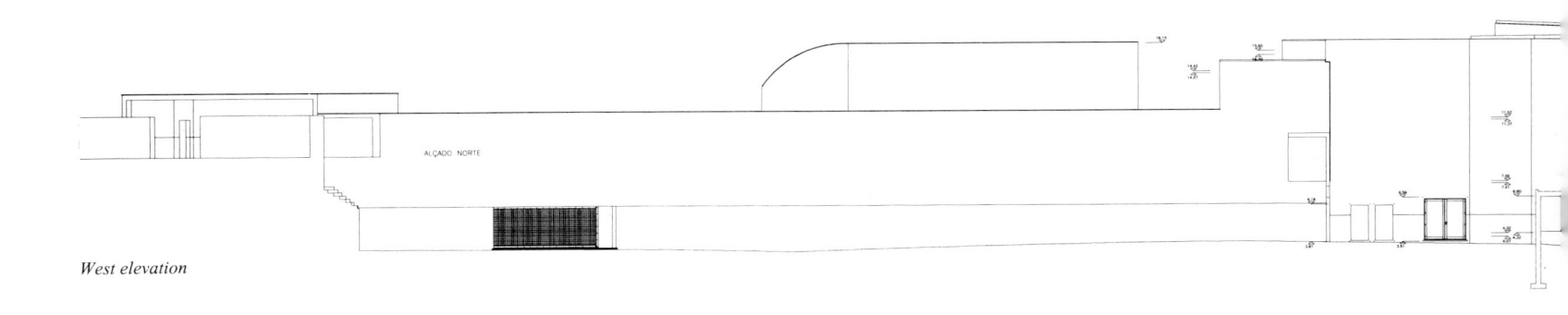

West elevation

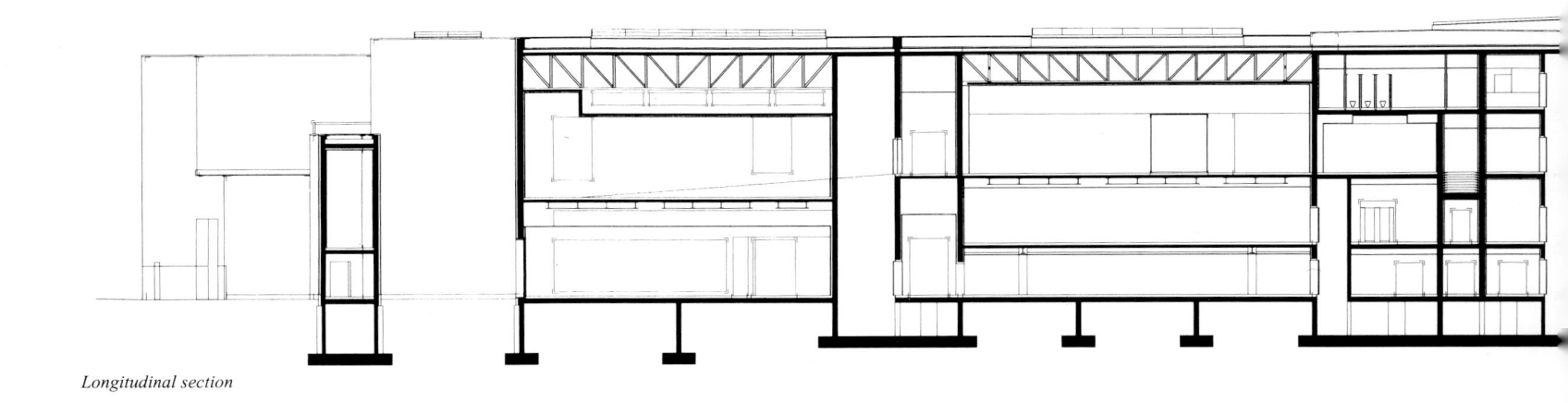

Longitudinal section

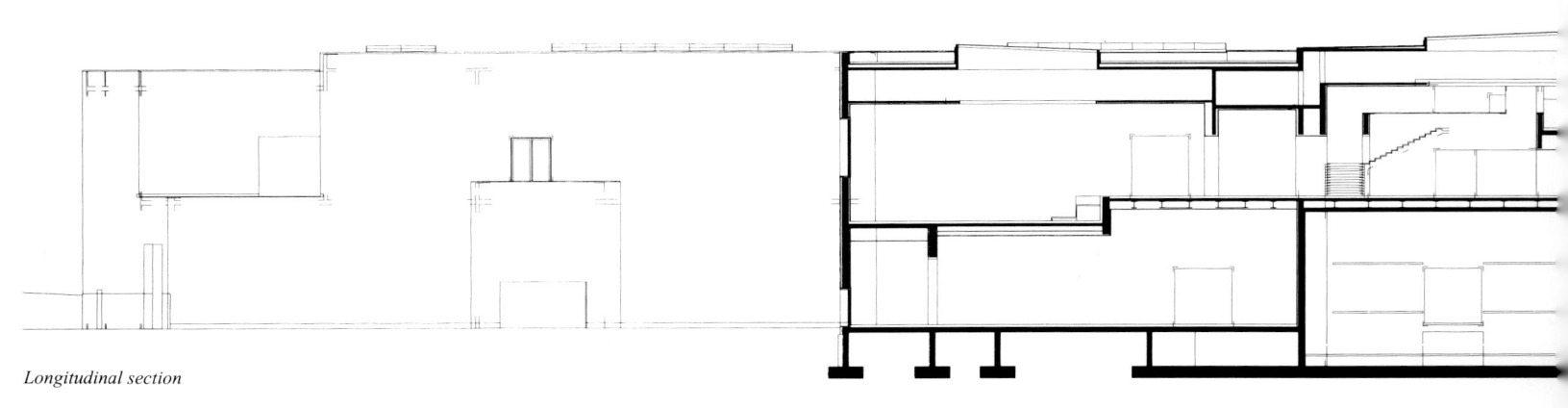

Longitudinal section

151

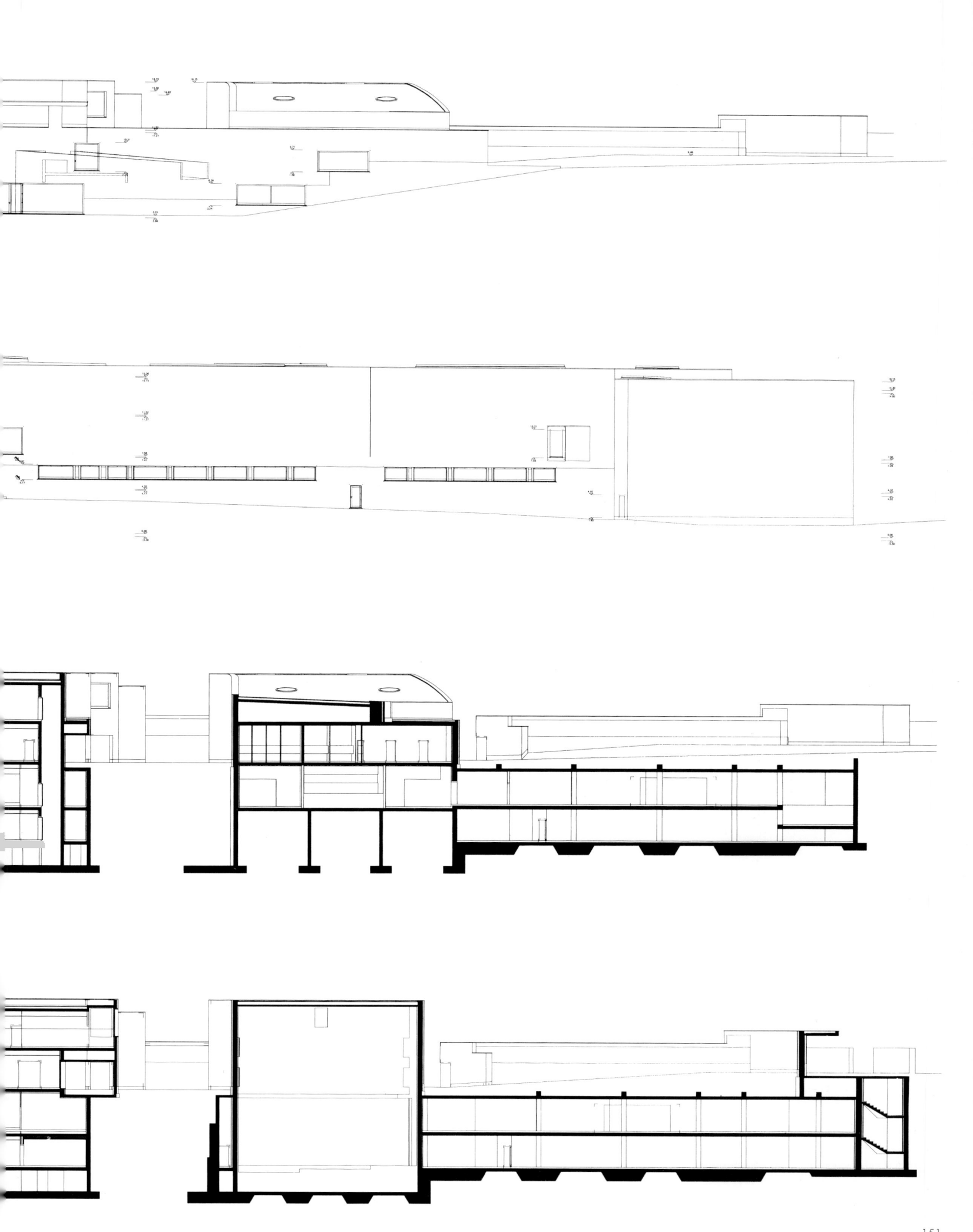

Section A-A

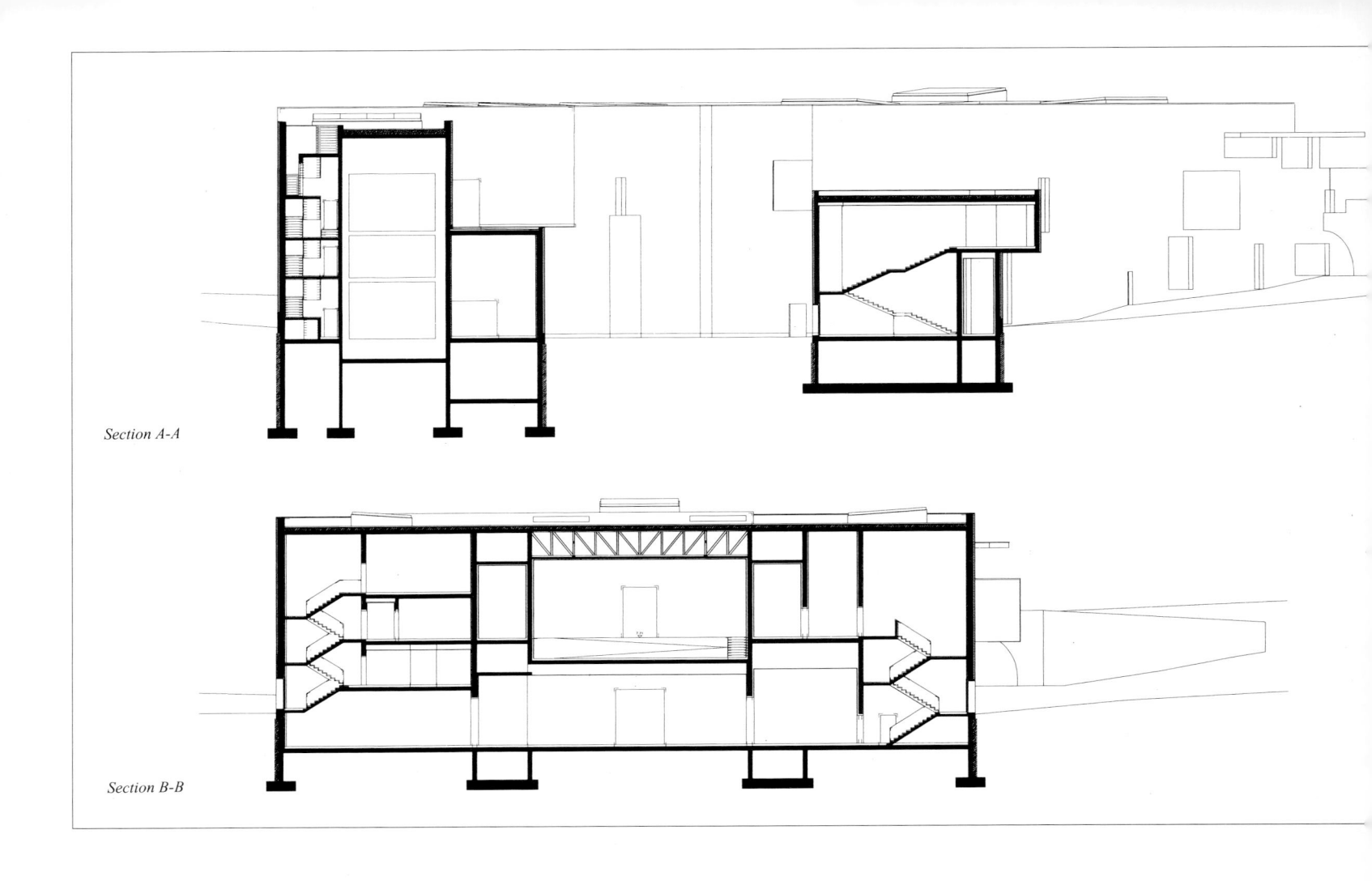

Section B-B

は出来ない。間に木立があるからです。ですから、記憶に頼らざるを得ない。正面から入って来れば、2つの建物を一度に見なかったとしても、その関係は非常に明快です。

この公園は、住宅、フォーマルな庭園、自然の草木、ロマンティックな湖、そして農園で構成されています。美術館は2階までしかなく、展示作品のために非常に天井の高い空間になっています。エントランスの近くにある2層吹き抜けた中央アトリウムの隣に、小さなブックショップとレストランがあります。ある意味でこれは、やはりアトリウムのある既存住宅への言及です。同じような種類のエレメントを取り込みたかったのです。次に、地下階があります。最後に来る部屋は、彫刻庭園でもあるパティオとつながっています。美術館職員のための駐車場が地下にありますが、公共用ではありません。われわれがそのまま残した並木がありますが、いくつかの場所で、植物を植え足す必要がありました。大体が、美術館の全体像を一目で見ることは出来ません。これは重要なことなのです。なぜかといえば、私たちは、建物が支配的な要素になって欲しくなかったからです。

GA：つまり、仰々しいファサードをつくろうという気持ちはなかったのですね。

シザ：その通りです。まさにその反対です。公園のなかにある建物をつくりたいと思いました。このプロジェクトを私はそのようにみていました。ある意味でこれは、古い住宅との間で起こったことと同じです。どちらの場合も、建物は非常に豊かな内部体験を得るに十分な大きさがありましたから、外に対しあまり強調した表現をとる必要はなかったのです。またこの地区には小さな住宅がありますから、大きなファサードはインパクトが強すぎました。

GA：この美術館は、これまで話してきたもののなかで三つ目にあたります。これを他の二つとどのように関係づけられていますか。

シザ：この美術館では、単に展示作品だけではなく、建物を生かすことにより大きな重点を置いています。たとえば、オーディトリアムはこの街において、重要な役割を演じることになるでしょう。ある時点では、もっと大きなものにすること、700人の会合に対応できるものにすることについて話し合いました。計画資金を得る方法を探そうという傾向の反映だったかもしれません。結局、当局はこの考えをあきらめましたが、これは私には幸いでした。スケールの点で操作するには、公園のなかには大きすぎるものでしたから。敷地は非常に魅力的で静かな公園です。ですから、建物は街の日々の生活との交流と、もっとダイレクトに結びつけられるべきものです。もちろん、展示作品も同様に重要になるでしょうが。美術館は既に、他の美術館と組んで、世界を巡回する展覧会の一役を担っています。収蔵品はたいしたものはありませんが、適切な作品取得計画も開始されています。しかし、美術館そのものの生命が展示作品を越えて拡大することが重要なのです。たとえば、レストランは従来より、公共に開放されています。

GA：オーディトリアムや展示スペースについて、何か特にやろうとしたことはありますか。

シザ：特別にはありません。コンポステラの美術館に非常によく似たいくつかのエレメントがあり、他のスペースははるかに伝統的な展示空間です。もちろん、多様な空間がありますし、連続性の感覚もあります。プログラムから切り離された断片をつくりたくはありませんでした。基本的な統一感があります。すべてコンクリート造です。基部は花崗岩で、上部は、ほとんどがスタッコ仕上げ。内部には木、大理石、スタッコを使用しています。

GA：目下、どの段階にあるのですか。

シザ：内部の間仕切りと仕上げにかかっています。今年の末には開館したいということです。私の意見では、全部を思い通りにやるには十分な時間ではないのですが、これは世の常です。すべてを決定するのに何年もかかりながら、今や、すべてを瞬時に進めることを望んでいる。

GA：決定プロセスがそんなに長引くのはなぜ

other spaces which are much more traditional gallery spaces. Of course there is a good variety of spaces and a sense of continuity. I didn't want to detach pieces of the program. There is a basic unity. It is all concrete construction. The base is granite and with the upper portions mostly finished in stucco. Inside we used wood, marble and stucco.

GA: So what stage is it in now?

Siza: They are working on the interior partitions and finishes. They want to open by the end of the year. In my opinion this isn't enough time to do everything right, but that is human nature. It took years to make all of the decisions and now they want everything in a moment.

GA: Why do you think the decision making process is so drawn out?

Siza: Today there is this fear of architecture. This extends to all kinds of building. This is not without reasons, but people are very afraid. A lot has been destroyed for the sake of terrible buildings so naturally people have become suspicious of building. Today, when you have the opportunity to build a significant building, you will always find opposition because of the many bad examples that have come before.

GA: Henri Gaudin once got a commission to renovate a Rodin Museum in Paris, but it was terminated because the neighbors were afraid that the project would destroy their gardens.

Siza: It is crazy. Because at a certain point the desire to preserve and defend becomes a huge obstacle for creation. With this project we had a lot of problems with commissions that argued that the museum would have a negative impact on the park. A lot of the arguments were made by landscape architects and ecologists. It's very funny when you look at a city and see the terrible things that have been built and nobody says anything about this.

だと思われますか。

シザ：今，建築に対する不信感が広がっているのです。これは，あらゆる種類の建物に及んでいます。理由は無いのですが，人々はとても怖がっています。ひどい建物であるために，多くが取り壊されてきましたから，建てることに懐疑的になるのは自然なことです。今日，重要な建物を設計する機会を得ると，過去に生まれたたくさんの悪例があるゆえに，常に，反対に合うことになります。

GA：アンリ・ゴーダンはかつてパリのロダン美術館の改装を依頼されたのですが，中止されました。周囲の住民が，このプロジェクトは彼らの庭を破壊するだろうと恐れたからです。

シザ：馬鹿げたことです。ある点で，保存や防衛への願望は，創造に対する巨大な障害となりますから。このプロジェクトでも，美術館が公園に悪い影響を及ぼすだろうと主張する委員会との間に多くの問題がありました。主張の多くはランドスケープ・アーキテクトとエコロジストからのものでした。街をよく見ると，ひどい建物がたくさん建っているのに，誰もこれについては何も言わないのは，おかしなことです。

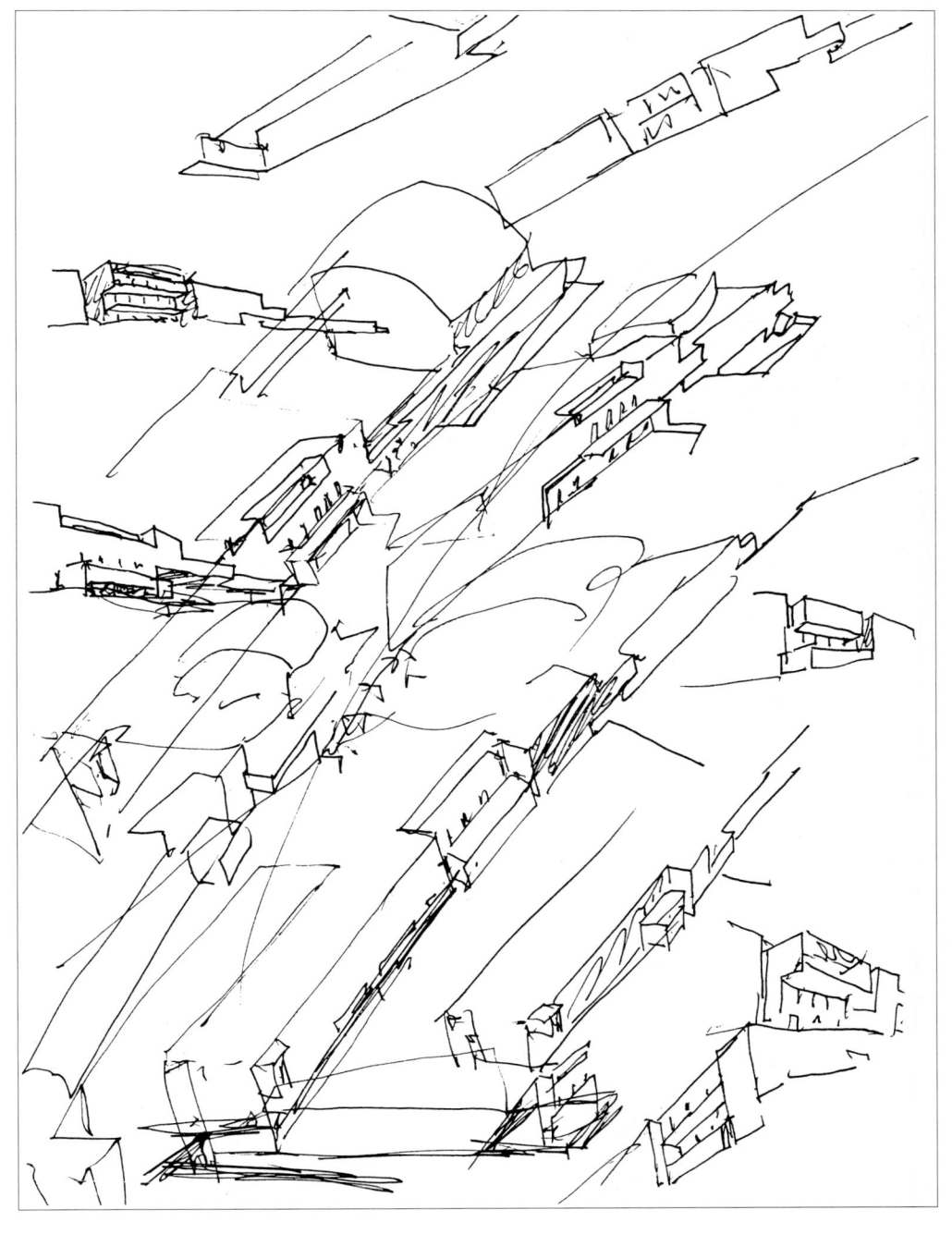

Section E-E

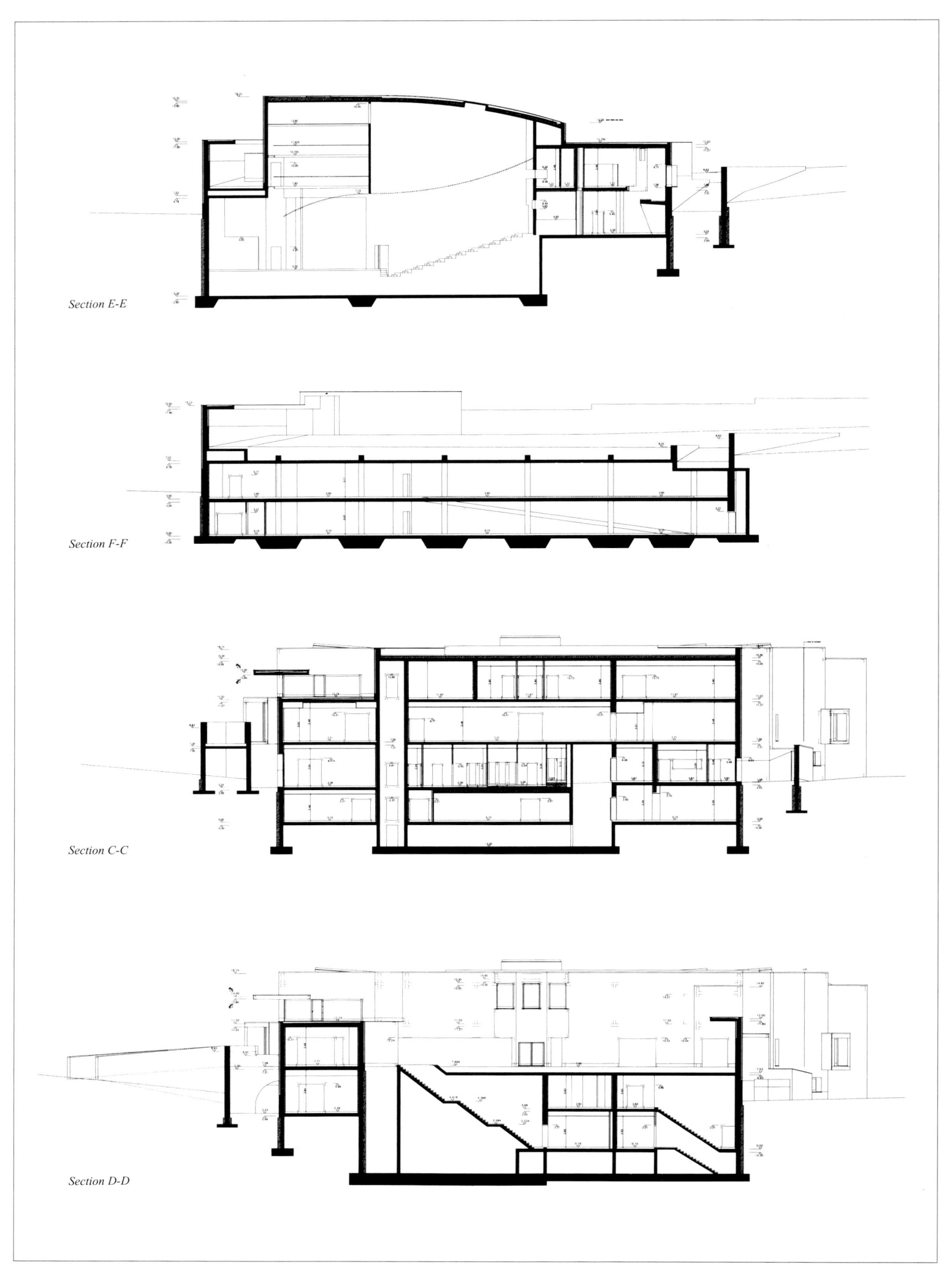

Section F-F

Section C-C

Section D-D

155

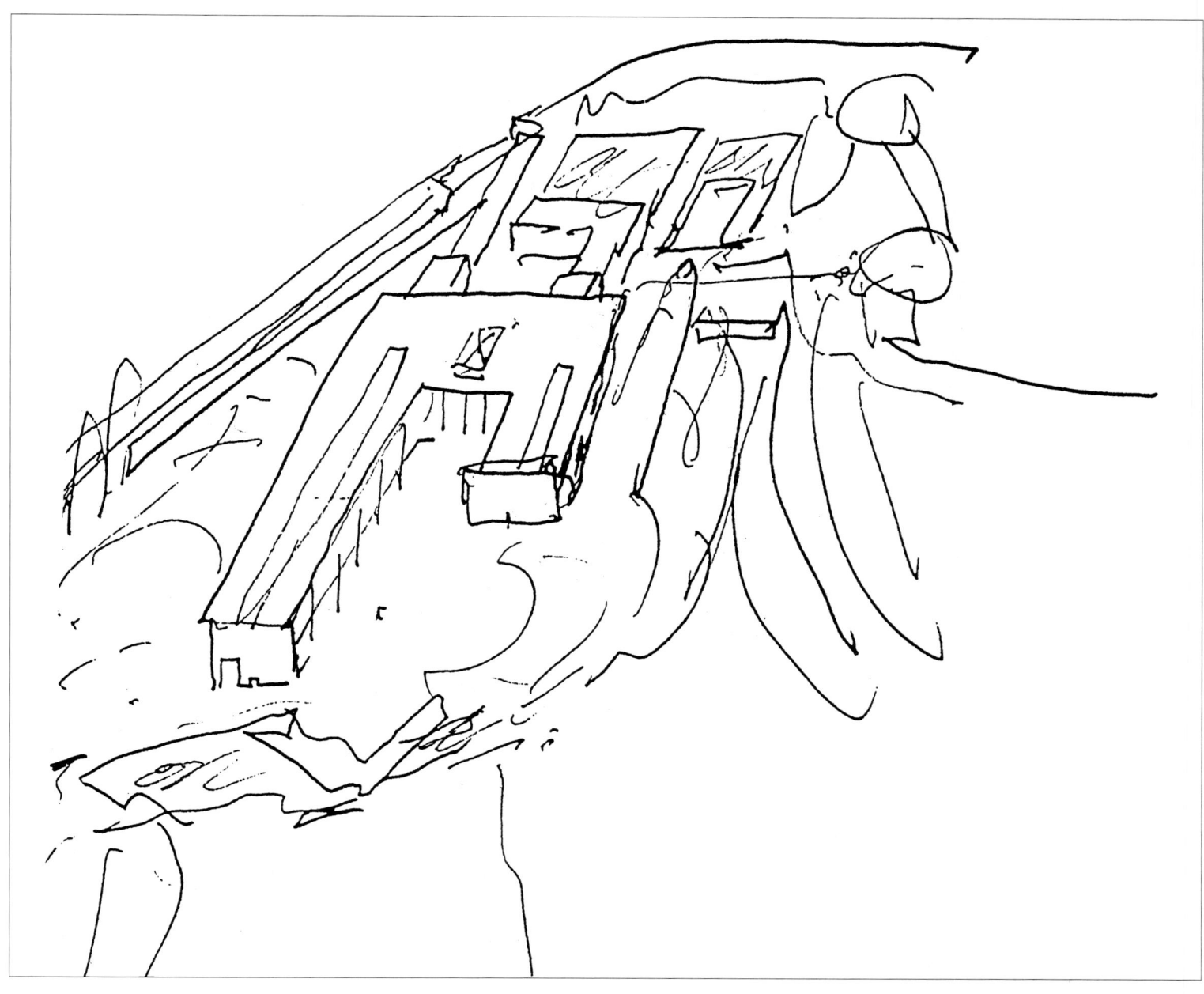

Faculty of the Media Science, Santiago University

サンティアゴ大学情報科学学部

Santiago de Compostela, Spain

Client: Santiago University Design period: 1993–96 Construction: 1997 Architects: Álvaro Siza Arquitecto, Lda—Carlos Seoane, Marco Rampulla, principals-in-charge Project team: Cristina Ferreirinha, Edison Okumura, Luís-Diaz Mauriño, Gonzalo Benavides Structural engineers: G.O.P.—Jorge Silva, João Maria Sobreira Mechanical engineers: Costa Pereira, Raul Serafim General contractor: Constructora San José Structural system: reinforced concrete structure

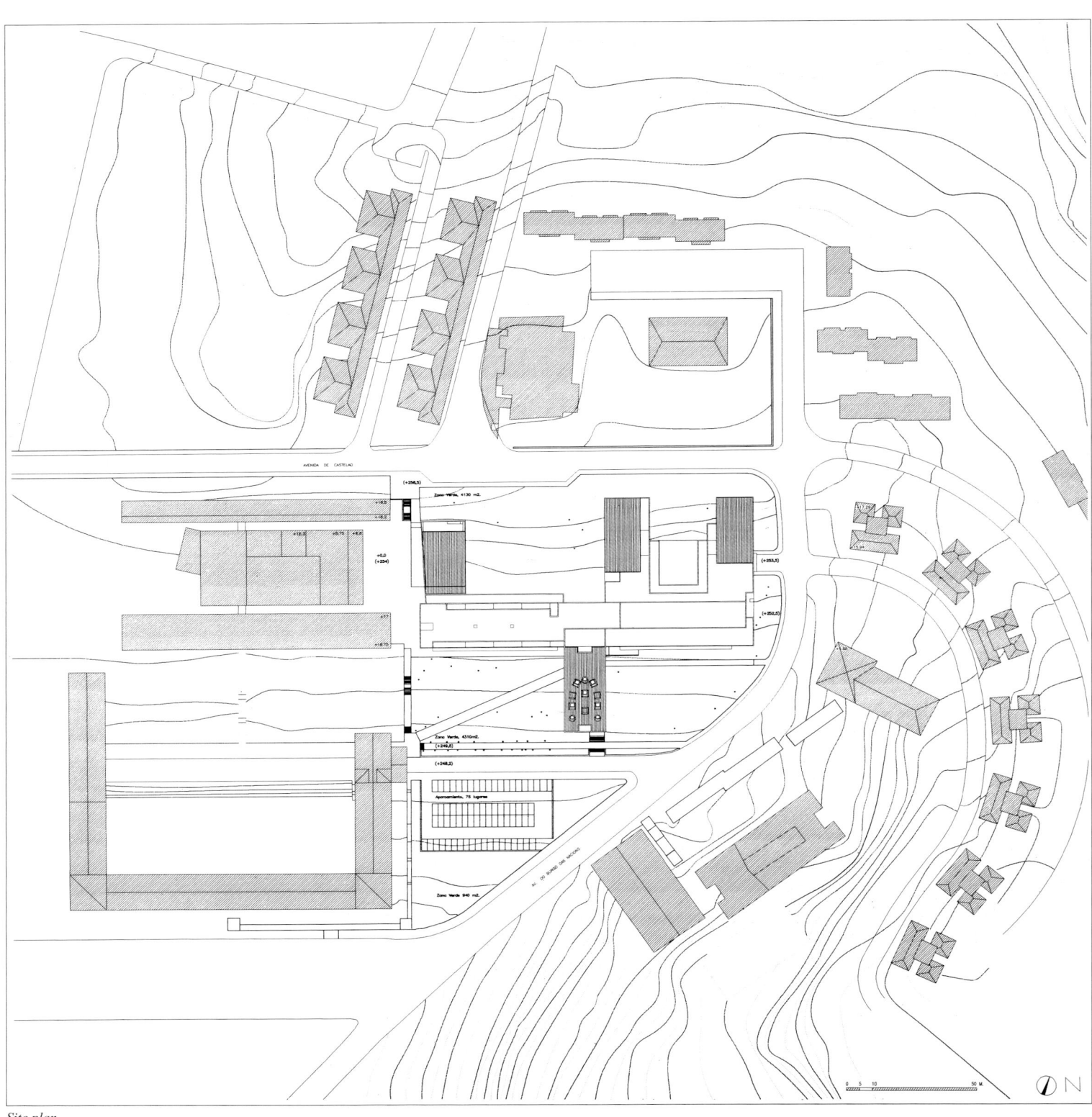

Site plan

Level +1.4m

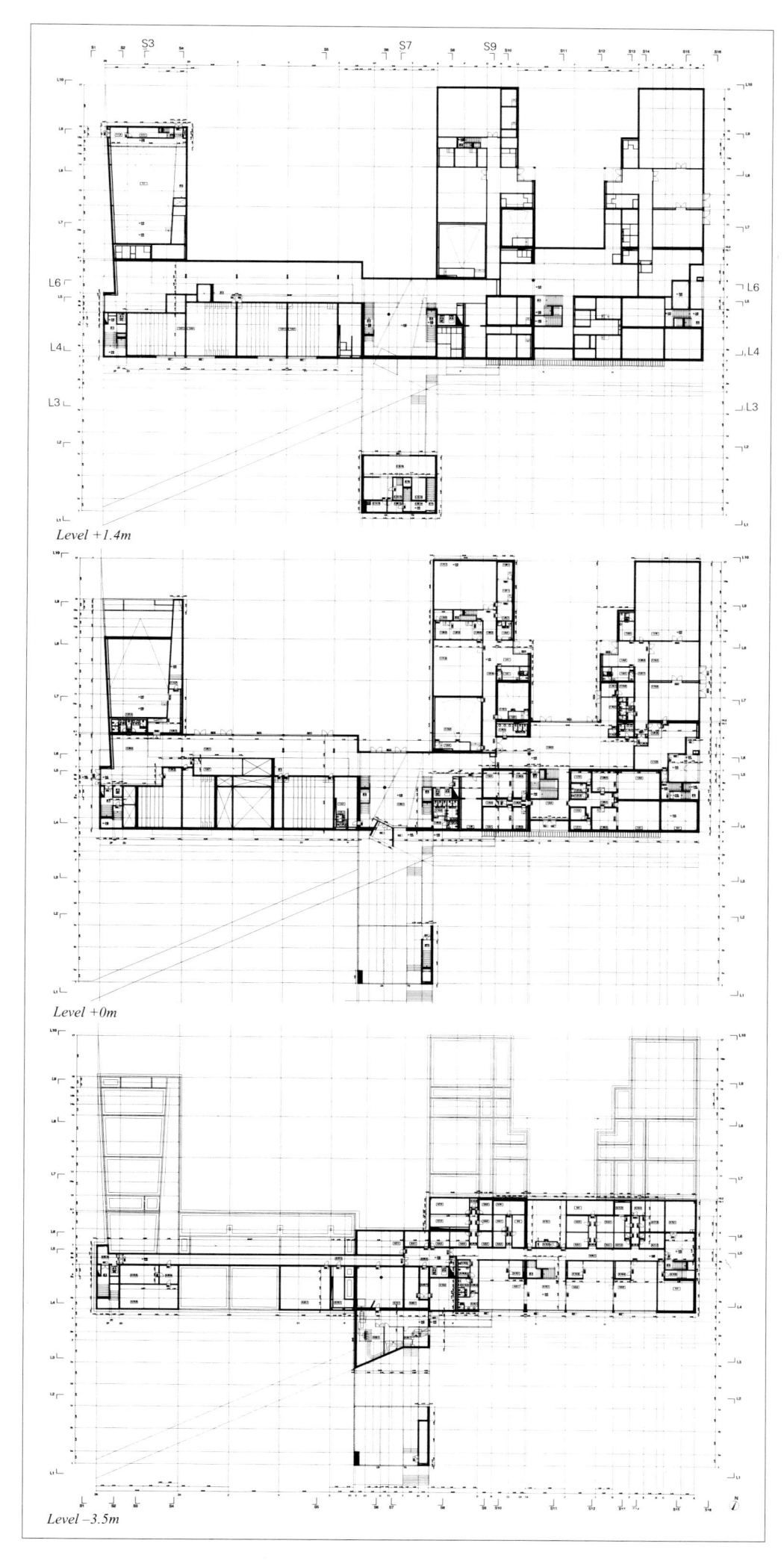

Level +0m

Level −3.5m

GA: How did this project begin?

Álvaro Siza: The start was interesting because Santiago University created a plan for a campus in a free space, a park. It was a megastructure, a single building, like the University of Berlin, with everything connected. But then they built dorms for students, and the idea of making one building was gone, which I think this was a good thing. Then they contacted me about the design of a building for the faculty of journalism. I respected the geometry of the plan, but I designed a detached building. I made part of the building in the same orientation as the existing one, and then I opened patios to the street so the garden extended inside and light could come in. There is a detached volume on two pillars and you actually pass underneath this structure to enter the building.

A library is located in the middle and acts as a conceptual center. Then you have a big gallery that spins you off to the different parts. There are studios for film and photography, and also an auditorium. Of course there are also classrooms on different floors. Floors are connected by ramps and the gallery is open to the gardens.

GA: You consciously used a similar shape here for the auditorium and the library. What's the logic behind that?

Siza: Perhaps the shape of the auditorium

GA：このプロジェクトはどのような具合に始まったのですか。

アルヴァロ・シザ：スタートは面白いものでした。サンティアゴ大学はキャンパスをフリー・スペース，つまり公園のなかに計画したのです。それはメガストラクチャー，単体の建物で，ベルリンの自由大学のようにすべてがつながっていました。しかし，次に彼らは学生の寄宿舎を建て，一つの建物というアイディアは消え去りました。それは良い考えだったと思うのですが。次に，彼らは情報科学の学部建物の設計について私に接触してきたのです。もとの計画のジオメトリーは尊重しましたが，私は分離した建物を設計しました。建物の一部を既存建物の方位に合わせましたが，次に，道に対してパティオを開きました。これによって庭が内部を広げ，光は屋内に入ってくるでしょう。2本の柱の上に切り離されたヴォリュームが乗っていて，実際に，この構造物の下を通り抜けて建物に入るのです。

図書館が真ん中に位置し，コンセプト上の中心として働きます。次に広いギャラリーがあり，ここから様々な方向へ振り分けられます。映画と写真のスタジオがあり，オーディトリアムもあります。もちろん各階に教室がある。各階はスロープでつながり，ギャラリーは庭に面して開いている。

is more understandable in terms of its use. The library is more difficult to explain. But when you have two floors connected by a void, my feeling is that the ceiling upstairs should not be flat. It should be more evocative. In this case, the shape also comes from a sense of composition: a kind of relationship from one side to the other. The shapes of the volumes also help to indicate the main collective spaces within the building. The three places where people are brought together to interact are the library, the auditorium, and the gallery. So I felt that it was important to articulate the relationship between these spaces. There are both interior and exterior reasons, and perhaps some things that I cannot explain. The finishes are the same with my recent museum projects. There is granite at the base and stucco above. It is very important that the base be solid, not just in terms of how the building meets the ground, but also for the purposes of maintenance. Here in Portugal, building maintenance is not as good as it should be and so I need to use a strong materials.

GA：ここではオーディトリアムと図書館に同じ形を意識的に使っていますね。この背後にあるロジックはどんなものなのですか。

シザ：たぶん，オーディトリアムの形はその用途が解りやすいということからきています。図書館の方はもっと説明が難しい。しかし，ヴォイドでつながれた2つの階があるとき，私の感じたのは，上の階の天井はフラットであるべきではないということです。それはもっと喚起的なものであるべきです。この場合，その形は構成感覚，一方の側から他方の側への一種の関係性にも由来しています。このヴォリュームの形態はまた，建物内の主要な集合空間を示唆する助けにもなっています。皆が一緒になって交流するその3つの場所は，図書館と，オーディトリアムとギャラリーです。つまり，私はこの3つの空間の間の関係を分節することが重要だと感じていました。内部にも外部にもその理由が存在しますが，たぶん私には説明出来ない何かです。仕上げの材料は最近の美術館プロジェクトと同じものです。基部に花崗岩，その上がスタッコ。基部がソリッドなものであるのはとても大切です。単に，建物を地上とどのように接するようにするかという点からばかりでなく，メンテナンスの面からもそうなのです。ポルトガルでは建物のメンテナンス事情は，あるべき水準にはありませんから，耐久性のある材料を使う必要があるのです。

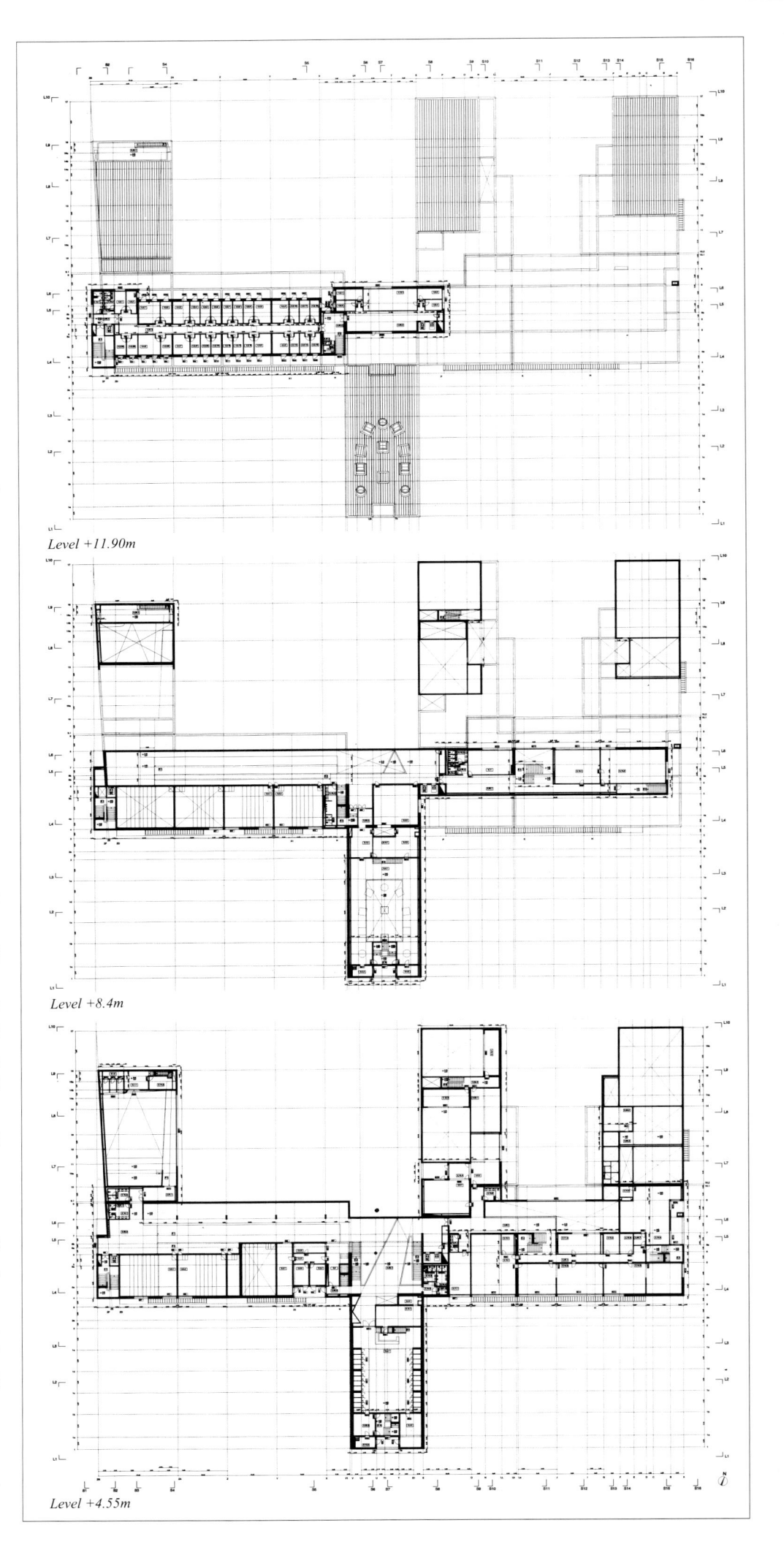

Level +11.90m

Level +8.4m

Level +4.55m

East elevation

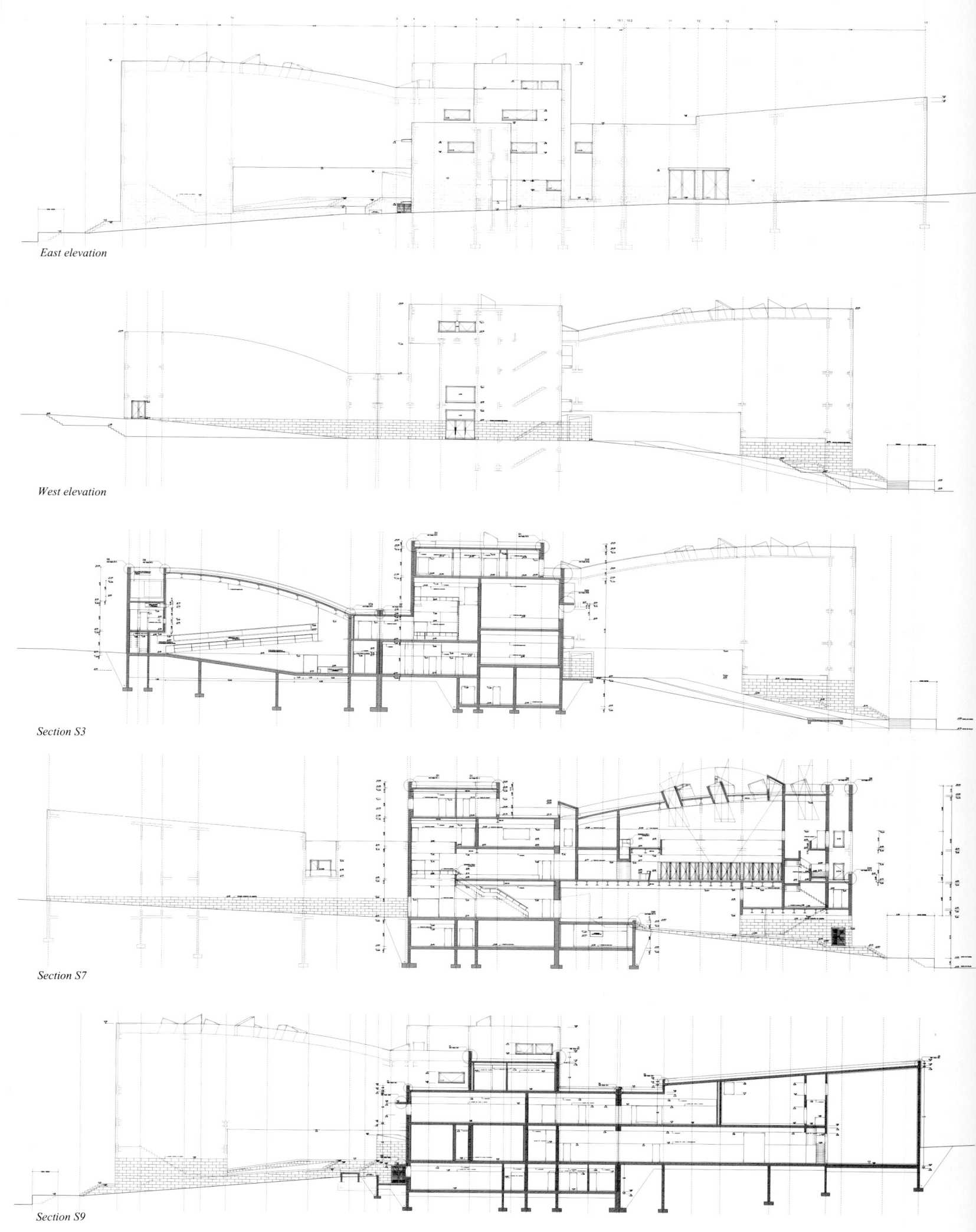

West elevation

Section S3

Section S7

Section S9

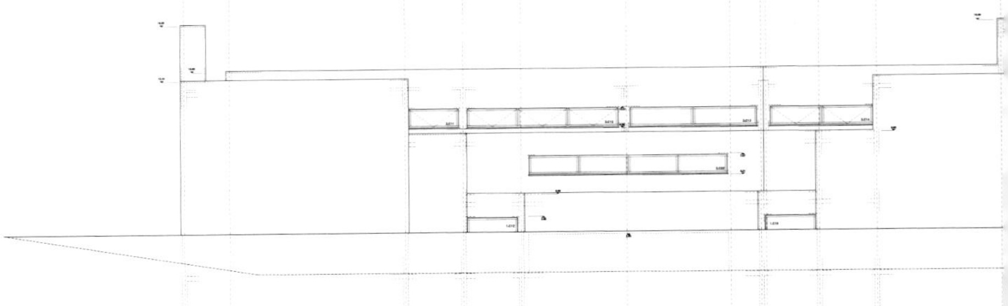

DESCRIPTION

The Information Sciences Faculty building will be located in the Burgo das Nações, forming an integral part of the new university campus, on a lot defined in the relevant Partial Plan. This lot is bounded in the north by Rua Castelão, in the south and east by the Avenida do Burgo das Nações, and in the west by the steps which connect these two streets.

The main part of the building is a linear organization running in the west-east direction, respecting the southern alignment of the Philology Faculty. It has three floors (ground floor and two upper floors in the half of the building on the west side, and a basement, ground floor and one upper floor along the rest of the length). Its dimensions are 17.5 m × 127 m.

This division of the roof structure into different levels is the result of the adaptation to the topography and the constraints of the program. In the larger volume there are nine amphitheater-style lecture halls, which are accessible by ramp, lift and stairs and, on the top floor, the lecturers' offices. The smaller volume houses the radio and visual media studios and the audio-visual laboratories.

All the spaces are arranged along a north-facing gallery. The main atrium is located between the two areas already mentioned (the lecture halls and the audio-visual facilities). The gallery also provides access to the three perpendicularly located buildings, between 7 and 10 meters in height, which define patio areas opening onto Rua Castelão. The volume situated at the far west of the gallery houses the auditorium (300 places). The other two volumes, at the far east of the lot, complete the audio-visual facility, housing the television and film studios.

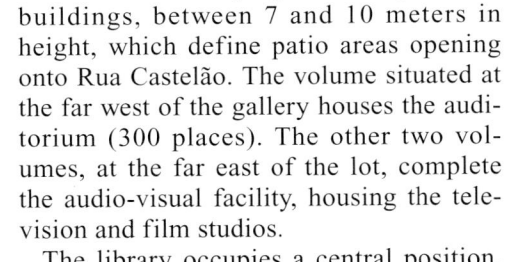

The library occupies a central position, being accessible from both levels of the atrium. Its volume defines a spacious entrance gateway.

The stairs, lifts and toilet facilities are placed in a balanced arrangement along the circulation gallery in a way that complies with the various relevant regulations.

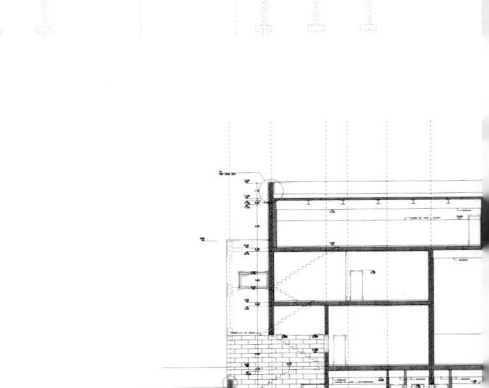

North elevation

Section L6

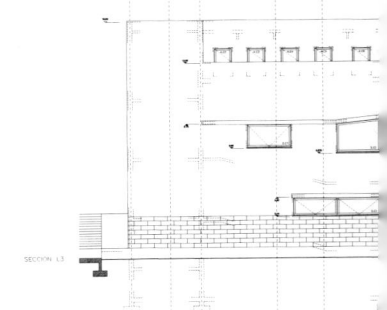

Section L3

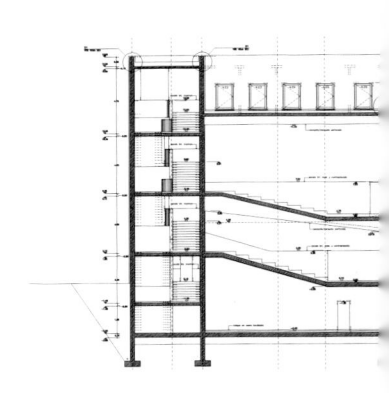

Section L4

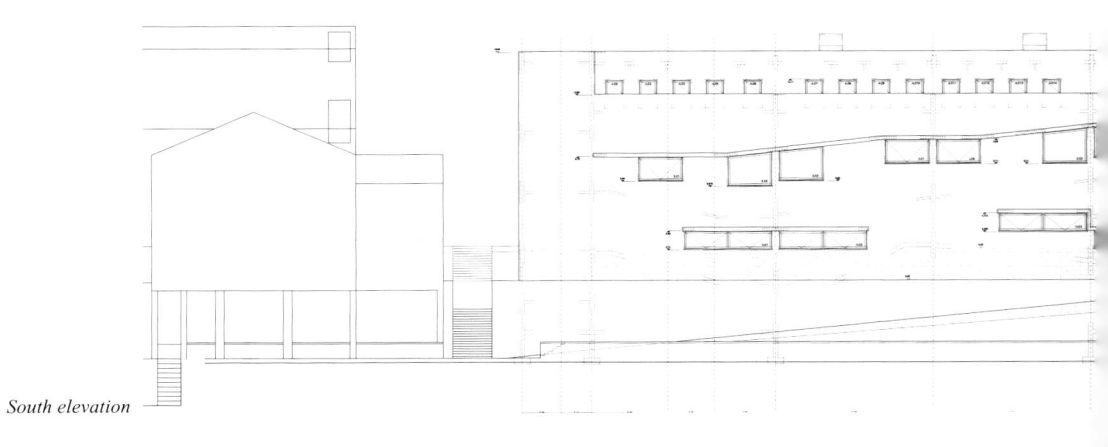

South elevation

<解説>
情報科学学部の建物はブルゴ・ダス・ナソインスに設置されることになろう。それは，適切な部分計画によって区画された敷地で，新しい大学キャンパスの一部を構成する。この区画は，北をカステラーン通り，南と東をブルゴ・ダス・ナソインス通り，西をこれら2つの通りを結ぶ階段によって囲まれている。

建物の主要部は，南側の言語学部棟（文献学）との整列を尊重しながら，東西に走るリニアーな構成である。建物は3階建てで（西側半分は地上階，上層2階で構成され，建物長さの残りの部分に沿っては，地階，地上階，上層1階で構成されている）。幅17.5m，長さ127mである。

いくつかの異なったレベルへと分割された屋根構造は，地形とプログラムの制約に適合させた結果である。大きい方のヴォリュームには，斜路，リフト，階段から入れる，階段教室形式のホールが9つと，最上階に講師のオフィスがある。小さな方のヴォリュームには，ラジオと視覚メディアのスタジオ，そして視聴覚ラボが配されている。

スペースはすべて，北に面したギャラリーに沿って配置されている。主アトリウムは上述した2つのエリア（講義ホールと視聴覚施設）の間に位置している。このギャラリーは，高さ7mから10mの，垂直方向に位置し，カステラーン通りに向けて開いたパティオを縁取る3つの建物へのアクセスを提供する。ギャラリーの西端部に位置するヴォリュームにはオーディトリアム（300席）が置かれている。敷地の東端に位置する，他の2つのヴォリュームには視聴覚施設に加えて，テレビと映画スタジオがある。

図書館が中央部を占め，アトリウムの両方の階から入ることが出来る。そのヴォリュームは広々としたエントランス・ゲートウェイを明快に輪郭づけている。

階段，リフト，洗面所は，動線を構成するギャラリーに沿って，様々な適切な規制に従いながら，均衡をとって配置される。

0 1m   5m   10m

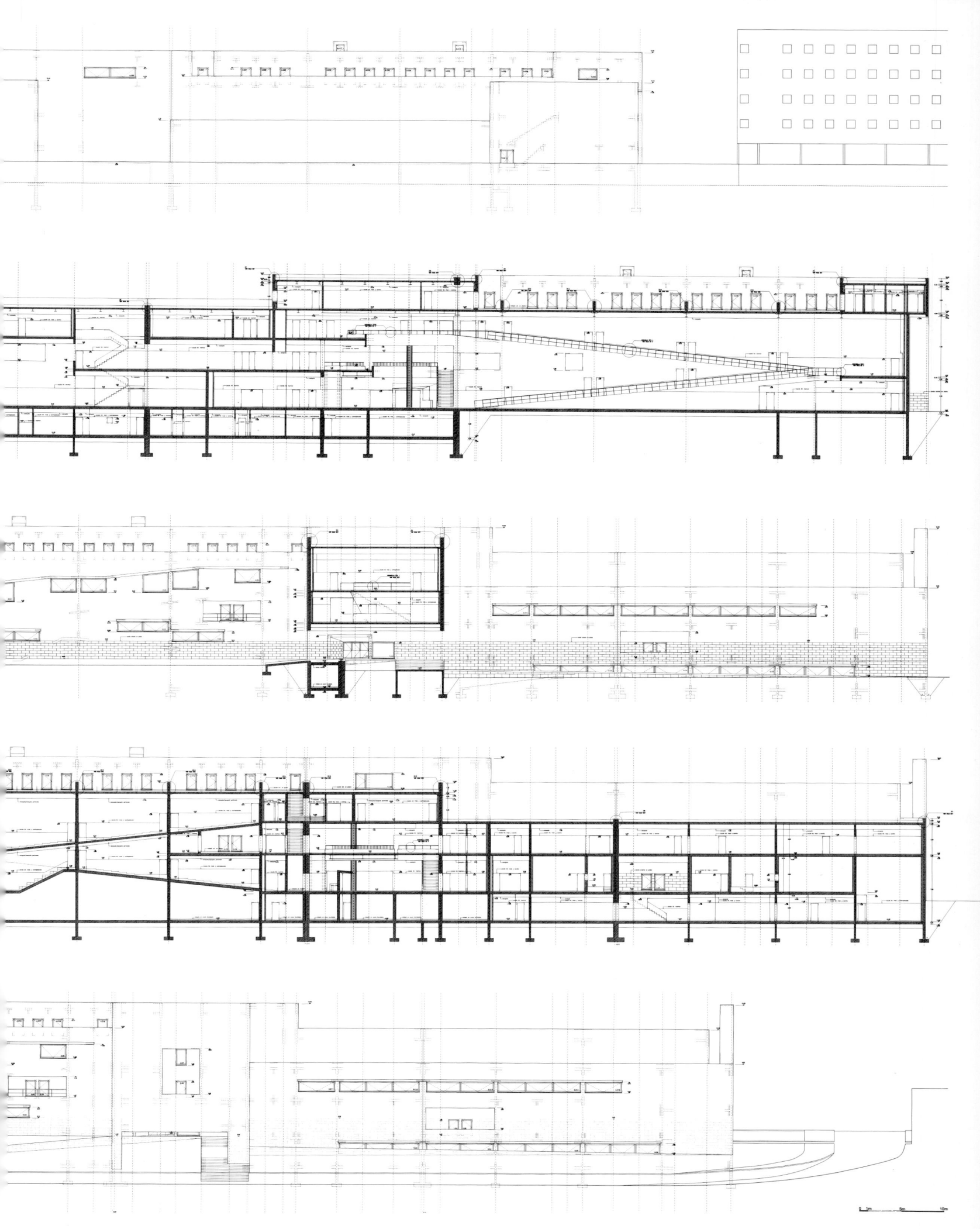

161

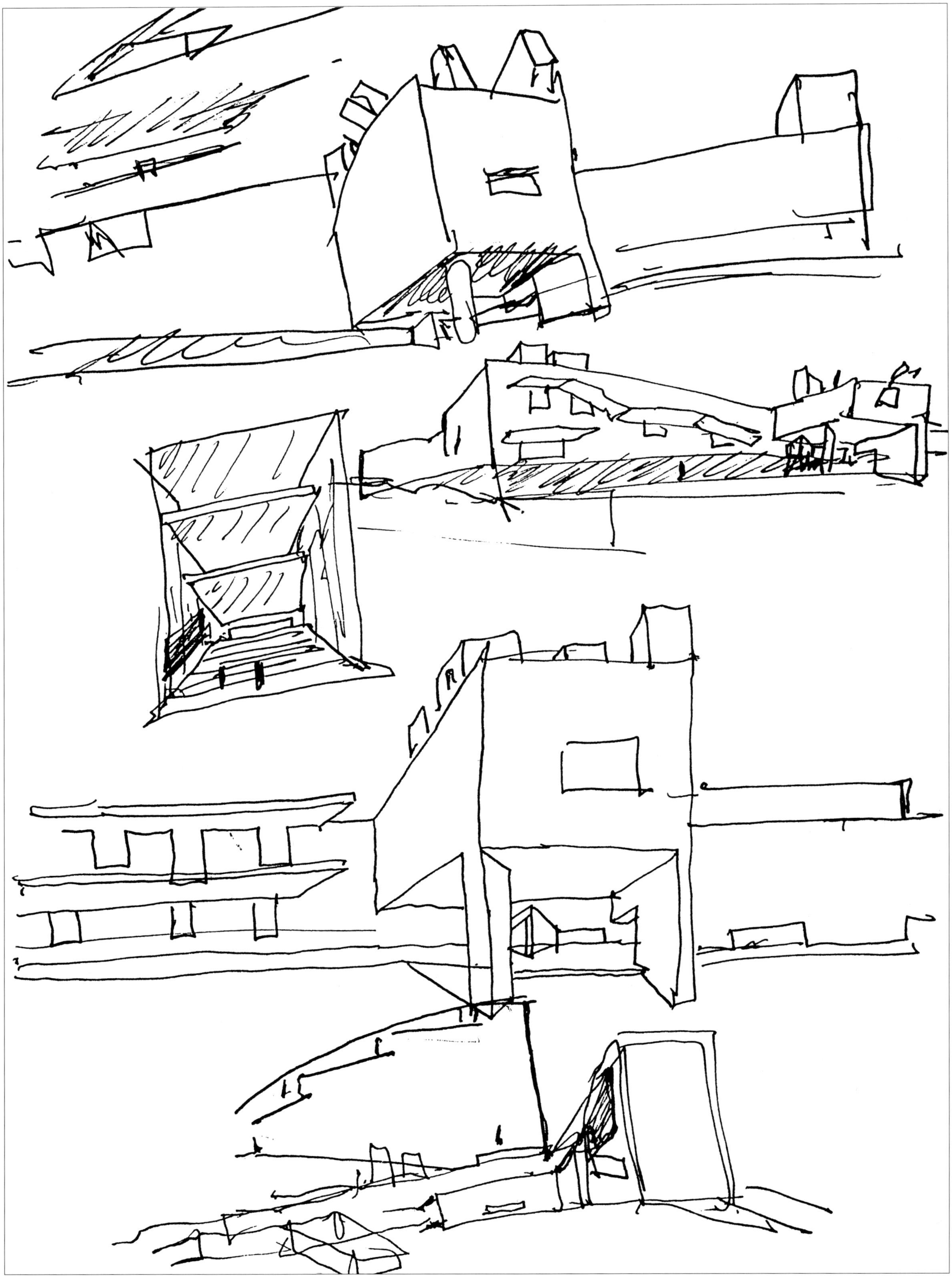

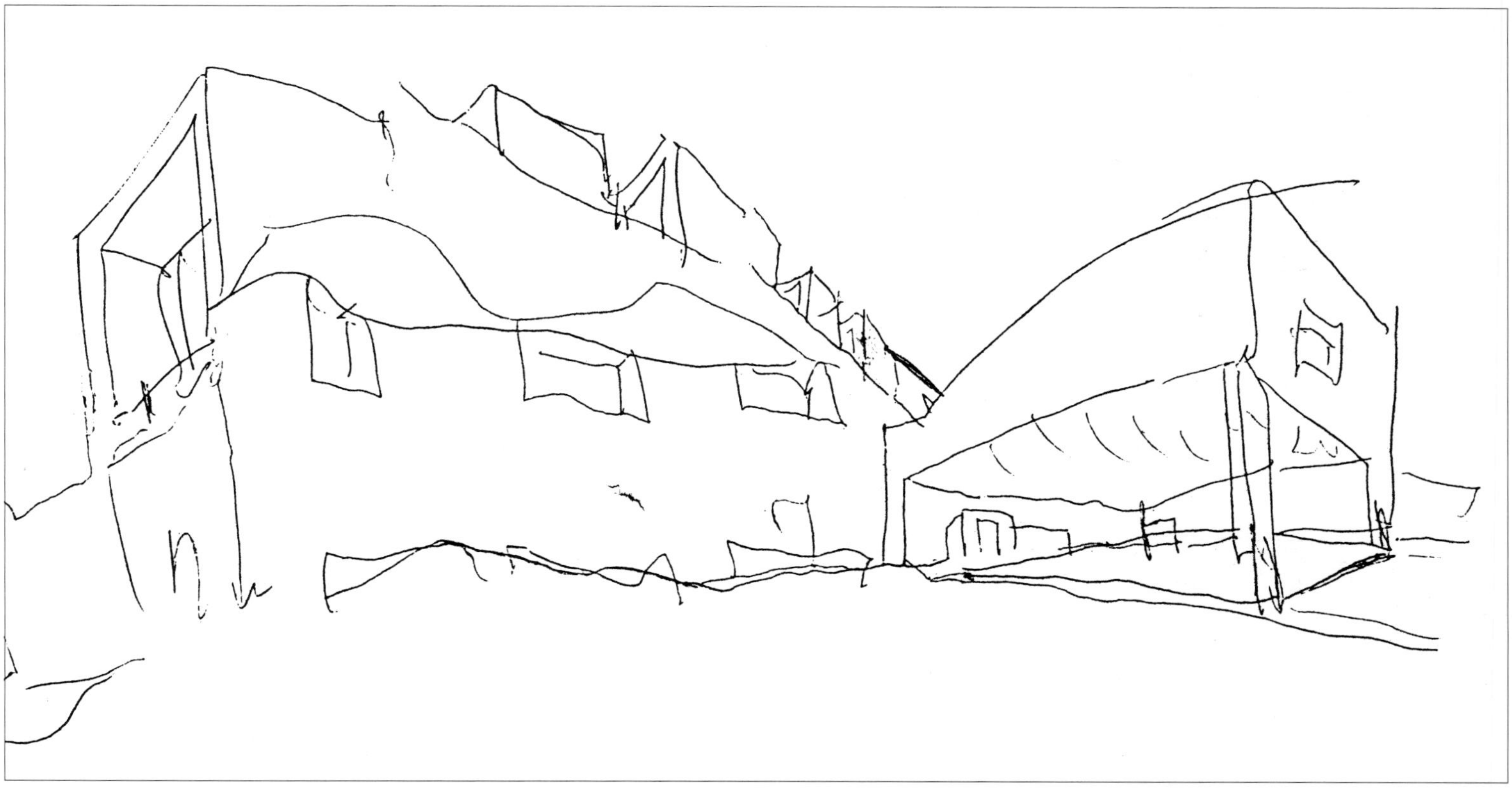

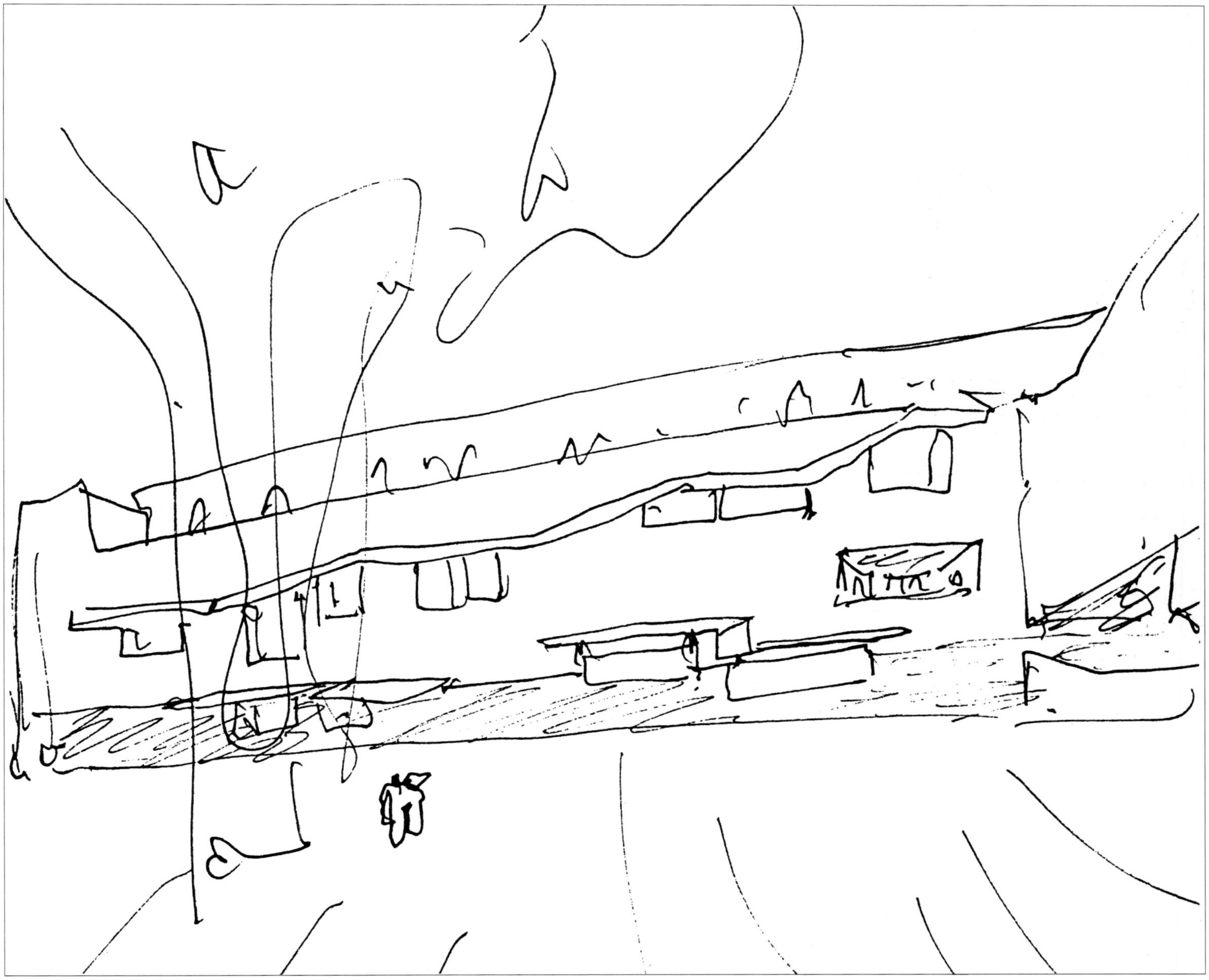

Cultural Center of the Precinct of Revellin
レヴェリン文化センター

Ceuta, Spain

Client: Municipality of Ceuta Design period: 1997–98 Architects: Álvaro Siza Arquitecto, Lda—Hana Kassem, Lia Kiladis, principals-in-charge Project team: Daniela Antonucci, Paul Scott Structural engineer: G.O.P.—João Maria Sobreira Mechanical engineer: G.E.T.—Alfredo Costa Pereira Acoustical engineer: Daniel Commins Stage design: Fravio Tirone Structural system: reinforced concrete structure

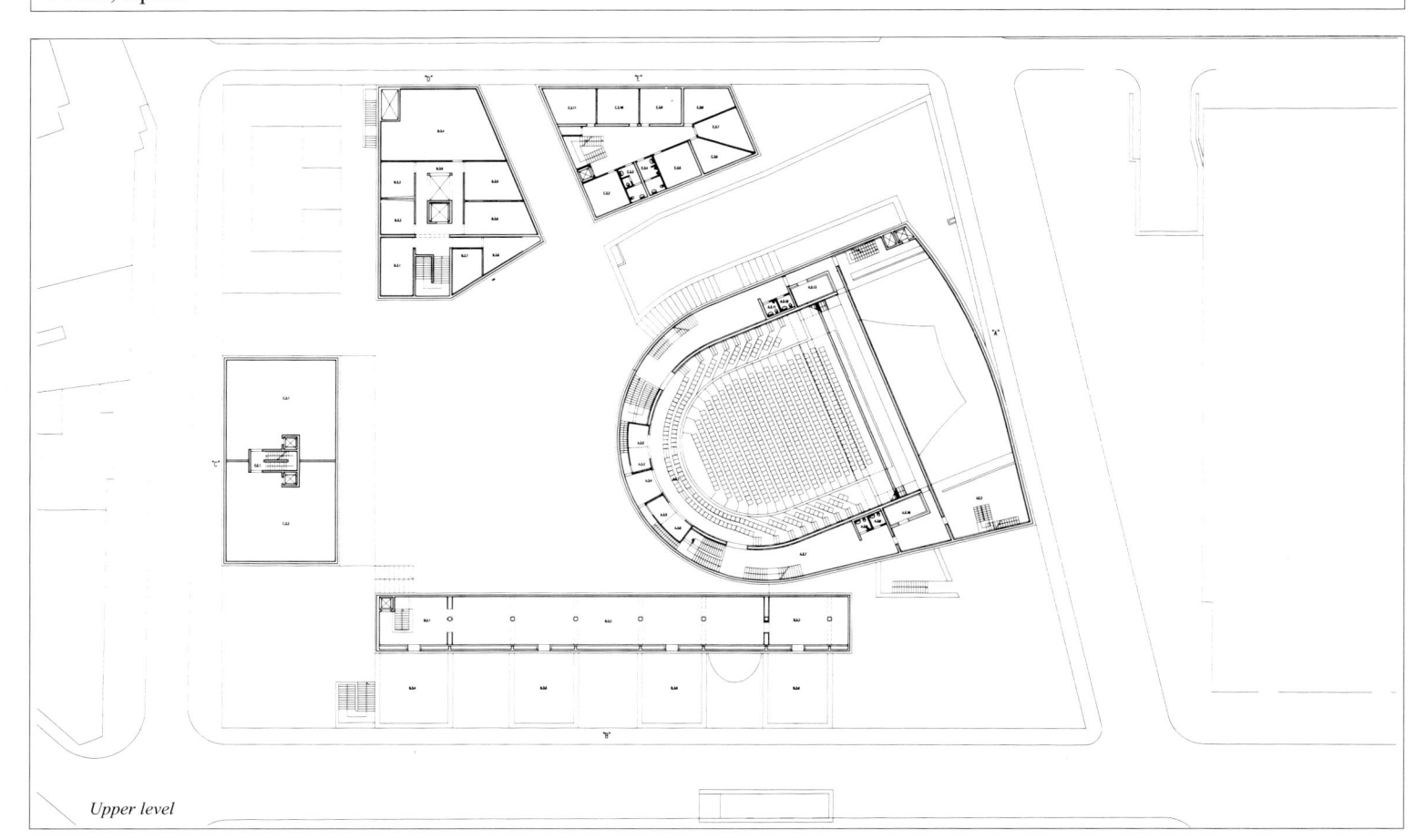

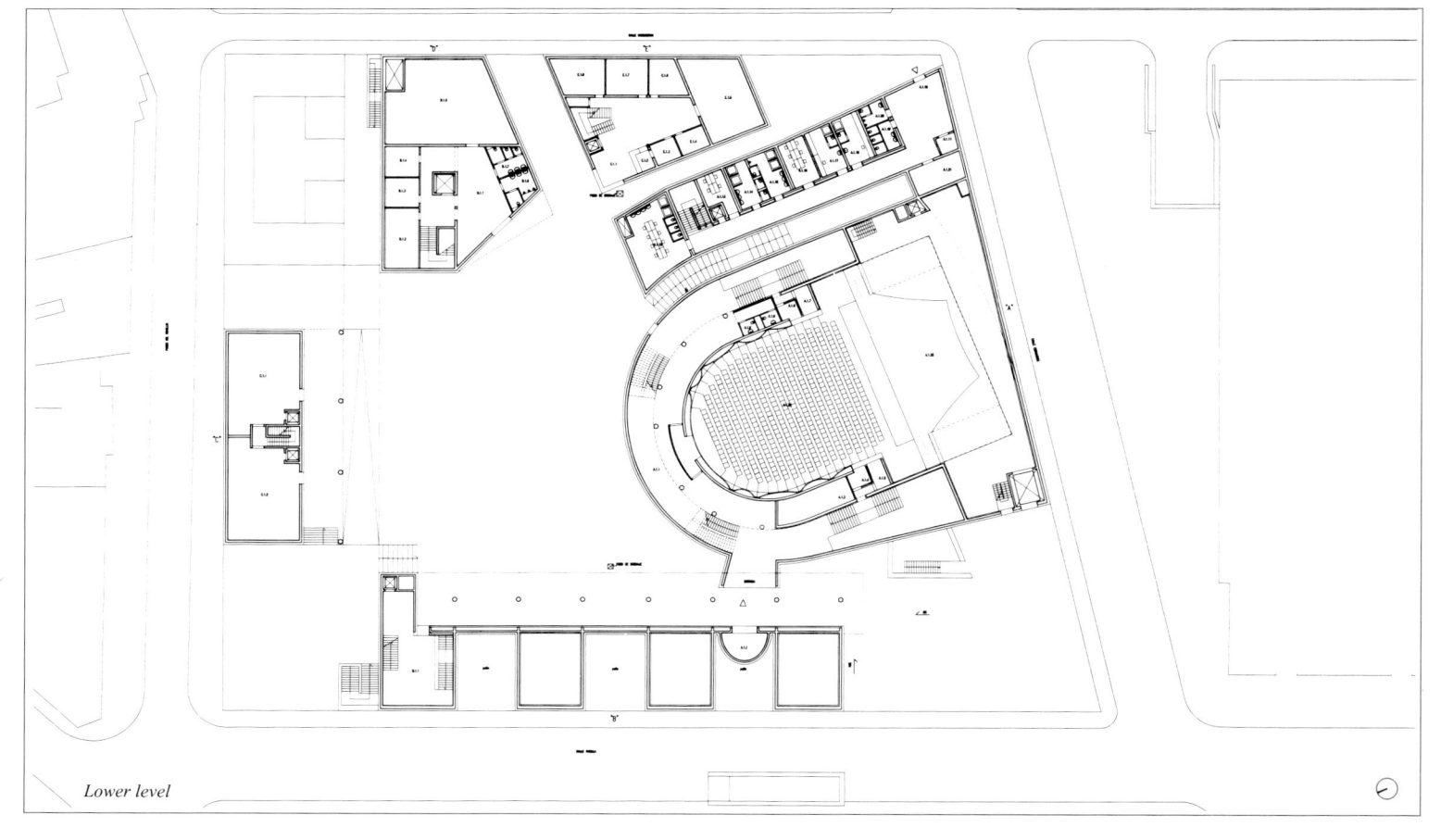

Upper level

Lower level

GA: How did you get this commission?
Álvaro Siza: I've done several projects in Spain. And I have many old friends who are Spanish architects. One of them in Madrid proposed the renovation of the Portuguese fort in this town. Then he proposed that the town invite me and they thought it would be interesting to have a Portuguese architect work on the project.

You see, this was in fact the first Portuguese town in North Africa. The Portuguese created other towns along the coast at strategic points for the maintenance of the ships and for bringing on supplies. But in the middle of the 17th century, the king of Spain became the king of Portugal. The two countries were unified for about 60 years after which they split again. During this process, Ceuta became Spanish again and remains so today. So the town has a big connection with the sea. It was an outpost so they had to defend this little territory from the land. You have walls to defend from inland forces. It's a western town of modest buildings. But geographically it is very beautiful. The main monument, of course, is the fortress walls.

In the center of town there is a vast open space where a big building was demolished long time ago. I was called upon to help reorganize this space. First they wanted to make a park. But now they want to create some cultural facilities centered around an auditorium. They didn't have a clear idea. In the end they decided to make two schools, one for music and one for languages, with some commercial buildings. What I proposed was a main volume of an auditorium that would help restore the existing tissue around this area.

The tradition in Morocco, as you may know, is not so much in large urban spaces, but smaller more intimate spaces, like patios. So I wanted to create something along those lines. I created patios for the activities. The auditorium has a gallery for art upstairs and also some meeting rooms. Together these could be used for an organized conference or they could be used separately. Underground you have two levels of parking. One of the difficult things designing spaces around the structural requirements of the parking.
GA: How did you go about organizing the spaces?
Siza: The orientation of the auditorium comes from the street grid. This also creates the form of the other buildings. There were problems of scale, of the articulation of spaces, and of the axes of the grid.
GA: Does the town have any particular qualities you tried to draw from?
Siza: Not much in the way of historical buildings. Here you have some churches but not many. There are mostly small buildings, some are rationalist and some in Art Nouveau. Most of the buildings are very average 19th century buildings. The atmosphere is a little bit like a South American colonial town. Of course the presence of the sea is very important and the landscape is very beautiful. The atmosphere is pretty interesting. You don't see many Muslims like you do in Morocco, but the small-scale spaces are very similar. The street life is very intense and the atmosphere of the market-places is very interesting. It is a very peaceful and quiet kind of life there. I like it very much. The only difficulty was in finding people to work with there. It is so relaxed no one is ever in their offices.

GA：この仕事はどういうふうに始まったのですか。
アルヴァロ・シザ：スペインでいくつかのプロジェクトをやっていました。そして、スペインには古くからの建築家の友人がたくさんいます。マドリッドに住む友人の一人が、セウタにあるポルトガルの要塞跡の改造を提案したのです。それから彼は私を招くように町に推薦し、町は、このプロジェクトをポルトガル人の建築家にまかすのも面白いと考えたのです。

ご存知のように、ここは、事実、北アフリカにおける最初のポルトガルの街でした。ポルトガルは、船の修理と補給に必要な海岸沿いの戦略地点に次々に街をつくって行きました。しかし17世紀半ばにスペイン王がポルトガル王になり、2つの国は再び分裂するまで約60年間、統一されていたわけです。この経過のなかで、セウタは再びスペイン領となり、そのまま今日まできている。ですからこの街は海との大きなつながりがあるのです。ここは前哨地でしたから、この小さな領土を周囲の国から守る必要がありました。内陸からの武力から守るために壁がつくられたわけです。質素な建物から成る西の街です。しかし、地理的にはとても美しい。主要なモニュメントはもちろん要塞の壁です。

街の中心には非常に広いオープン・スペースがあります。ここは以前には大きな建物が建っていたのですが、ずいぶん前に取り壊されました。私はこの空間を再構成するように頼まれたわけです。町は最初、公園をつくりたいと考えていました。しかし、今は、オーディトリアムを中心に囲んでいくつかの文化施設をつくりたいということなのです。明快なアイディアは持っていませんでした。結局、音楽と語学の学校を2つといくつかの商業施設をつくることが決まりました。私の提案は、この地域を囲む既存の街並みを修復するのを助けることになるであろうオーディトリアムを主要な建物とするものでした。

モロッコの伝統では、ご存知かもしれませんが、大きな都市空間はそれほどなく、パティオのようなもっと小さな、こじんまりした空間が多いのです。ですから、私はこの線に添った何かをつくりたかったのです。さまざまな活動のためのパティオをつくりました。オーディトリアムには上階にアート・ギャラリーがあり、いくつかの集会室もあります。全部を使って組織された会議も開けますし、ばらばらにも使えます。地階には2層の駐車場があります。駐車場の構造的要求に基づいて空間を設計するのは難しかったことの一つです。
GA：空間構成についてはどのように進められたのですか。
シザ：オーディトリアムの方位は道路のグリッドに由来しています。これはまた、他の建物の形態もつくりだしている。スケール、空間の分節、グリッドの軸線などの問題がありました。
GA：この街には、引き出したいと思われた、何か特別な性格がありましたか。
シザ：歴史的建造物という点ではそれほどあるわけではないのです。教会がいくつかありますが、多くはありません。街の大体が小さな建物で、いくつかは合理主義者のもの、いくつかはアール・ヌーヴォーのものです。ほとんどの建物はごく標準的な19世紀のものです。その雰囲気はいくぶん、南アフリカのコロニアル・タウンに似たところがあります。もちろん、海の存在はとても重要で、風景は非常に美しいのです。雰囲気はとても興味深いものです。セウタではモロッコにおけるほどイスラム教徒を多く見かけることはありませんが、小さなスケールの空間の面ではイスラムととてもよく似ています。道路での人々の活動には非常に激しいものがあり、市場の雰囲気は実に楽しい。とても平和で、静かな生活があります。私は大好きですね。ただ一つ困るのは、一緒に働く人を見つけるのが難しいことです。あまりにのんびりしていて、オフィスに人がいることが無い。

North elevation

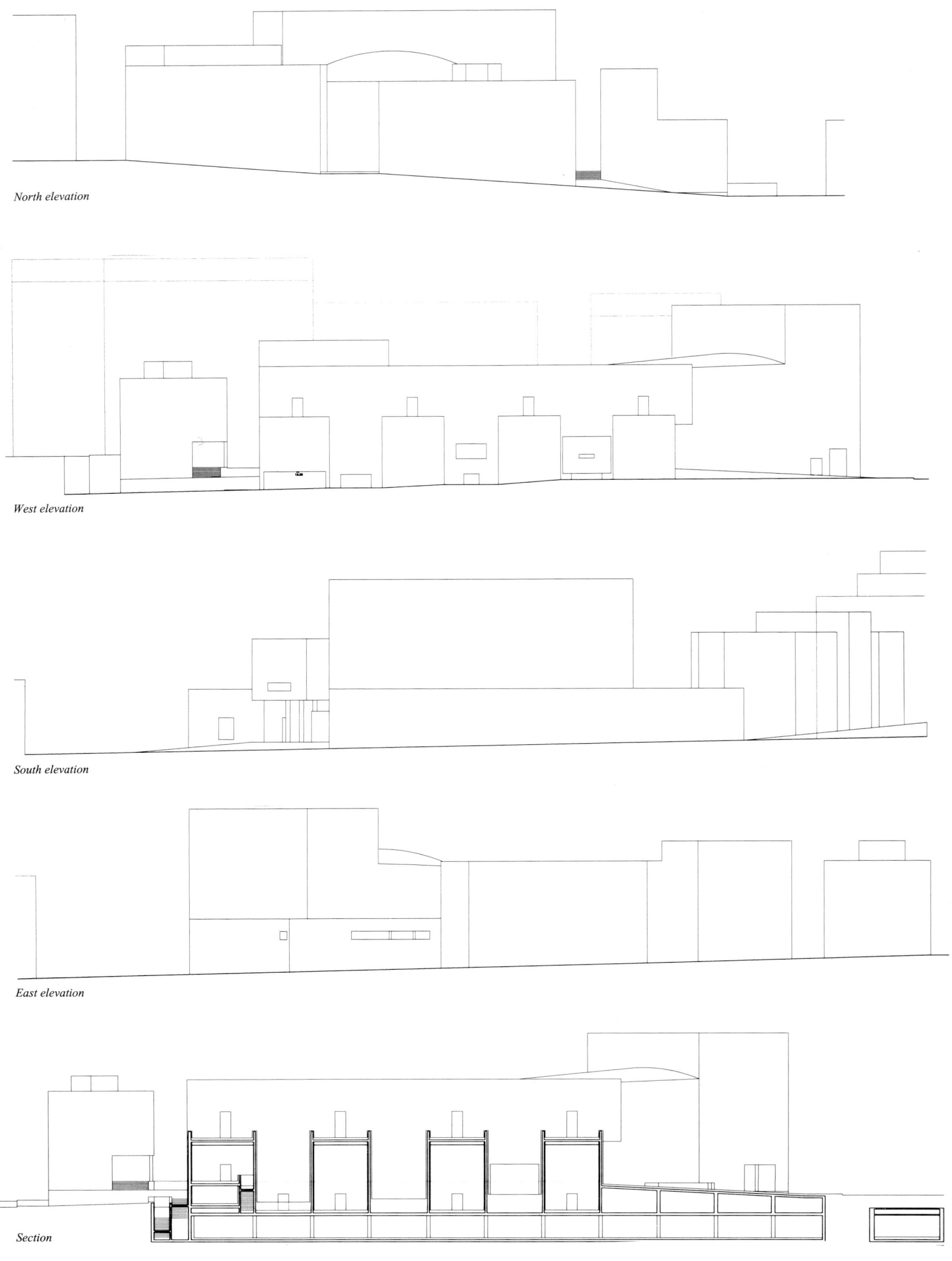

West elevation

South elevation

East elevation

Section

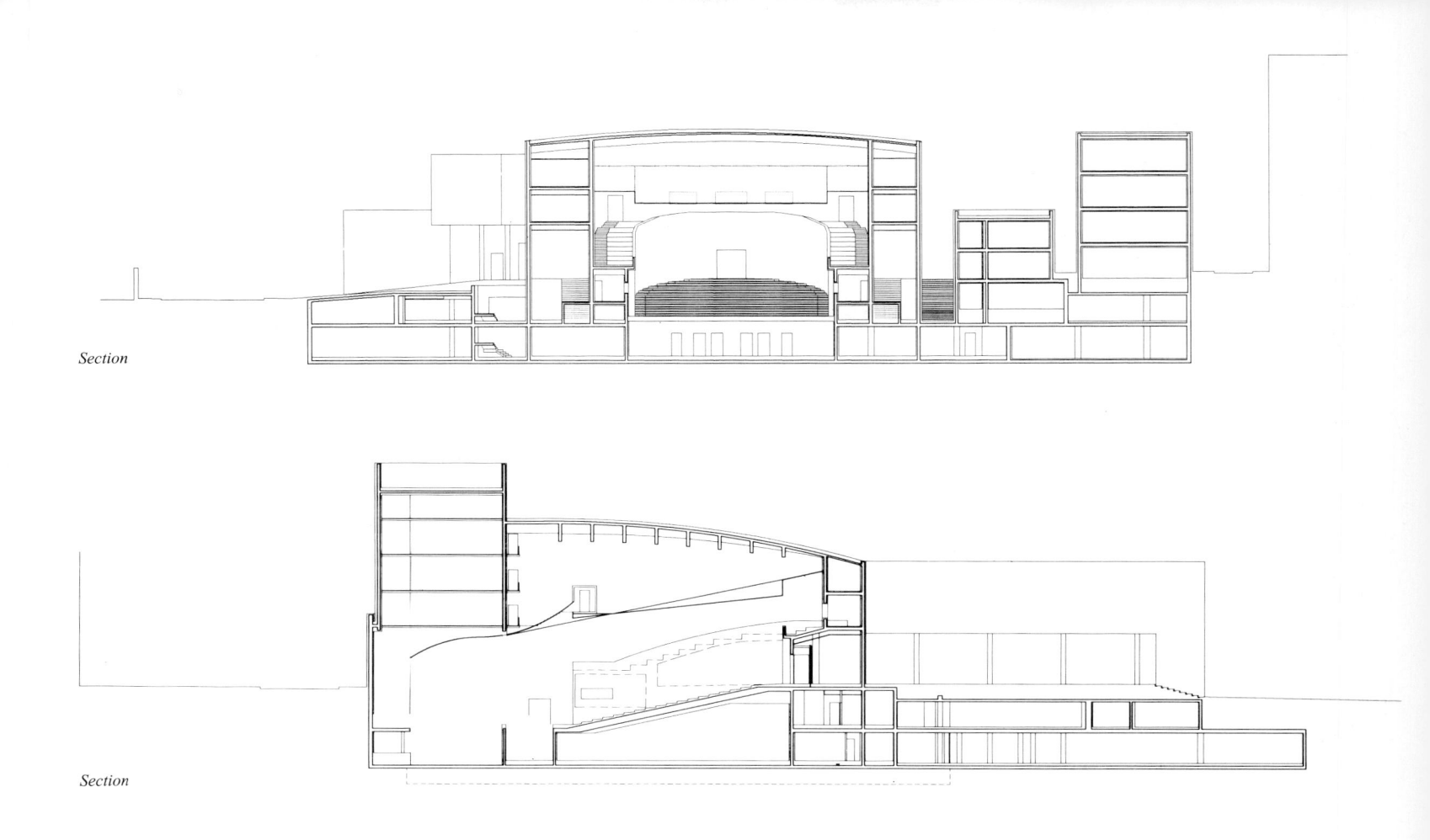

Section

Section

DESCRIPTION
Siting
The Cultural Center of the Revellin neighborhood is located in the historical and geographical center of the city of Ceuta, where the urban fabric is the most dense. The project occupies one square block of the city, bounded by Calle des Ingenieros to the east, a new extension of Calle Cervantes to the south, Calle Padilla to the west, and the tree-lined Paseo del Revellin to the north. On the north-west corner of the site sits the neo-classical Municipal Museum, housing archaeological and cartographic works and possessing a clear view of the harbor from its terrace.

The remainder of the sloping site, once occupied by a public market, is now vacant. It is bounded on all four sides by buildings of various heights, styles, and functions which, through their own orientation and the strength of their interstitial spaces, inform the morphology of the new building. The project takes into consideration both the necessary continuation of the urban fabric and the public nature of this open urban space in the development of its built form.

Spatial Organization and Accesses
The design takes its cues from the surrounding geography, respecting the rhythm of the urban topography of the area and enhancing its situation through a play or pedestrian and vehicular accesses to and through the project site. The majority of the buildings sit on a plinth which forms a public plaza, Pedestrian accesses are carved in from the existing passages stepping down from Plaza de España to the east, and at the south-west and north-west corners of Calle Padilla. As in other parts of the city, the pedestrian is invited into the passage between buildings, where he is rewarded with a quiet respite in an open court, as well as access to all buildings of the site.

Following the large curved wall which nudges the open court, and drawn by a simple colonnade, one is led to the entry of the theater. Access to the congress center is located at the near end of the colonnade, under the volume of the gallery space which shadows the west end of the site.

The congress hall can also be entered directly from Calle Padilla, by a small ramp between two volumes of the halls themselves. Entry to the parking below also occurs along this side. Underneath the entire plaza are located two levels of public and private parking, the main entry of which previously exists and is shared by the "Ceuta Center" building to the south.

Geometry and Volumetrics
The five buildings which compose the project are each placed with one side along the perimeter of the block, deferring to the inherently urban nature of the site. The volume of the theater dominates in both size and shape, its curvilinear form distinguishing the block from its neighbors and calling attention to the particular function which it houses. The stage tower rises as if peels away from Calle Cervantes, marking the complex from afar as the tallest volume on the site. The wall at pedestrian level respects the street edge, while the axis of the stage and hall is turned to align perpendicularly to the streets which push into the site from the east. Accordingly, the artists' wing, which sits alongside the hall, is oriented along this axis. Together the three visible volumes which compose the theater—stage, hall, artists' wing—express the fundamental relationship through which performing arts operate.

The four separated boxes of the congress center anchor the sloping site at its west level, on axis with Calle Padilla, and, like the volume of the theater, clearly delimit their function as large open rooms. Below ground, each hall is accessed along a shared corridor, which joins the public lobby of the theater. An interior public space is thus carved from the conjunction of the two buildings, in the coolness of a subterranean environment sheltered from

<解説>
敷地：
レヴェリン文化センター地区は，セウタの歴史的地形的な中心部にあり，都市構成の密度が最も高い場所である。プロジェクトは，方形の一街区を占め，東をインジェニロス通り，南をセルヴァンテス通りの新たな延長部，西をパディラ通り，北を並木のあるレヴェリン通りに囲まれている。敷地の北西角には新古典様式の市立博物館が建ち，ここには考古学関係，地図製作関係の品物が収蔵され，テラスからは港が広々と望める。

斜面となった敷地の建物以外の部分には，かつて市場が立ったが，現在は空き地である。その四面は，様々な高さ，様式，機能の建物に囲まれ，それぞれの方位，隙間空間の力を通して，新しい建物の形態構造を告知する。このプロジェクトは，建築形態の展開において，必要とされる都市ファブリックとの連続性，またその敷地であるオープンな都市空間の持つ公共的性格の両方を考慮にいれて計画されている。

空間構成とアクセス：
デザインは，周囲の地形からヒントを得ており，周辺地域の都市の地勢が備えているリズムを尊重し，敷地に至り，そこを通り抜けて行く歩行路や自動車路とのからみあいを通してその状況を強調する。建物の大半は，公共広場を形成する基壇上に座している。歩行者のアクセスは，スペイン広場から東に，そしてパディラ通りの南西と北西の角へと階段を刻んで降りて行く既存通路から彫り込まれている。街の他の部分のように，歩行者は建物の間の通路に誘われ，そこに入って行くとオープン・コートのなか，一息つける静かな場所を与えられる。

オープン・コートを軽く押している，湾曲する大きな壁に沿って進むと，単純な列柱に引き込まれて，劇場のエントランスに導かれる。会議センターへのアクセスは，列柱の端部近く，敷地西端に影を落とすギャラリー・スペースのヴォリュームの下にある。

会議場へは，その2つの会議場の間に位置する小さなスロープによって，パディラ通りからも直接入れる。広場全体の下には2層にわたる公共及び専用の駐車場があり，ここは以前の主入り口で，南側の"セウタ・センター"の建物と共有されている。

ジオメトリーと容積：
プロジェクトを構成する5つの建物は，敷地固有の都市的性格に従って，それぞれ一面をブロック周縁に沿って配置される。劇場のヴォリュームは，大きさ，形態ともこの場を支配し，その曲線的形態はこのブロックを周辺から際だせ，その内包する特殊な機能に注目を引き寄せる。舞台を収めたタワーはセルヴァンテス通りから皮をむくように立ち上がり，敷地内の最も高い建物として，このコンプレックスの遠くからの目印となる。歩行者レベルの壁は道路の縁を尊重し，一方，舞台とホールの軸線は，東側から入り込んでいる道路に対し垂直に整列するように向いている。それに応じて，ホールの脇に位置するアーティスト・ウィングはこの軸線に向けられる。劇場を構成する，目に見える3つのヴォリューム——舞台，ホール，アーティスト・ウィングは舞台芸術が演じられる際の基本的な関係を表現している。

会議センターの4つに分かれた箱形の建物は一番低い所，パディラ通りと軸線をそろえて建ち，斜面の敷地を留めている。それらは，劇場のヴォリュームのように，その機能を広い開放的な空間として明快に境界づけている。地盤面下では各ホールは，劇場のパブリック・ロビーに至る，共有廊下に沿って入る。内部のパブリック・スペースは，このように2つの建物の連携から生まれている。そこは，地下の環境で涼しく，この地方の大体が暑い気候からの避難所となる。

音楽学校，語学学校，商業ビルは，それぞれのジオメトリーを，密度のある都市ファブリックとこの新しい，重要な場所の間の仲介者の役割を果たしている。敷地自身がもともと備えている手がかりから引き出している。市立博物館

169

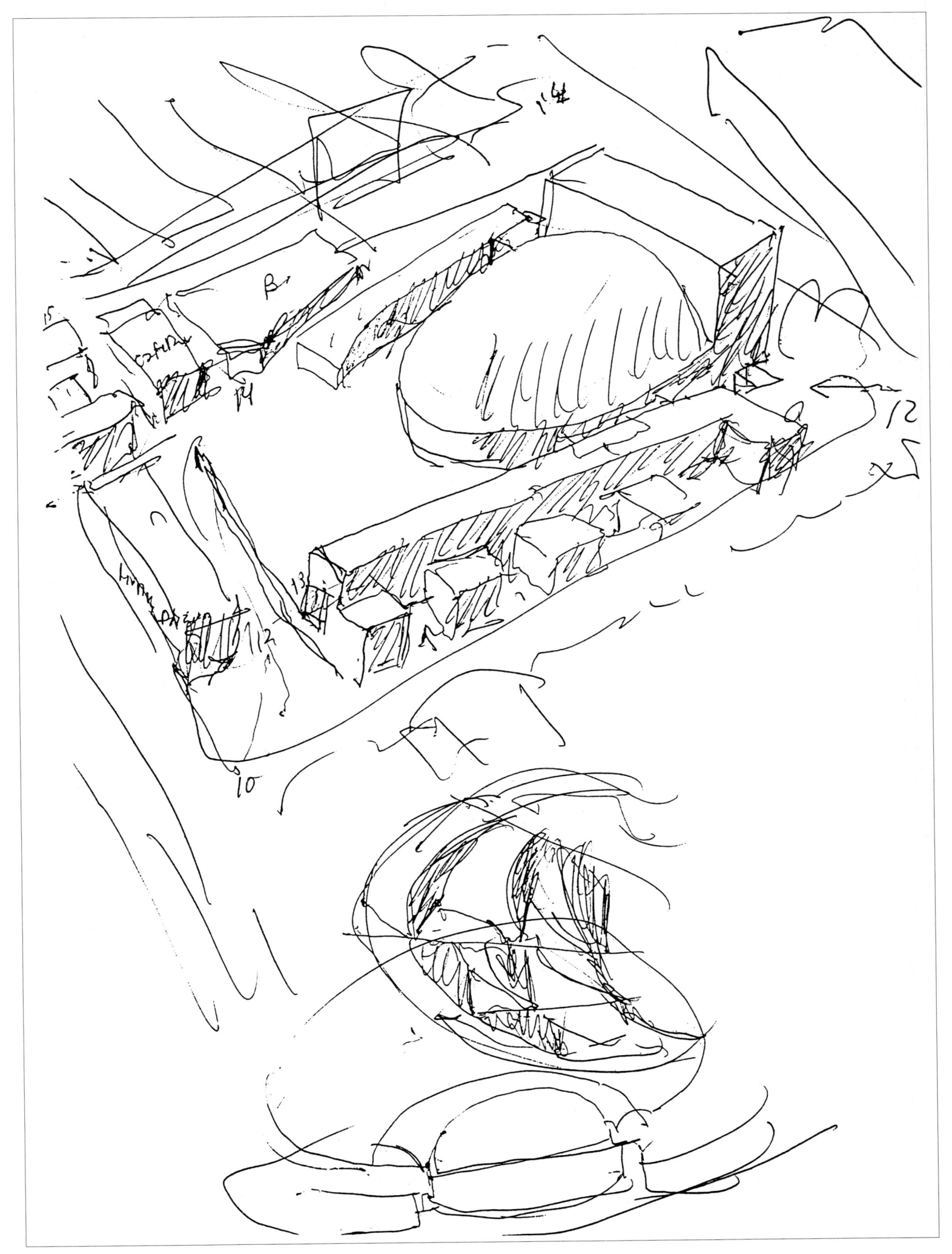

the normally hot climate of the region.

The Music School, Language School, and commercial building derive their respective geometries from the pre-existing clues of the site itself, acting as mediators between the dense fabric of the city and this new, important place. The Municipal Museum is re-integrated into its immediate surroundings and, in dialogue with the new buildings, helps to raise the civic importance of this quarter of the city.

Program
—Theater: Practice area and dressing rooms for orchestra members, artists' lounge, storage for scenery, lighting and instruments, support spaces for technical staff, mechanical rooms, and access to stage machinery and the orchestra pit compose the lowest level of the theater building (floor 1). At ground level (floor 0) are the stage, the lowest levels or theater seating, and public areas including bars and

restrooms. A row of artists' suites and the green room lead directly to the stage area. Public entry to the theater is located on the first floor (floor 1), where tickets can be purchased before entering the building. The main body of seating is completed at this level with space for 494 patrons. Also at this level are entrances to translation booths, cloakroom, and restrooms, accessed from the lobby space around the hall. The artists' entrance and wing of dressing rooms are located to the east of the stage, and a loading area is positioned to the west. Secondary exits from the theater are located on either side of the hall, and lead directly to the exterior plaza.

A final row of office suites completes the artists' wing on the second floor. The balcony level of seating (140 seats) is located on the third floor. At the rear of the hall are the technical cabins for sound, light, and projection. An open gallery area surrounds the perimeter of the hall at the uppermost public floor (level 4). Technical bridges occupy the stage tower at level 5.

—Congress Center: The lowest level of the congress center, at ground level, provides entry to the building and each of its three double-height lecture halls, a lobby area with cafe and restroom facilities, and vertical circulation to the upper levels. Midway up, at the first floor, is located the entrance from the plaza. Above this, at the third floor and running the length of the building, is a large gallery space, punctuated by four exterior terraces.

—Commercial Building: A symmetrical plan allows for two commercial spaces at each of the three levels of the building, with entrances stepping up from plaza level and vertical circulation running between the two stores and storage in the basement.

—Music School: Entrance to the school occurs at plaza level, with administration offices, a multipurpose hall, and restrooms at the first level. Seminar and practice rooms, the library, professors' room, and restrooms are located on the second level. A double-height orchestra and chorus room, two chamber music rooms, and additional classrooms are located on the third level.

—Language School: Entrance to the school is located from the plaza, with administrative offices and large hall at the first level. Seminar rooms, classrooms, and the library are located on the second floor. Further classrooms are located on the third and fourth floors. Restrooms are provided at each floor.

—Parking: A total of 167 public spaces and 126 private spaces are provided over two levels, plus public restroom facilities on each level. Staff, technical, and handicap access to the theater and congress hall, are also accommodated through the parking area.

Technical Equipment

The stage opening will have the capacity to change from a traditional width of 18 meters up to 25 meters in width, with a height of nine meters. The levels of the stage and proscenium will be divided into platforms which can adjust between one and three meters in height, so that many types of spectacles—from traditional opera to symphony concerts to modern dance—can be accommodated on the stage.

Construction and Finishes

Exterior spaces will be paved with traditional small cut stones. The exterior finish of the building will have a stone base and stucco above. In the parking, the pavement will be stone, the walls will be covered with 14 × 14 tiles up to 1.68 meters with stucco above, and the stairwells will be finished in marble. At the interior, floors will be finished in wood and stone. Walls will have a stone wainscot with stucco above. All openings will be framed in painted wood. The roof of the auditorium will be covered in lead or ceramic roof tiles.

はその近接する周辺環境に再統合され，新しい建物と対話を交わし，街のこの地区の都市的重要性をつくりあげる助けとなる。

プログラム：

—劇場：オーケストラ団員の練習場と更衣室，アーティスト・ラウンジ，舞台装置室，照明，器具，技術スタッフ用サポート・スペース，機械室，舞台設備とオーケストラ・ピットへの経路が，シアター・ビルの低層階（レベル−1）にある。地上階（レベル0）は舞台，客席の低い方の部分，バーと洗面所を含むパブリック・エリアである。芸術家用の楽屋の列と温室が直接，舞台エリアへ続いている。劇場への一般用エントランスは1階（レベル1），ここで建物に入る前に切符を買うことになるだろう。客席の主要部分は494人のパトロンのためのスペースのあるこのレベルで完結する。この階はまた，同時通訳ブース，クローク，洗面所への入り口でもあり，ホールを囲むロビーから入れる。出演者の入り口と化粧室ウィングは舞台の東側に位置し，搬送エリアは西側に位置する。劇場からの補助的な出口はホールの両脇にあり，外部広場へ直接通じている。

オフィス・スイートの最終列が，アーティスト・ウィングの2階を完結する。客席のバルコニー・レベル（140席）は3階に位置する。ホールの後背部は音響，照明，映写の技術室。最上部のパブリック階（レベル4）にあるホール周縁をオープン・ギャラリーが囲んでいる。テクニカル・ブリッジが舞台棟のレベル5を占めている。

—会議センター：会議センターの一番低いレベルである地上階は，建物とそのなかにある2層吹抜けの3つのレクチュア・ホールへのエントランス，カフェと洗面所の付いたロビー・エリア，上階への垂直動線が配されている。半階分上がった1階には広場からのエントランス。この上に位置する3階には，建物の全長にわたって広いギャラリー・スペースがあり，その間に4つの外部テラスが差し挟まれている。

—商業ビル：左右対称のプランは建物の3つの階それぞれに2つの商業施設を配置することが出来る。広場レベルから階段で上がるエントランスが付き，2つの店舗の間に垂直動線が置かれ，倉庫が地下階にある。

—音楽学校：エントランスは広場レベルに，事務局オフィス，多目的ホール，洗面所が1階にある。セミナー及び練習室，図書室，教授室，洗面所が2階にある。2層吹抜けのオーケストラと合唱室，室内楽室2つ，付加的な教室が3階にある。

—語学学校：エントランスは広場レベルにあり，1階は管理事務オフィス，大ホール。セミナー室，教室，図書室が2階。3，4階も教室である。洗面所は各階にある。

—駐車場：公共用167台分，専用126台分の駐車スペースが2層にわたって配置され，各階に公共の洗面所が置かれている。劇場および会議ホールへの，職員，技術者，ハンディキャップのある人のためのアクセスも駐車場内にある。

技術設備

舞台の開口は，従来の18m幅から25m幅まで拡大出来ることになろう。高さは9m。舞台とプロセニアムは高さを1mから3mまで調節できるプラットフォームに分割されている。これによって，伝統的なオペラから交響楽，現代舞踊まで多様な公演に対応可能となる。

建設と仕上げ

外部空間は伝統的な小さく切り出した石を敷き詰める予定。建物外面は，基部が石で，上部がスタッコ仕上げ。駐車場は石敷，壁は1.68mの高さまで，14cm角のタイルを貼り，その上はスタッコ塗り。階段室は大理石仕上げ。内部の床は木と石で仕上げる。壁は石の羽目板に上部はスタッコ仕上げ。開口部はすべてペイント塗りの木枠とする。オーディトリアムの屋根は鉛かセラミックタイルで覆うことになるだろう。

ÁLVARO SIZA VIEIRA
アルヴァロ・シザ

1933	Born in Matosinhos (near Oporto), Portugal ポルトガル，ポルト近郊マトジィニョスに生まれる		1990–	Santa Maria Church of Marco de Canavezes and Parochial Center, Marco de Canavezes マルコ・ドゥ・カナヴェーゼスの教会と教区センター
1949–55	Studied at School of Architecture of Oporto (ESBAP) ポルト造形美術高等学校（ESBAP）で学ぶ		1992	Pritzker Prize by Hyatt Foundation of Chicago シカゴのハイアット財団よりプリツカー賞
1954	Finished his first built project 最初のプロジェクト完成		1993	National Prize of Architecture by Portuguese Architects Association ポルトガル建築家協会より国内建築賞
1955–58	Collaborator of Fernando Távora フェルナンド・ターヴォラのもとで働く		1994	Dr. H.P. Berlagestichting Prize ベルラーゲシュティヒティンク賞
1961–66	Swimming Pool, Leça da Palmeira レサのスイミング・プール			Gubbio Prize/Associazione Nazionale Centri Storico-Artistici グッビオ賞
1966–69	Taught at School of Architecture of Oporto (ESBAP) ESBAPで教鞭を執る		1995	Gold Medal from Nara World Architecture Exposition 奈良国際建築展覧会ゴールドメダル
1971–74	Pinto & Sotto Mayor Bank, Oliveira de Azemeis ピント＆ソット・マヨール銀行			International Award "Architetture di Pietra" by Fiera di Verona ヴェローナ，「石の建築」国際賞
1973–77	Bouça Social Housing, Oporto ボウサの集合住宅		1995–97	Rectory of University of Alicante, Spain アリカンテ大学管理／教室棟
1976	Appointed Professor of "Construction" (ESBAP) ESBAP「建築構法」教授			Expo '98 Portuguese Pavilion, Lisbon Expo'98ポルトガル・パヴィリオン
1982	Prize of Architecture from the Portuguese Department of International Association of Art Critics 国際芸術批評家協会ポルトガル支部より建築賞		1996	Secil Prize of Architecture セシル建築賞
1986–93	Setúbal Teachers' Training College, Setúbal セテューバル教育大学		1997	Manuel de la Dehesa Award by Menendez Pelayo University, Santander, Sapin メネンデス・ペラヨ大学よりマヌエル・デ・ラ・エーサ賞
1987–93	Faculty of Architecture, University of Oporto, Oporto ポルト大学建築学部棟		1998	Praemium Imperiale, Japan 高松宮殿下記念世界文化賞
1987	Award from Portuguese Architects Association ポルトガル建築家協会賞		at present	Visiting Professor at École Polythechnique Fédérale de Lausanne, University of Pennsylvania, Los Andes University of Bogotá and Graduate School of Design of Harvard University and continues to teach at School of Architecture, University of Oporto 現在，ポルト大学建築学部で教鞭を執るかたわら，ローザンヌ工科大学，ペンシルヴァニア大学，ボゴタのロス・アンデス大学，ハーヴァード大学大学院デザイン学部客員教授を勤める。
1988–93	Galician Center for Contemporary Art, Spain ガリシア現代美術センター			
1988–95	Main Library, University of Aveiro, Aveiro アヴェイロ大学図書館			
1988	Gold Medal of "Colegio de Arquitectos" of Spain スペイン建築家協会ゴールドメダル			Member of American Academy of Arts and Science, Honorary Fellow of RIBA, AIA, Académie d'Architecture de France and European Academy of Science and Arts アメリカ芸術科学アカデミー会員，RIBA，AIA，フランス建築アカデミー，ヨーロッパ科学芸術アカデミー名誉会員
	Gold Medal of Alvar Aalto Foundation アルヴァ・アアルト財団ゴールドメダル			
	"Prince of Wales Prize" in Urban Design by Harvard University for Quinta da Malagueira Residential District, Évora (1977) ハーヴァード大学都市計画学科よりキンタ・ダ・マラゲイラの住宅開発地区（1977）に対し「プリンス・オブ・ウェールズ賞」			
	"European Award of Architecture" by Economic European Community/Mies van der Rohe Foundation, Barcelona, for Borges & Irmãn Bank, Vila do Conde (1978–86) ヨーロッパ経済共同体／バルセロナ・ミース・ファン・デル・ローエ財団よりボルジェス＆イルマーン銀行（1978–86）に対し「ヨーロッパ建築賞」			

Álvaro Siza Arquitecto, Lda. Collaborators 1998

Architecture staffs: Avelino Silva, Bárbara Carvalho, Chiara Porcu, Clemente Semide, Cristina Ferreirinha, Daniela Antonucci, Edison Yutaka Okumura, Edite Rosa, Elisário Miranda, Francesca Montalto, João Pedro Xavier, Jorge Carvalho, José Luís C. Gomes, Lia Kiladis, Luis Antas de Barros, Lisa Penha, Marco Rampulla, Michael Gigante, Miguel Nery, Pedro Rogado, Raffaele Leone, Roberto Cremascoli, Rui Castro, Taichi Tomuro, Tatiana Berger **Secretarial staffs:** Teresa Godinho, Dinora Rodrigues **Computer assistant:** António Dias

Photographic credits—Taichi Tomuro, pp. 28, 29

GAドキュメント・エクストラ11＜アルヴァロ・シザ＞
1998年9月17日発行／企画・編集・撮影：二川幸夫／インタヴュー：二川由夫（和訳：菊池泰子）／デザイン：細谷巌／発行者：二川幸夫
制作：ジーエー・デザインセンター／印刷・製本：大日本印刷株式会社／発行：エーディーエー・エディタ・トーキョー／東京都渋谷区千駄ヶ谷3-12-14
Tel: 03-3403-1581／Fax: 03-3497-0649／e-mail: ga-ada@fb3.so-net.ne.jp　http://www02.so-net.ne.jp/~ga-ada/／禁無断転載／ISBN4-87140-231-2 C1352
取次店：トーハン・日販・大阪屋・栗田出版販売・誠光堂・西村書店・中央社・太洋社

173

57

Latest Issue 新刊

Cover : Eychaner/Lee House by Tadao Ando

世界の村と街：インドネシア 撮影：小松義夫	**VILLAGES AND TOWNS: INDONESIA** Photos by Yoshio Komatsu
安藤忠雄 アイキャナー/リー邸	**TADAO ANDO** Eychaner/Lee House
レム・コールハース ボルドーの住宅	**REM KOOLHAAS** Maison à Bordeaux
シャルロット・ペリアン パリのステュディオ	**CHARLOTTE PERRIAND** Renovation of Twin Studio Apartments
アンジェリル/グラハム/フェニンガー/ショル HT96.4	**ANGÉLIL/GRAHAM/PFENNINGER/SCHOLL** HT96.4
アルベルト・カラチ＆ダニエル・アルヴァレス ネグロ・ハウス	**ALBERTO KALACH & DANIEL ALVAREZ** Negro House
リカルド・レゴレッタ リカルド・レゴレッタ邸	**RICARDO LEGORRETA** Ricardo Legorreta's House
齋藤裕 蓴居	**YUTAKA SAITO** Shun-kyo
坂茂 壁のない家	**SHIGERU BAN** House Without Walls
窪田勝文 Y-HOUSE	**KATSUFUMI KUBOTA** Y-HOUSE
ディーン/ウルフ スパイラル・ハウス	**DEAN/WOLF** Spiral House

English and Japanese text／Size: 300×228mm／160 total pages. 72 in color／￥2,848

表記価格に消費税は含まれておりません。

Latest Issue 新刊

55

Cover: Getty Center by Richard Meier

リチャード・マイヤー ゲッティ・センター ロサンジェルス, U.S.A.	**RICHARD MEIER** **Getty Center** Los Angeles, California, U.S.A.
レンゾ・ピアノ バイエラー財団美術館 バーゼル, スイス	**RENZO PIANO** **Beyeler Foundation Museum** Riehen (Basel), Switzerland
磯崎新 群馬県立近代美術館現代美術棟 群馬県高崎市	**ARATA ISOZAKI** **Museum of Modern Art, Gunma—Contemporary Art Wing** Gunma, Japan
安藤忠雄 綾部工業団地交流プラザ 京都府綾部市	**TADAO ANDO** **Ayabe Community Center** Kyoto, Japan
安藤忠雄 TOTOセミナーハウス 兵庫県津名郡	**TADAO ANDO** **TOTO Seminar House** Hyogo, Japan
MZRC フランス・スタジアム サン・ドニ, フランス	**MZRC STADE ARCHITECTURE** **Stade de France** Saint-Denis, France
メカノ デルフト工科大学図書館 デルフト, オランダ	**MECANOO ARCHITEKTEN** **Library of the Delft University of Technology** Delft, The Netherlands
原広司 宮城県図書館 宮城県仙台市	**HIROSHI HARA** **Miyagi Prefectural Library** Sendai, Miyagi, Japan
リカルド・レゴレッタ サン・アントニオ中央図書館 テキサス, U.S.A.	**LEGORRETA ARQUITECTOS** **San Antonio Main Library** San Antonio, Texas, U.S.A.

English and Japanese text／Size: 300×297mm／132 total pages. 54 in color／¥2,848

表記価格に消費税は含まれておりません。

La Maison de Verre

EDITED & PHOTOGRAPHED by Yukio Futagawa **TEXT & DRAWINGS by** Bernard Bauchet **TEXT by** Marc Vellay

Pierre Chareau

ガラスの家：ダルザス邸

企画・撮影＝二川幸夫
文・図面＝ベルナール・ボシェ／翻訳：三宅理一

再版出来ました。
printed and available now.

Built in the center of Paris, La Maison de Verre is neither a work which can be overlooked for it avant-garde qualities, nor as a landmark in the history of Modern Architecture. This volume attempts to give an overall picture of this major work with photographs and survey drawings.

1932年，パリのサンジェルマン大通りに近い，古いアパートの1，2階に嵌め込まれた＜ガラスの家＞は，スチールとガラスブロックの大胆な構成で，近代建築史上，その前衛性からも注目すべき建築である。光の浸透というテーマがどのような構成の原理と空間構成のテクニックのうえに成立しているのか。特別撮影の写真と実測図面により解明する。

English and Japanese text／Size: 300×307mm／180 total pages, 42 in color／¥5,806

表記価格に消費税は含まれておりません。